George Procter

History of the Crusades

George Procter

History of the Crusades

ISBN/EAN: 9783337320379

Printed in Europe, USA, Canada, Australia, Japan

Cover: Foto ©ninafisch / pixelio.de

More available books at **www.hansebooks.com**

Proctor's
History of the Crusades

COMPRISING THE

Rise, Progress and Results

OF THE

Various Extraordinary European Expeditions for the Recovery of the Holy Land from the Saracens, and Turks.

BY

Major George Proctor.

OF THE ROYAL MILITARY ACADEMY, SANDHURST, ENGLAND.

With 150 Illustrations.

PHILADELPHIA:
THE KEYSTONE PUBLISHING CO

At the present time, when a misunderstanding concerning the Holy Places at Jerusalem has given rise to a war involving four of the great Powers of Europe, the mind naturally reverts to the period when nearly all the military power of Europe made a descent on Palestine for the recovery of them from the possession of the infidels. It would seem that the interest in these places is still alive; and the history of the Holy Wars of Palestine during a considerable portion of the Middle Ages, may be supposed to form an attractive theme for the general reader.

of the Crusades" has been carefully revised, some additions made, a series of illustrative engravings, executed by first-rate artists, introduced, and the edition is now respectfully submitted to the public.

The editor, in the performance of his duty, has been struck with the masterly, clear, and lucid method in which the author has executed the work—a work of considerable difficulty, when we consider the long period and the multiplicity of important events embraced in the history; nor has the editor been less impressed with the vigorous style, and the happy power of giving vividness, colour and thrilling interest to the events which he narrates, so conspicuous in Major Proctor's history. No other historian of the Crusades has succeeded in comprising so complete and entertaining a narrative in so reasonable a compass.

AMERICAN EDITOR.

CHAPTER I.

The First Crusade.

Section I.
Causes of the Crusades.. *Page*

Section II.
Preaching of the First Crusade..

Section III.
Peter the Hermit.—The Crusade undertaken by the People..........

Section V.
The First Crusaders at Constantinople ....*Page* 79

Section VI.
The Siege of Nice 96

Section VII.
Defeat of the Turks.—Seizure of Edessa...................... 105

Section VIII.
Seige and Capture of Antioch by the Crusaders............ 119

Section IX.
Defence of Antioch by the Crusaders............................ 130

Section X.
Seige and Capture of Jerusalem by the Crusaders......... 153

CHAPTER II.

The Second Crusade.

Section I.
State of the Latin Kingdom.. 176

Section II
Origin of the Orders of Religious Chivalry..................... 194

Section III.
Fall of Edessa.—Preaching of the Second Crusade......... 205

CONTENTS.

CHAPTER III.

The Third Crusade.

Section I.
The Rise of Saladin .... *Page* 224

Section II.
Battle of Tiberias, and Fall of Jerusalem 238

Section III.
The Germans undertake the Crusade 248

Section IV.
Richard Cœur de Lion in Palestine 257

CHAPTER IV.

The Fourth Crusade.

Section I.
The French, Germans, and Italians unite in the Crusade 285

Section II.
Affairs of the Eastern Empire 298

Section III.
Expedition against Constantinople 311

CHAPTER V.

The Last Four Crusades.

Section I.
History of the Latin Empire of the East.................Page 342

Section II.
The Fifth Crusade... 361

Section III.
The Sixth Crusade... 380

Section IV.
The Seventh Crusade... 401

Section V.
The Eighth Crusade... 428

CHAPTER VI.
Consequences of the Crusades 453

ILLUSTRATIONS

CRUSADERS in sight of Jerusalem	FRONTISPIECE
The Holy Sepulchre	TITLE
Head-piece to Preface	PAGE 3
Head-piece to Contents	5
Head-piece to Illustrations	9
Pope Urban II. preaching the First Crusade, at the Council of Clermont	13
Head-piece to Chapter I.	17
Ornamental Letter	17
A Norman Knight	21
The Normans conquering Sicily	22
Charlemagne	26
Mohammed	30
Early Career of Mohammed	31

ILLUSTRATIONS.

	PAGE
Robert Guiscard ordering his ships to be burned	88
Tail-piece	40
Peter the Hermit	41
Ornamental Letter	41
Peter the Hermit and the Patriarch of Jerusalem	42
Peter the Hermit preaching the First Crusade	45
Norman Armour	55
Ornamental Letter	55
Peter the Hermit leading the First Crusaders	58
Tail-piece	64
Armour	65
Henry IV	68
Godfrey of Bouillon	69
Siege of Rome	71
Robert of Normandy and his Father	72
A Crusader	79
Ornamental Letter	79
The Emperor Alexius	90
Regalia	96
Ornamental Letter	96
Tail-piece	104
Head-piece	105
Ornamental Letter	105
A Turkish Encampment	110
Baldwin seizes Edessa	116
Tail-piece	117

ILLUSTRATIONS.

	PAGE
Antioch	118
Ornamental Letter	118
Kara Hissar	124
Capture of Antioch by the Crusaders	128
Robert of Normandy slaying the Turk	129
Head-piece	130
Ornamental Letter	130
Bishop Adhemar blessing the Crusaders	141
Tail-piece	152
Jerusalem	153
Ornamental Letter	153
Mount Sion	157
Godfrey of Bouillon	161
Capture of Jerusalem	164
Godfrey of Bouillon elected King of Jerusalem	172
Tail-piece	175
Ascalon	176
Ornamental Letter	176
Tancred	181
Funeral of Baldwin I., King of Jerusalem	188
Ruins of Tyre	190
Tail-piece	193
Institution of the Order of the Knights of St. John of Jerusalem	194
Armour	194
Ornamental Letter	195

ILLUSTRATIONS.

	PAGE
Grand-Master of the Knights of Malta	198
Grand-Marshal of the Knights of Malta	199
Malta	201
Knights Templars	203
Head-piece	205
Ornamental Letter	205
Queen Eleanor of Aquitaine	211
St. Bernard preaching the Second Crusade	211
Tail-piece	213
Head-piece	214
Ornamental Letter	214
Conrad III	217
Passage of the Meander	218
Louis VII. defending himself against the Turks	219
Damascus	221
Tail-piece	223
Arab Encampment	224
Ornamental Letter	224
Noureddin marching on Antioch	228
Shiracouch	231
Saladin	236
Tail-piece	237
Head-piece	238
Ornamental Letter	238

ILLUSTRATIONS.

	PAGE
Head-piece	248
Ornamental Letter	248
Frederic Barbarossa	252
Head-piece	257
Ornamental Letter	257
Richard Cœur De Lion	260
Rhodes	262
Siege of Acre	264
Movable Towers	265
Capitulation of Acre	266
Tower and Battering-ram	266
Richard Cœur de Lion at Antioch	267
Richard I. at Asotus	272
Hebron	275
Richard Cœur de Lion at Jaffa	280
General View of Jerusalem	284
Head-piece	285
Ornamental Letter	285
Henry VI., Emperor of Germany	287
Place of St. Mark's, Venice	293
Street in Constantinople	298
Ornamental Letter	298
Isaac Angelus	304
Tail-piece	310
Dandolo, Doge of Venice	311
Ornamental Letter	311

ILLUSTRATIONS.

	PAGE
Theodore Lascaris	327
Ornamental Letter	327
Desecration of the Churches	334
Tower of St. Mark's, Venice	335
Ceremony of raising an elected King on a buckler	337
Tail-piece, Gethsemene	341
Baldwin I., Emperor of the East	342
Ornamental Letter	342
Baldwin II	354
Head-piece	361
Ornamental Letter	361
William Longespee, Earl of Salisbury	364
Capture of Damietta by the Crusaders	367
Emperor Frederic II	372
Head-piece	380
Ornamental Letter	380
Richard, Earl of Cornwall	382
Frederic II	385
Zingis Khan	391
Tail-piece	400
View on the Nile	401
Ornamental Letter	401
Blanche of Castile	403
Haco, King of Norway	404
Ships of the 13th Century	405
St. Louis in captivity	416

ILLUSTRATIONS.

	PAGE
St. Louis entering Ptolemais	419
Tail-piece	427
Head-piece	428
Ornamental Letter	428
Death of St. Louis	431
Edward I. of England	432
Attempt to assassinate Edward	435
Funeral of Robert Guiscard	452
Head-piece	453
Ornamental Letter	453
Tail-piece	464

HISTORY OF THE CRUSADES.

CHAPTER I.

The First Crusade.

FROM A.D. 1095 TO A.D. 1099.

SECTION I.—CAUSES OF THE CRUSADES.

THE term CRUSADE is derived from the French word *Croisade*, and is employed to designate that series of extraordinary expeditions undertaken by the Western nations of Europe, during the eleventh and twelfth centuries, for the recovery of the Holy Land from the Saracens and Turks. The space of time consumed in these strange enterprises extends over nearly, if not quite, two hundred years, and in whatever light we contemplate them, they constitute one of the most interesting chapters that is to be found in the annals of mankind. Nothing like them had been seen before in either the ancient or the modern world, and nothing like them has been seen since; and it is the object of the present volume to investigate the causes which led to them, to describe the incidents by which they were accompanied, and to estimate the consequences that followed from them.

The predisposing circumstances which led to those famous enterprises, and thereby impressed such singular features on the history of the period, are to be sought rather in the general aspect and feelings of society during the ages immediately antecedent, than in the occurrence of any particular events. Amid the lawless violence which preceded and attended the settlement of the feudal system, the voice of religion could seldom be heard above the perpetual din of armed rapine; and her influence, instead of being habitually exercised over the consciences of men, was felt only with startling remorse in some brief interval of sickness or calamity. Then, the rude and superstitious warrior, with the same untempered energy of passion, was prepared to rush at once from the perpetration of atrocious crime to seek its atonement in exercises of the severest penance. Equally among churchmen and laity, the devotional spirit of the times, such as it was, knew no other mode of reconcilement with offended Heaven, than in these acts of mortification. But, if many sought to expiate their guilt in the passive austerities of the cloister, it was more congenial to the restless and enterprising character which marked the Northern mind, to embrace the encounter with fatigue and peril, as the surest test and the most acceptable tribute of repentant faith. The Romish clergy, therefore, probably only indulged instead of creating a popular inclination, when, in the eighth and ninth centuries, they began to commute the more ancient penances enjoined by the canons of the church, for pilgrimages to Rome, to the shrines of various saints, and above all to Jerusalem. The desire of visiting the places where celebrated events have occurred, seems, indeed, a curiosity too deeply implanted in our nature to belong to any particular time or condition of man; but the associations connected with the hallowed scene of human redemption were calculated to sanctify this feeling with peculiar interest, and had rendered journeys to Jerusalem not uncommon in some of the earliest ages of Christianity. When this practice was communicated to the Gothic nations, the love of pilgrimages gradually became almost a universal passion; and though its objects were deformed by the grossness of superstition, and its course much diverted to Rome itself, and to those shrines in different countries at which pretended mi-

Compostella, in Spain, the stream of mistaken yet sincere devotion continued to set steadily toward the shores of Palestine.

But the impulse which, above all others, had a tendency to increase the ardour for pilgrimages, arose from a growing belief, early in the tenth century, that the end of the world was at hand. It was imagined that the thousand years mentioned in the Apocalypse would speedily be fulfilled; that the reign of Antichrist approached; and that the terrors of the last judgment would immediately follow.[*] In proportion as this erroneous interpretation of sacred prophecy gained wider credence, the Western World became violently agitated with fearful forebodings of the destruction which awaited the earth; every delusive form of propitiation for sin, in penance and pilgrimage, was eagerly embraced; and, as it was concluded that to visit the scenes of redemption was both a meritorious and a preservative act, multitudes annually flocked to Jerusalem, to revive and recover those hopes of salvation which withered under the remembrance of habitual guilt. When an expedient so quieting to the consciences of men in a state of society

---

[*] *Chron.*Guil.Godelli, (in *Recueil des Historiens Français*, vol. x.,) p 262. De Vic et de Vaisette, *Hist. de Languedoc*, vol. ii. p. 86–117, &c As Robertson has remarked, (*Hist. of Charles V.*, vol. i. note 13,) even many of the charters of the tenth century have for preamble, "*Appropinquante mundi termino,*" &c., (seeing that the end of the world is at hand.)

A Norman Knight.

equally fruitful of crime and superstition, had once been discovered, inducements were not wanting for its repetition; and the custom surpassed and survived its original impulse and occasion. Throughout the tenth and eleventh centuries, the passion for pilgrimages was ever on the increase; and it is recorded of a single company which visited the Holy Sepulchre, about the middle of the latter age, that its numbers were no fewer than seven thousand persons.*

The Normans conquering Sicily.

Foremost among the devotees, as among the warriors of the times, were the Normans. That singular and high-spirited people, in every respect the most remarkable of the barbarian races, had no sooner become converts to Christianity, than they strangely infused into their religious profession the same wild and enthusiastic temper, the same ardour for adventurous enterprise, which had distinguished their pagan career. The conquest of Southern Italy, which originated entirely in the casual return of their pilgrims from the Holy Land through that theatre of Saracen warfare,* is, in itself, a striking memorial both of their addiction to such religious journeyings, and of the

---

* Leo Ostiensis, *Chron. Mon. Cassin*, lib. ii. c. 37. Giannone, *Istoria di Napoli*, vol. ii. p. 7

equal readiness for either devout or martial achievement by which they were animated. Traversing Italy in the route between their own land and the Mediterranean ports which communicated with Palestine, in small but well-armed bands, the Norman pilgrims were prepared alike, either to crave hospitality in the blessed name of the Cross, or to force their way at the point of the lance. Their victorious establishment in Italy tended to increase their intercourse with the East; their daring assaults upon the Byzantine empire, though foreign to our present subject, attest their undiminished thirst of enterprise; and we shall find the sons of the Norman conquerors of the Sicilies and England figuring among the chief promoters and warriors of the First Crusade.

Such a union of religious and martial ardour, however, was by no means confined to the Normans; and the eleventh century was marked, throughout Western Europe, by the general expansion of a spirit, of which the organized result may be numbered among the most active and powerful causes of the crusades. This was the institution of CHIVALRY. The rude origin of a state of manners so extraordinary in itself, and so restricted to the descendants of the great Northern race,* is obviously to be found in those ceremonies which, among their ancestors in the German forests, attended the assumption of arms by the youthful

---

not, in rather an elaborate passage, cited the Achilles of Homer as a beautiful portraiture of the chivalric character "in its most general form." On this position it may, in the first place, be remarked as singular, that Mr. Hallam should number "a calm indifference to the cause in which he was engaged" among the qualities of the Homeric hero, as suggesting a parallel with the knightly character; of which, enthusiastic and loyal devotion in enterprise formed the peculiar attributes. In the next place, the resentment of Achilles for the loss of Briseis merely as his captured *property*, is utterly repugnant to that principle of respectful idolatry for the fair, which every true knight cherished as an indispensable article in his creed of love and honour. In fact, the most irreconcilable distinction between the manners of the classical and Gothic ages rests, as we have before had occasion to remark, on the totally opposite estimation of woman. Finally, his conduct of Achilles, both in suffering the inferior herd of Greeks to strike the corpse of Hector, and in dragging the lifeless body of the noble and fallen antagonist at his chariot wheels, would have been held utterly abhorrent from chivalric ideas of courtesy; and Mr. Hallam, a few pages farther on, has quoted a passage from a chronicler of the thirteeeth century, which denounces the act of insulting the dead body of an enemy as the lowest depth of infamy. Thus, altogether, to say nothing of the absence of that dedication of the sword to the cause of Heaven, which, mistaken as it was, gave a religious impression to the knightly character, the portraiture of Achilles is completely destitute of those qualities of loyalty, devotedness to woman, and courtesy to enemies, which Mr. Hallam himself justly specifies as virtues essential to chivalry. That lofty energy of the soul which is inspired by contempt of death and thirst for glory, and displayed in daring and magnanimous achievement, constitutes, indeed, the vital essence of heroism under every form of society; but into this lifespring of action, common to the Grecian and the Gothic warrior, it was the singular peculiarity of the chivalric spirit to infuse the triple incentive and sentiment of religious,

warrior.* In subsequent ages the same forms of martial investiture, with little addition or variation, were preserved among the conquerors of the Roman empire, and perpetuated in every kingdom which they had founded. In the Lombard annals; in a recorded act, as well as occasionally in the capitularies of Charlemagne; and in the chronicles of the Anglo-Saxon era, are to be found sufficient evidence† of a common practice in the ceremonial investiture of knighthood. We may here overleap the chain of circumstances which, in later connection with feudal and social obligations, imparted to the spirit of chivalry, which in the outset was only essentially martial, its more graceful virtues of loyalty and honour, courtesy and benevolence, generosity to enemies, protection to the feeble and the oppressed, and respectful tenderness to woman. To trace the growth of these beautiful attributes of chivalry, as a moral and social system, belongs not to our present inquiry; and it will suffice to notice in this place that admixture of religious ideas and duties with a military institution, which converted it into a ready engine of superstitious excitement, and singularly

---

suggested, the Homeric representation, abounding as it does in native sublimity of conception, might, with more propriety, be selected for a sufficient example of the contrast between the heroic character in the two great romantic ages of the ancient and modern world.

* Tacitus, *De Moribus Germanorum*, c. 18.

† Paulus Diaconus, *De Gestis Langobard*, c. 23, 24. *Vita Ludovici Pii*, ad Ann. 791. Malmsbury. lib. ii. c. 2.

Charlemagne.

disposed the public mind of Europe for any enterprise of fanatical warfare.

The exact epoch at which chivalry acquired a religious character, it is neither easy, nor is it material, to ascertain. In the age of Charlemagne, and in his empire at least, the form of knightly investiture was certainly unattended by any vows or ecclesiastical ceremonies.* But, in the eleventh century, it had become common to invoke the aid of religion in the inauguration of the knight; his sword was laid on the altar, blessed, and even sometimes girded to his side, by the priest; and his solemn vow dedicated its use to the service of Heaven, in the special defence of the church, as well as the general protection of the weak and the oppressed. The more complete conversion of the whole process of investiture into a religious ceremonial; the previous vigils, confession, prayer, and receipt of the sacrament; the bath and the robe of white linen, as emblems of purification; all those preparations, in short, by which the entrance into the knightly career, was designedly assimilated to that into the monastic profession, formed the growth of rather later times.† But there is abundant proof of the success of the church, before the Crusades, in infusing some religious principle into the martial spirit of chivalry.‡ For this, justice has scarcely been extended to the motives of the Romish clergy by different classes of writers, who, whether from indignation at the real corruptions of that church, or from hostility to the cause of Christianity itself, can discover only unmingled evil in the ecclesiastical policy of the Middle Ages. But, apart from the lower and more interested purpose, in itself surely not unjustifiable, of converting the

---

* *Vita Ludov. Pii, ubi suprá.*
† Du Cange, *Glossarium in vv. Arma, Miles,* &c.

martial temper of lawless communities into a means of defence for the church, the clergy of the eleventh century appear to have laboured with a zeal and sincerity above suspicion, in mitigating a spirit which they could not subdue. Their efforts to soften the ferocity and harmonize the feelings of the times by their reprobation of private wars and judicial combats, are deserving of all praise;* and there seems no reason to doubt that, in covering the ceremonies of chivalry with the sanction of religion, their policy was originally animated by a principle equally praiseworthy. In the same knightly vows which they demanded or registered at the altar, engagements to abstain from secret perfidy and open wrong, to shield the oppressed, and to do justice to all Christian men, were at least mingled with the obligation of fidelity and protection to the church itself. The ultimate extension of these pledges into the imaginary duty of warring to the utterance against all infidels, was, indeed, as incompatible with the generally peaceful designs of the clergy, as it was repugnant to every genuine precept of the gospel. But, in a period so turbulent that even the ordinary social virtues could be no better exercised and protected than at the sword's point, a warlike and ignorant race passed, by an easy and obvious transition, into the monstrous error of believing that the sincerity of their faith and the cause of divine truth were to be proven and upheld by the same carnal weapon.

This doctrine was too congenial both to the fierce manners and superstitious feelings of the laity to need the suggestions of the ecclesiastical order for its excitement, and it may well be questioned whether the clergy directed or merely shared or obeyed the impulse of the times. They who can see nothing in the pilgrimizing and crusading madness of the tenth and eleventh centuries but the influence of a crafty system of ecclesiastical policy, attribute to the clergy a far greater superiority of intellect over the spirit of their age than they apparently possessed, only to fix the deeper stigma upon the abuse of their power. It is not only more probable in itself, but more consistent with historical evidence, to conclude that they were fervently imbued with the fanaticism which they are accused of having coolly excited: a vast number of prelates and inferior ecclesiastics shared in the toils and dangers of pilgrimages and Crusades; and the sincerity of the preachers and the warriors of those expeditions must, in general, be tried by the same standard of mistaken enthusiasm. In every sense, indeed, it was the union of religious and martial principles, first effected in the chivalric institutions, which prepared and prolonged the fanatical madness of Europe; the profession of arms became hallowed by its presumed dedication to the service of Heaven; and

Mohammed.

brated writer, in pronouncing chivalry to have been at once both a principal cause and an enduring consequence of the Crusades.*

Such, then, through the united influence of martial and superstitious feelings, were the circumstances which predisposed the nations of Western Europe for any enterprise of fanatical warfare. The immediate occasion of the Crusades must be related in retrospect to the fall of Jerusalem, and the affairs of both the Byzantine and Mohammedan empires. During a long interval of above four centuries, between its capture by Omar, and by the Seljukian Turks,† Jerusa-

---

* Gibbon, *Decline and Fall, &c.* vol. xi. p. 41.
† Jerusalem was captured by the Caliph Omar, A. r. 637, and by

CAUSES OF THE CRUSADES. 31

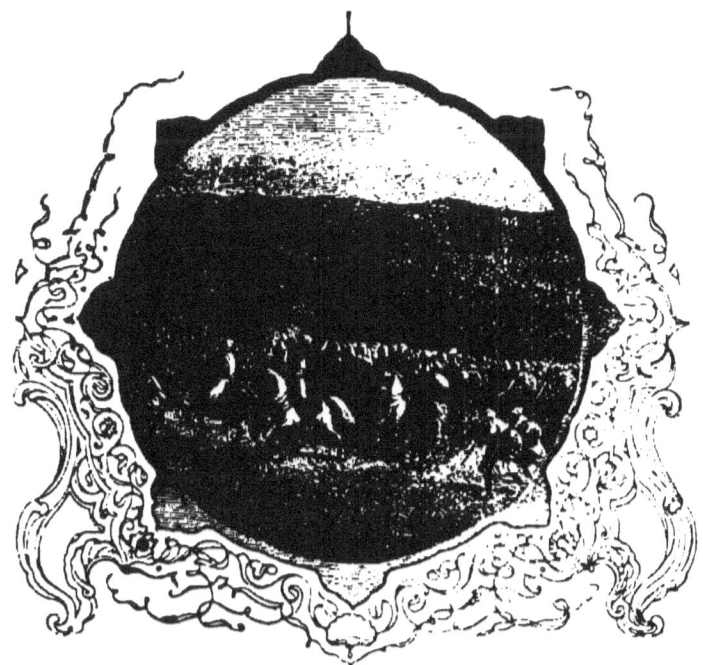

Early career of Mohammed.

lem had shared the vicissitudes of Saracen revolution, and the treatment both of its Christian inhabitants, and of the pilgrims who thronged to its sacred places, was variously affected by the temper of its Mussulman lords. After the fierce spirit of intolerance, which animated the Saracens in their early career of proselyting conquest, had subsided, and during the more tranquil period of the Khalifate, no obstacle was opposed either to the exercise of worship by residents, or to the resort of devout strangers. The spot which

---

Togrul Beg, the grandson of Seljuk, a Turkoman chieftain, whence the name Seljukian, A. D. 1076.

tradition had assigned to the Holy Sepulchre, together with the Church of the Resurrection originally built by Constantine the Great,* were left in possession of the Christians; and, satisfied with the exaction of a small tribute from every inhabitant and pilgrim, the Saracen governors even encouraged the periodical increase of population which swelled their revenues. The reign of Haroun Al Raschid was especially marked as a period of undisturbed communication between the Latin world and Jerusalem; and the transmission of the keys of the city to Charlemagne by that Khalif, though assuredly not designed as a surrender of its sovereignty, was an elegant expression of esteem for the emperor of the Western Christians, and a pledge of secure access for his subjects.†

When, in the tenth century, Jerusalem fell under the dominion of the Fatimite Khalifs of Egypt, the resort of pilgrims to Jerusalem was equally protected by the first two princes of that dynasty, who were not insensible to the benefits of the commercial intercourse of the same fleets which conveyed these devout passengers. But when the frenzy of Hakem, the third Fatimite Khalif, instigated him to destroy, or, at least, greatly to injure, the Church of the Resurrection and the Rock of the Sepulchre, the horrors of a perse-

---

* Eusebius, *in Vitâ Constantin.* lib. iii. c. 25.

† Eginharti *Vita Caroli Magni*, p. 80, 81. Willermus Tyrensis Archiepiscopus, (*Gesta Dei per Francos,*) p. 630.

cution which he at the same time inflicted on the
Christians of Jerusalem, interrupted the devotional
visits of their Western brethren; and the report of his
sacrilegious tyranny first excited that indignation of
the Latin world at the possession and profanation of
the Holy Sepulchre by infidels, which afterward burst
into action with an energy so tremendous. Before
the institutions of ·chivalry were sufficiently matured
to feed this kindling spirit, the death of Hakem, and
the return of his successors to a more tolerant policy,
again opened the shores of Palestine to the devotion
of Europe; the Church of the Resurrection rose from
its ruins; the Holy Sepulchre was repaired; and the
custom of pilgrimage, stimulated by its temporary
repression, was renewed with tenfold ardour. An immense tide of population flowed from every Western
country toward Jerusalem; and, in the language of a
contemporary chronicler, the innumerable multitude of
pilgrims comprehended the lowest and middle orders
of the people, counts, princes, and dignified prelates,
and even women, as well of noble as of poorer condition.*

During the remaining period of the Fatimite dominion in Palestine, these pious visitants continued to
experience from the Mussulman tyrants of the land, in
the alternations of policy and caprice, just sufficient
protection to encourage their concourse, with abundant

---

* Glaber, lib. iv. in *Recueil des Hist. Français*, vol. x. p. 50.

injuries to exasperate that desire of vengeance which they communicated to the whole Western world. Precisely when this feeling, nourished by the general dispositions in the social state of Europe to which we have referred, had acquired full strength, it was forced into impetuous action by one of those sudden and violent vicissitudes of revolution, to which Asia, in every age of her history, has been subject. In their rapid career of conquest, the Seljukian Turks, in an uncertain year toward the close of the eleventh century, became the masters of Palestine.* Those recent and fierce converts to Islamism, appearing as the champions of the Abassidan Khalifs of Bagdad, were animated with equal hatred against the Fatimite possessors and the Christian tributaries of Palestine; and their entrance into Jerusalem was marked by an indiscriminate massacre. The fanatical cruelty of a race of barbarians, with the sanguinary precepts of the Koran freshly engrafted on their native ferocity, was untempered, like that of the more civilized Saracens, by any motives of toleration; the Christian clergy in Jerusalem were frequently tortured and imprisoned in mere wanton fury, or for the sake of the ransom which their sufferings wrung from their brethren; and the Latin pilgrims, who, in defiance of danger, were still urged by pious impulses to visit the Holy Land, were exposed in their journey through it, and in their de-

---

* Willermus Tyr. p. 638.

votions at the Sepulchre, to every variety of insult and spoliation from the savage and greedy Turks. The reports which they circulated on their return, both of the afflictions of the church of Jerusalem and of their own endured wrongs, agitated all Christendom with an universal sentiment of mingled horror, shame, and vengeance, at the profanation of the holy places of Jerusalem, the imaginary disgrace of suffering the scenes of human redemption to remain in the hands of sacrilegious infidels, and the conviction that the punishment of their impious atrocities was a duty enjoined equally by religion and by honour.*

While these feelings were shared with deep sincerity alike by the great body of the clergy and laity of Western Europe, events had arisen in the state of the Byzantine empire, which gave the papal see an immediate motive of political interest in directing the strong impulse of the age to a religious war. When the victorious career of the Seljukian Turks, under Alp Arslan,† began to threaten the safety of Constantinople itself, the Emperor Michael VII., in the extremity of his distress and terror, grasped at a faint hope of succour by addressing himself to the ruler of the Latin church. Through a mission to Pope Gregory

---

* Willermus Tyr. p. 634.
† Alp Arslan, "the valiant lion," was the nephew and successor

THE FIRST CRUSADE.

Gregory VII.

VII., he exposed the common danger of Christendom from the new growth of the Mohammedan power, declared his reverence for the papal authority, and implored its exercise for his aid among the princes of the West. Such an application, which seemed to promise the submission of the Greek church to the papacy, opened views of aggrandizement, too congenial to the towering ambition and adventurous spirit of Gregory to be received with indifference; and he strenuously exhorted the sovereigns of Europe, by encyclical epistles, to arm against the infidels. In these letters the principal recommendation was the union of the two churches of Christendom for a general armament against the Turks; but in a single passage announcing that fifty thousand warriors had already declared their willingness to be led to the redemption of the Holy Sepulchre, is first* plainly shadowed out the great subsequent design of the Crusades.†

The proposal of Gregory VII. was not yet, however, directed with sufficient singleness of purpose to the shores of Palestine to inflame the kindling enthusiasm of the West; and the opportunity of maturing his daring project was reserved for his successor and imitator, Urban II. A renewal of the supplication which had been addressed to Gregory was produced by the increasing distress of the Eastern empire; and the subsequent connection of its affairs with the first crusade requires that we should here briefly trace the thread of the Byzantine annals from the accession of Alexius Comnenus. That prince, at the outset of his reign, found his dominions assailed simultaneously on opposite extremities by the arms of the Normans of Italy and the Seljukian Turks. The invasion of Greece by Robert Guiscard, the first Norman Duke of Calabria, with the magnificent design of conquering the Eastern empire, demanded the earliest care of Alexius; and, though

---

* It is usual to infer that the first design of a crusade was contained in an encyclical letter of Pope Sylvester II. at the commencement of the eleventh century. But the object of his epistle (*Recueil des Hist. Français*, vol. x. p. 425) does not appear to have gone beyond the obtaining of some pecuniary succour from Christendom for the distressed church of Jerusalem.

Robert Guiscard ordering his ships to be burned.

his resistance was gallant and vigorous, his defeat by the Norman in the great battle of Durazzo, shook the tottering fabric of Byzantine power to its centre. In this war Robert Guiscard ordered his ships to be burned on the hostile shores of Illyria, to prevent his soldiers from having any hopes of retreat; and this, too, in the face of an almost innumerable host of the Eastern empire gathered together for the defence of Durazzo. The distraction of an Italian war arrested Guiscard in the subjugation of Greece, and, perhaps, saved Constantinople from his assaults:* but his enterprise had favoured the progress of the Turks in the eastern provinces of the empire; and Alexius was compelled to purchase their forbearance by the formal cession of

---

* Anna Commena, *Alexias*, lib. iii.–v. &c. Galfridus Malaterra,

Asia Minor. The establishment in that wealthy region, of the subordinate Seljukian kingdom of Roum or of the Romans—a title in itself insulting to the proud pretensions and fallen majesty of the successors of Constantine—contracted the eastern frontiers of their empire to the shores of the Bosphorus and the Hellespont. The residence of Solyman, the Sultan of Roum, was fixed at Nice in Bythynia, within a hundred miles of Constantinople; and the Turkish outposts were separated only by the strait from the imperial capital. A hollow pacification did not prevent Solymon from meditating the passage of that channel; and his preparation of a naval armament filled Alexius with reasonable alarm for the safety of the European remnant of his dominions.* Following the example of Michael VII., he addressed the most earnest entreaties for succour to the Pope and the temporal princes of Western Christendom.† The independent partitions of the Seljukian conquests on the death of Malek Shah, and the decline of the Turkish power through intestine dissensions, relieved the pressure on the Byzantine empire; and Alexius was enabled even to recover some portion of Asia Minor from the successor of Solyman; but his envoys were

---

* For the history of the Turkish conquest of Asia Minor, &c., vide De Guignes, vol. i. p. 244, vol. ii. p. 1–12. Also the original account of William of Tyre, lib. i. c. 9, 10.

† Guibert Abbat. *Hist. Hierosol.* p. 475, 476. (*Gesta Dei per Francos.*)

yet resident at the Papal Court, when, by an instrument apparently far more powerless, that spark was struck into the enthusiasm of Europe which threw its combustible elements into one general conflagration of religious warfare.

Peter the Hermit.

SECTION II.

PREACHING OF THE FIRST CRUSADE.

THE name and story of the extraordinary individual who lit up this unquenchable flame of fanaticism, must be familiar to every reader. Peter the Hermit was a poor gentleman of Picardy, who, after following in arms his feudal lord, Eustace de Bouillon, and vainly attempting to improve his fortunes by an alliance with a lady of noble family, had, in some moment either

Peter the Hermit and the Patriarch of Jerusalem.

of disappointed ambition or of awakened remorse for deeper guilt, escaped, from a profitless service and a distasteful marriage, to the refuge of the cloister. But the resistless fervour of spirit, which afterward produced effects so memorable, led him shortly to desert the monastic profession for a life of absolute solitude; and to the character of an anchorite he next superadded that of a pilgrim to the Holy Land. The scenes which he witnessed, the sufferings which he endured, in this expedition, were of a nature to confirm the mental distemper which had been nourished in his cell. At Jerusalem his indignation was excited by the cruelties of the Turks to the Christian residents and pilgrims: his piety was shocked at the

sulted by those barbarian infidels. He fancied himself inspired by Heaven to effect its deliverance from their hands; and, in a conversation with the Patriarch of Jerusalem, he declared his purpose to rouse the princes and people of the West to avenge the disgrace of Christendom.* He possessed many qualities which, notwithstanding an unpromising exterior, peculiarly fitted him for the task to which he thoroughly devoted himself. He was inspired with the genuine spirit of enthusiasm: regardless of bodily privation and fatigue, steadfast in purpose, ardent in imagination, and, above all, animated by that admixture of pious intentions with personal vanity, which has deluded the fanatic of every age. When he first emerged from obscurity, and burst upon the world as the preacher of a religious war, he is described as emaciated by self-inflicted austerities and wayfaring toil; diminutive in stature; mean in appearance; and clad in those coarse weeds of a solitary, from whence he derived his surname of the Hermit. But his eye beamed with fire and intelligence; he was fluent in speech; and the vehement sincerity of his feelings supplied him with the only eloquence which would have been intelligible to the popular passions of his times.†

Having obtained from the Patriarch of Jerusalem letters of credence and supplication for the cause which he had undertaken, Peter, on his return to Europe, repaired at once to the Papal Court, and found in Urban II. an astonished but ready listener to his magnanimous project. The pope recognised, and, perhaps, sincerely credited, the Divine authority of his mission; but the views of Gregory VII. were not forgotten by his successor; and motives of ambition, sufficiently strong to induce his assent, must have been suggested by the embassy of Alexius, and the desire of extending the authority of the Papal See over the churches of the East. The probability that schemes of mere worldly policy were at least mingled with the religious impressions of Urban II. is increased by the assertion of a well-informed writer of his times,* that he had recourse to a temperate counsellor, who had in his own person proved the weakness of the Byzantine empire. This was Boemond, natural son of Robert Guiscard, who had attended his father in his daring invasion of Greece, and whose ambitious spirit was now impatiently restrained within the narrow limits of a Neapolitan fief. The Norman prince,

---

Sed major in exiguo regnabat corpore virtus. Vivacis enim ingenii erat, et oculum habens perspicacem; gratumque, et sponte fluens ei non deerat eloquium. (This man was little in stature and contemptible in appearance; but there reigned within that slight body a very courageous spirit. He possessed a lively genius, and had a quick, clear eye; nor was he wanting in agreeable and ready eloquence.)

whose selfish and wily character strikingly developed itself in the subsequent events of the Crusade, was little influenced by the devotional fervour of the age; and, if his advice determined Urban to direct the enthusiasm of Europe to the shores of Palestine, we may readily believe the chronicler that it was founded more upon political than religious considerations.*

However this may have been, the Hermit of Picardy quitted the Papal Court strengthened by the approbation and the promises of the spiritual chief of Christendom; and, travelling over Italy and France, he everywhere proclaimed the sacred duty of delivering the sepulchre of Christ from the hands of the infidels. Unless we bear in mind the prodigious influence of those superstitious and martial feelings which together absorbed the passions of a fierce and ignorant age, it is difficult to conceive the recorded effects of the Hermit's preaching; and language has been exhausted in describing, after contemporary authorities, the innumerable crowds of all ranks which thronged cities and hamlets, churches and highways, at his voice; the tears, the sighs, the indignation excited in these multitudes by his picture of the wrongs of their Christian brethren, and the sacrilegious defilement of the Holy Sepulchre; the shame and remorse which followed his reproaches at the guilty supineness that had abandoned the blessed scenes of redemption to the insults of infidels; the eager reception of his injunctions to every sinner to seek reconcilement with Heaven by devotion to its cause; and the rapture which his denunciations of vengeance against the Saracen enemies of God awakened in the stern hearts of congregated warriors. The fanatical austerity of the preacher, which was proclaimed in his withered form, his squalid attire, and his abstemious diet; the voluntary poverty which distributed to the indigent the arms vainly designed for its own relief; the rude eloquence of speech and gesture, which flowed from impassioned sincerity, were all in deep unison with the religious sentiments of his hearers: the appeal to arms roused, with irresistible strength, that double excitement of devotion and valour which animated, as with a blended and inseparable principle, the Christian chivalry of Europe.*

The pope had dismissed the Hermit with the assurance that he would strenuously support his great design; and the enthusiasm which Peter had awakened by his preaching was restrained from bursting into action, only by eager expectation of the fulfilment of the pledge. At Piacenza, Urban first convoked the prelates of Italy and the neighbouring regions; four thousand inferior clergy, and thirty thousand lay persons, are computed to have flocked to the scene;

---

* Willermus Tyr. p. 688. Guibert, p. 482. **Fulcherius Carnotensis**, (*Gesta Dei per Francos*,) p. 381.

[A. D. 1095, March;] and, the legates of the Eastern Emperor having been admitted into the assembly to expose the dangers which menaced their country and all Christendom from the progress of the Turks, and to implore the aid of the nations of the West against the infidels, it was resolved to promote the demand, and to mature the design of a holy war, by the authority of a more general Council.* Urban was directed, in his choice of a place for its assemblage, by the partialities of birth, by the predominant martial and religious spirit of his native country, France, and by the special invitation of Raymond, Count of Thoulouse. Clermont, the capital of Auvergne, was appointed for the seat of the Council, at which the pope in person presided, and an immense multitude of clergy and laity of all ranks, from France, Italy, and Germany, gave their attendance. [Nov. 1095.] During the first week after the opening of the Council, its deliberations were chiefly engaged in the enactment of some general provisions for the improvement of morals and the repression of private war; but, on the ninth morrow of the session, the pope himself ascended an elevated pulpit in the open air, and preached the sacred duty of redeeming the sepulchre of Christ from the infidels, and the certain propitiation for sin by devotion to this meritorious service. His fervent exhortations were addressed to a multitude already deeply imbued with fanatical purpose; his inference of a divine command for the holy war was interrupted by one universal and tumultuous cry of "It is the will of God;" and the slightly varied acclamations of *Deus vult, Dieux el volt,* and *Deus lo volt,* expressed the common enthusiasm of the clergy and the people, while it marks the pure retention of the Latin tongue in the familiar speech of ecclesiastics, and the popular corruptions which it had undergone into the two great northern and provençal dialects of France. At the instant when their cries resounded throughout the vast assembly, the figurative injunction of Scripture to the sinner, to take up the cross of Christ, suggested to Urban the idea that all who embraced the sacred enterprise should bear on their shoulder or breast that symbol of salvation. The proposal was eagerly adopted; the Bishop of Puy first solicited the pope to affix the holy sign in red cloth* on his shoulder; and the example being immediately followed, the cross became the invariable badge of the profession, while it gave an enduring title to the warfare of the *Croissé* or Crusader. The first temporal prince who assumed the cross was the Count of Thoulouse; and his offers, through his ambassa-

---

* It has been observed by Gibbon, after Du Cange, that although in the first Crusade red was the general colour of the cross, different hues were subsequently adopted as national distinctions: red by the French, green by the Flemings, and *white* by the English. Yet the red cross of St. George was early our national emblem, and still proudly floats on that banner which "a thousand years has braved the battle and the breeze."

dors, to devote his powerful resources, as well as his person, to the cause, were hailed with admiration. Before the Council broke up, Adhemar, the Bishop of Puy, was invested by Urban with full authority as papal legate for the conduct of the expedition; and the following spring was appointed for the period of its departure to the East.*

The decision of the Council of Clermont was welcomed throughout the Latin world with joyful assent; and Europe echoed with the clang of warlike preparation for the sacred enterprise. France, Italy, and Germany were inspired with a common ardour; the same spirit was communicated to the British Islands, and penetrated the remoter region of Scandinavia;† and, if Spain did not equally respond to the call, it was only because the Christian chivalry of Castile and Arragon were already occupied on a nearer theatre of religious hostility, in the long contest with their Sara-

---

* Willermus Tyr. p. 639–641. Guibert, p. 478–480 Fulcher. p. 382. Baldricus Arch. (also in *Gesta Dei*,) p. 79–88. Labbé, *Concilia*, vol. x.

† Malmsbury whimsically involves his picture of the universal extent of the crusading ardour, in an allusion to national habits: "The Welshman forsook his hunting; the Scot his companionship with vermin; the Dane his carouse; and the Norwegian his raw fish," p. 416. Among the distinguished personages who joined the first Crusade from our own island, were Stephen, the English Norman Earl of Albemarle, Odo, Bishop of Bayeux and Earl of Kent, (Dugdale, *Baronage*, vol. i. p. 28, 61,) and perhaps (*L'Art de Vérifier les Dates*, vol. i. p. 842) a son of Malcolm Ceanmore, King of Scot-

cen enemies.* In every country, and among all ranks and conditions of men, the master passions of fanatical and martial zeal were fed by various impulses of action. The chief inducement, beyond doubt, was a canon of the Council of Clermont, by which the performance of the crusading vow was accepted as a full equivalent for all ecclesiastical penances. This decree is memorable in itself as having first suggested, or at least rapidly extended, the idea of granting plenary indulgences: the sale of which for money was afterward converted, by the cupidity of the popes, into so profitable an expedient for replenishing their coffers, and became the most scandalous practical corruption of the Romish Church.†

To the feudal nobility and their followers, the commutation of penances for a military enterprise was peculiarly grateful. The anathemas of the church

---

* The sacred and meritorious character of the warfare against the Spanish Saracens had been already recognised by the popes. In the conquest of Toledo, (A. D. 1085,) Alfonzo VI. had been assisted by many foreign knights; and, when pressed in the following year by the African Saracens, he was succoured by the chivalry of France. It has even been contended (Mailly, *Esprit des Croisades*, vol. ii. p. 91) that their auxiliary expedition should be numbered as the first of the Crusades; and there is no doubt that is was considered as a holy war, and must have familiarized the French nobles with the idea of such enterprises—though its memory has been eclipsed by the superior importance of the subsequent design for the redemption of the Sepulchre.

† Labbé, *Concilia*, vol. x. p. 507. Mosheim, *Eccles. Hist. Cent.* xii P. 2. c. 3. Muratori, *Antiq. Med. Ævi. Diss.* lxviii.

against private wars, the enforcement of the truce of God, and the prohibition to bear arms, or to mount on horseback, which the clergy often employed as a form of penance, were all grievous to an order in whom the love of arms and rapine struggled with the terrors of superstition.* An injunction to religious warfare, which relieved their fears, while it promised free indulgence to their favourite pursuits, was gladly embraced as the very easiest mode of reconciling their usual course of life with expiation for its disorders; and so admirable, in the judgment of the age, appeared this discovery of a mode of atoning for its prevalent crimes by their very repetition, that a chronicler emphatically eulogizes it as a new kind of salvation.* Nor were there wanting the worldly incentives of avarice, ambition, and renown, still further to animate the mistaken sense of religious duty. The exaggerated tales of pilgrims and traders were filled with pictures of oriental wealth; the subjugation of Asia seemed an easy and glorious achievemnt; and the chivalry of Europe already shared in imagination the countless treasures and fertile provinces of the gorgeous East.†

By the remaining classes of society, the same mingled influence of spiritual and temporal motives was equally felt. While numbers of the clergy sincerely

---

* "*Novum salutis genus.*" Guibert, p. 471; (a new kind of sal-

shared the general fanaticism, the conquest of Asia opened prospects of wealthy establishments to the higher order of ecclesiastics; the monks found at least a meritorious occasion of escape from the irksome restraint of the cloister, and the peasantry from feudal bondage to the soil. Under the pretence of a holy purpose which it was decreed sinful to prevent, debtors were protected both from the present demands of their creditors and the accumulation of interest during their absence; criminals were permitted to elude the pursuit of justice; and offenders of every degree, under the special safeguard which the church threw over the performance of their vows, were enabled to defy the vengeance of the secular law.* Lastly, even the speculations of an infant commerce assisted the general excitement; and the merchants of Italy, in particular, engaged with avidity in enterprises from which, in effect, they alone, by the establishment and extension of a lucrative maritime trade, derived any solid and durable advantage.

Yet all these were but the secondary motives of that one mighty impulse, under which all the ordinary considerations of life, all the ties which bind men to home and country, to kindred and possessions, were alike disregarded. To obtain funds for so distant and expensive an enterprise, princes and high nobles mortgaged, or even alienated their vast do-

---

* See Du Cange, *in v. Crucis Privilegium*, and the authorities

mains; warriors of inferior rank either wholly abandoned their feudal estates and obligations, or prepared to follow their lords in voluntary service; lands were everywhere converted into money; horses, arms, and means of transport were collected at exorbitant prices; and valuable property of all kinds was recklessly sacrificed on the most inadequate terms to colder or craftier dealers. Yet, even among such, the irresistible force of example often prevailed; the awakening conviction of duty, the thirst of glory, or the dread of reproach, was gradually imparted to every bosom not wholly insensible to religion and honour; and the prudent or designing purchaser in one hour, was himself the deluded seller in the next. Nor was the contagion of fanatical adventure confined to the chivalric order. Not only ecclesiastics deserted their benefices, and monastic recluses their cells, but mechanics and rustics forsook their occupations, and exchanged their implements of industry for weapons of offence; and women of all ranks, with an abandonment of the more timid and becoming virtues of their sex, which produced equal misery and scandal, either left their husbands behind them, or, with their children, swelled and encumbered the unwieldy masses of helpless pilgrims.* Moreover, the superstitious

---

* Guibert, p. 481. Albertus Aquensis, (*Gesta Dei per Francos,*) p. 185. Guibert has a passage which too curiously illustrates the madness of the prevalent fanaticism to be passed without notice in

confidence of atonement for past crimes, and the expectation of license for future enormities, equally attracted the vilest portion of mankind. Robbers, murderers, and other criminals of the deepest dye, professed their design to wash out their guilt in the blood of the enemies of God.* The aggregate of the immense multitudes who thus assumed the cross could scarcely be accurately computed, in an age so unfavourable for collecting the details of statistical calculation. By one chronicler it is vaguely estimated at six millions of persons; † by a less credulous contemporary it is denied that all the kingdoms of the West could supply so vast a host; ‡ but even the exaggeration proves that the original design of enthusiasm would have totally depopulated Europe; and, after making every deduction for the influence of delay, returning reason, and the accidents of life, in cooling the first burst of fanatical fervour, the numbers which actually fulfilled their purpose justify the assertion that whole nations rather than the mere armies of Western Christendom, were precipitated upon Mohammedan Asia.

---

carts, in which they placed their families and goods to perform the sacred journey; and it was *planè joco aptissimum* (very amusing) to hear the children inquiring, as they approached any city, whether that were Jerusalem, p. 482.

* Wilermus Tyr. p. 641. Albertus Aquensis, *ubi suprà.*
† Fulcherius Carnot. p. 386.
‡ Guibert, p. 556.

Norman Armour.

SECTION III

PETER THE HERMIT—THE CRUSADES UNDERTAKEN BY THE PEOPLE.

ONG before the season, the end of spring,* fixed by the Pope for the departure of the Crusaders had expired, the impatience of the ruder multitudes of people grew too violent for restraint. [A. D. 1096, March.] Soon after the commencement of the new year, an immense concourse of pilgrims, chiefly of the lowest orders, had thronged

---

* And not the "Feast of the Assumption in August," as Gibbon has stated. See the interesting version of the speech of Urban, in the Council of Clermont, as given by William of Malmsbury. The first detachment under Godfrey, Duke of Lorraine, set out by

around Peter the Hermit on the western frontiers of France, and urged him, as the original preacher of the sacred enterprise, to assume its conduct. Apparently unconscious of his utter unfitness for command, the fanatic rashly accepted the perilous charge; and, under his guidance, the accumulating torrent began to sweep over Germany.* Its immense tide overflowed the ordinary channels of communi-

---

* Before we accompany the disorderly march of the mob which thus commenced the First Crusade, it behooves us to specify our principal guides throughout the expedition. These are the original authorities contained in the great collection of Bongarsius, which he printed at Hanover, in two folio volumes, in 1611, under the general title of *Gesta Dei per Francos;* a designation which Jortin pithily proposed to change into *Gesta Diaboli*, &c. The actual eye-witnesses of the First Crusade, whose relations are to be found in the collection of Bongarsius, were, 1. Robert the Monk, (*Hist. Hierosolymitana;*) 2. Raymond de Agiles, chaplain to the Count of Thoulouse, during the Crusade, (*Hist. Francorum;*) and 3. Fulcher, also a chaplain, who accompanied the Count of Chartres, and afterward attached himself to Baldwin, brother of the great Godfrey, and second king of Jerusalem, (*Gesta Peregrinantium Francorum*); 4. next in the order of testimony is the work of an archbishop, Baldric, (*Hist. Hierosolym.,*) who assisted at the Council of Clermont, and whose relation, although he did not himself accompany the expedition, is declared to have been revised by an abbot who did so; 5. Albert of Aix, (*Hist. Hierosol. Expeditionis;*) and 6. Guibert, (the title of whose Chronicle, *Gesta Dei per Francos*, it was that Bongarsius adopted for the whole collection,) were contemporaries, and the latter was a keen observer and lively narrator; 7. and lastly, William, Archbishop of Tyre, already so often quoted, whose history, although he was not contemporary with the First Crusade, is, perhaps from the materials of information to which he had access, and the judgment with which he compiled them, the most valuable document in the whole collection.

cation; and devastation marked its course. The roads were obstructed by the multitude of passengers; the country through which they moved was oppressed by their excesses; the means of subsistence were exhausted by their wants; and Peter was compelled to exhort them to separate into smaller masses. Under the commaud of Gualtier, or Walter, a Burgundian knight, whose poverty procured for him the surname of *Sans-Avoir*, or the Pennyless, and who accepted the office of lieutenant to the Hermit, a body of twenty thousand pilgrims preceded the march of the main host through Hungary and Bulgaria toward Constantinople. The wretched quality of the adventurers who composed this advanced guard is sufficiently indicated by the fact that there were only eight horsemen in the whole number, and their conduct was as reckless as their condition was deplorable. Through Hungary, they were indebted for a safe though toilsome passage, to the friendly disposition of its king, Carloman, and Christian people; but, on their entrance into the still wilder regions of Bulgaria, which were governed by a lieutenant of the Byzantine empire, they encountered every possible obstacle, both from the treacherous policy of the imperial officers, who forbade the supply of their necessities, and from the ferocious temper of the natives. Hunger compelled the crusaders to resort to violence; the Bulgarians flew to arms, and the route of Walter and his followers was tracked in blood and flames. But in every day's march, the natives cut off hundreds of the miserable rabble; and the destruction of the whole host, before it reached the southern confines of Bulgaria, was so complete, that only Walter and a few survivors succeeded, by a flight through the forests, in reaching the Court of Constantinople.*

The second division of the crusading mob, under Peter the Hermit himself, amounting to forty thousand men, women, and children, followed on the traces of the first body. Aided by the good offices of the Hungarian king, their march through his country was abundantly supplied, and tranquilly pursued, until they reached Malleville, the modern Zemlin, on its southern confines, where the triumphant exhibition on the walls of the spoils of some of their precursors who had been slain in an affray with the inhabitants, roused them to a furious vengeance. The ramparts of the city were scaled; thousands of its people were slaughtered, and for several days the survivors were exposed to all the horrors of violation and rapine. The approach of Carloman with a large army to punish their perfidious ingratitude, accelerated the departure of the crusaders; and their hasty and disorderly passage of the Save exposed them to a heavy loss from the attacks of the savage hordes, who awaited their landing on the Bulgarian bank of that river. Though they finally repelled these new enemies, they found Bulgaria a wasted solitude. The natives had retreated to their fastnesses and strongholds; the fortified towns were closed against them; and the purchase of provisions for their march, under the walls of these places, was the only intercourse which the imperial officers would permit the inhabitants to hold with them. Their excesses again provoked a more open and fatal hostility. Enraged at some outrages, the people of Nissa pursued and massacred their rear-guard; the efforts of Peter could not dissuade the whole host from returning to avenge this quarrel; and, in an ineffectual attempt to renew the same scenes as at Zemlin, the assailants were repulsed from the walls with immense slaughter. The triumphant garrison and inhabitants issued forth upon them; a general and total rout ensued; and, in the onset, the sally, and the pursuit, above ten thousand of the crusaders perished. Their camp was abandoned and plundered; and despoiled of their baggage, of their money, and of their arms, the wretched herd of fugitives continued its journey toward Constantinople.*

When they had ceased to be formidable, their helpless misery extorted some compassion; Alexius interposed his protection, and their remains at length reached his capital, where they were reunited to Walter and the survivors of the first division. But they were no sooner refreshed, than they repaid their hospitable benefactor by new acts of insolence, licentiousness, and pillage; and Alexius gladly acceded to their desire to be transported across the Bosphorus. Under the conduct of Peter and his lieutenant Walter, they were landed in Asia Minor; but here, neither the exhortations of the Hermit could restrain their outrages against the religion and property of the subjects of Alexius, nor the advice of the emperor himself to await the arrival of the more disciplined chivalry of Europe, prevent their headlong advance. Peter, finding himself totally unable to control them, used a decent pretext for escaping back to Constantinople; but Walter, whose more martial spirit was really associated with qualities for command deserving of a better fate, was compelled to yield to their clamorous demand to be led against the infidels. Despite of his prudential warnings, they divided their forces to plunder the Turkish provinces, and reunited only on a report artfully circulated by the Sultan of Roum, that Nice, his capital, had fallen into the hands of an advanced body of their associates. Allured by the prospect of sharing in its spoils, they blindly rushed into the heart of a hostile country; but when they descended into the plain of Nice, instead of being welcomed by the sight of the Christian banners on its walls, they found themselves surrounded by the Turk-

covered with wounds, while vainly discharging, by intelligence and example, the twofold duties of the leader and the warrior. The disorderly multitude of his followers was immediately overwhelmed and slaughtered; a remnant, no more than three thousand, escaped the general destruction by flight to the nearest Byzantine fortress; and a huge mound, into which the savage victors piled the bones of the slain, formed an ominous monument of disaster for succeeding hosts of crusaders.*

The disorders and destruction of these first two divisions of the crusading rabble were, indeed, but a prelude to more atrocious scenes of guilt, and more enormous waste of human life. Stimulated by the example of Peter, a German monk, named Godeschal, preached the Crusade through the villages of his native land with so much effect, that he allured about fifteen thousand of the peasantry to follow him to the East. This third division took the same route as the two preceding; but, on their arrival in Hungary, they experienced a far different reception from its sovereign, who was justly exasperated at the outrages with which his hospitality had been repaid. At first he prudently supplied them with the means of accelerating their passage through his kingdom; but their march was attended with an aggravated repetition of

---

* Albert. p. 189–193. Baldricus Archiepiscopus, p. 89. Guibert, p. 485. Willermus Tyr. p. 645–647. Anna Comnena, p. 226, 227

the worst crimes which had been perpetrated by the followers of the Hermit; the whole population of Hungary rose in arms against them, and Carloman was at length provoked to deliver them over to the vengeance of his subjects. For this purpose he had recourse to a cruel act of perfidy, which deeply sullied the merit of his earlier forbearance. Before the walls of Belgrade, his promise of forgiveness and protection induced them to lay down their arms; and this act of submission was immediately followed by their ruthless massacre.*

But the numbers, the gross superstition, the licentious wickedness, and the miserable extirpation of these fanatical hordes, all sink into insignificance before the features displayed in the composition and conduct of the fourth and last division of the rabble of Europe. From France, from the Rhenish Provinces and Flanders, and from the British Islands, there gathered on the eastern confines of Germany one huge mass of the vile refuse of all these nations, amounting to no less than two hundred thousand persons. Some bands of nobles, with their mounted followers, were not ashamed to accompany their march, and share their prey; but their leaders are undistinguishable; and the most authentic contemporary records of their proceedings compel us to repeat the incredible assertion that their motions were guided

---

* Albert p. 194. Willermus Tyr. p. 648

by a goat and a goose, which were believed to be divinely inspired. If we impatiently dismiss a circumstance so revolting to every pious mind, and so degrading to the pride of human intellect, we find their actions as detestable as their superstition was blind and unholy. The unhappy Jews in the episcopal cities of the Rhine and Moselle were the first victims of their ferocity. Under the protection of the ecclesiastical lords of these commercial places, colonies of that outcast race had long enjoyed toleration and accumulated wealth. Their riches tempted the cupidity of fanatics, who professed a zeal for the pure religion of the gospel, only that they might violate its most sacred precepts of mercy and love. Under the pretence of commencing their holy war by extirpating the enemies of God in Europe, they sought the blood and spoils of a helpless and unoffending people. To the honour of the Romish Church, the Bishops of Mayence, Spires, and other cities, courageously endeavoured to shield the Jews from their fury and rapine; but their humane efforts were only partially successful, and thousands were either barbarously massacred, or, to escape the outrages and disappoint the cupidity of their enemies, cast themselves, their women and children, and their precious effects, into the waters or the flames. Sated with murder and spoliation, the ruffian host pursued its march from the Rhine to the Danube; and the continued in-

needed not the impulse of fanaticism for the commission of every atrocity. But it was at length overtaken by the vengeance of God and man. In the hour of danger, the unruly and wicked multitude proved as dastardly against an armed enemy as it had been ferocious toward the defenceless Jews. It effected the passages of the Danube only to encounter a tremendous defeat from the Hungarian army which had collected for the national defence; some sudden and inexplicable panic produced a general flight, and unresisted slaughter; and so dreadful was the carnage, that the course of the Danube was choked with the bodies, and its waters dyed with the blood of the slain. The contemporary chronicler, who was apparently best informed of their execrable crimes and well-merited fate, asserts that very few of the immense crusading multitude escaped death from the swords of the Hungarians or the rapid current of the river; and it is certain that, whatever remnant survived, saved their lives only by flight and dispersion.*

---

* Albert. Aquensis, p. 195, 196. Fulcher. p. 386 Willermus Tyr. p. 649, 650.

SECTION IV.

THE CRUSADE UNDERTAKEN BY KINGS AND NOBLES.

BEFORE twelve months had expired since the spirit of crusading was roused into action by the Council of Clermont, and before a single advantage had been gained over the infidels, the fanatical enthusiasm of Europe had already cost the lives, at the lowest computation, of two hundred and fifty thousand of its people.* But such were the stupid ignorance and headlong folly which misguided these wretched multitudes, and still more, so dark and grovelling was their superstition, so cruel and demoniacal their fanaticism, and so flagitious their licentiousness, that all pity for their fate is lost in the disgust and horror with which we recoil from the contemplation of brutality and guilt. The picture is relieved by no exhibition of dignified purpose or heroic achievement; the myriads who had perished in Hungary, in Bulgaria, and in Asia Minor, were animated by none of the loftier sentiments of the age; they were composed chiefly of the coarser rabble of every country; and in their destruction we behold only the offscouring of the popular ferment of Europe. But, while the first disasters of the Crusade were sweeping this mass of corruption from the surface of society, the genuine spirit of religious and martial enthusiasm was more slowly and powerfully evolved. With maturer preparation, and with steadier resolve than the half-armed and irregular rabble, the mailed and organized chivalry of Europe was arraying itself for the mighty contest; and a far different, a splendid and interesting spectacle, opens to our view. In the characters, the motives, and the conduct of the princely and noble leaders who achieved the design of the first Crusade, we are no longer presented with the revolting sameness of a mere brutal ferocity. Their zeal, although mingled with superstition, and not unstained by cruelty, was also elevated by the generous pursuit of martial fame, their resolves were inspired by the twofold incentive of spiritual duty and temporal honour; and their fanaticism was regulated by foresight and prudence. In entering on their purpose, they had, indeed, been more or less infected with the general madness of the age; but, in the guidance of the holy war, many of them proved themselves as politic in counsel, as skilful in expedients, and as patient and constant under difficulties, as they were adventurous in danger and courageous in combat. The wildness of their enterprise is condemned by our calmer reason; the justice of their cause may be impeached on every true principle of divine and human law; but, from the magnanimous devotion of their spirit, and the fearless heroism of their exploits, it is impossible to withhold our sympathy and admiration.

It has been deemed worthy of remark, that none of the principal sovereigns of Europe engaged in the first Crusade; but their absence was determined by the accidents of individual character and position. Pope Urban II. declined the personal command of the expedition, on the plea of his engrossing functions in the general government of the church, and his duty of repressing the schism 'created by the Antipope Clement; or, perhaps, on the more reasonable excuse of his age and infirmities;* but he deputed his spiritual authority to his legate Adhemar, the Bishop of Puy. The Emperor Henry IV., the personal enemy of Urban, and protector of the antipope, of course refused to recognise the authority by which the Crusade was preached. Philip I. of France was absorbed in sensual indulgence; and to renew the excommunication

---

* *Belli Sacri Hist.* (by an anonymous chronicler, in Mabillon, *Mus. Ital.* vol. i.) p. 135.

THE FIRST CRUSADE.

Henry IV.

already passed upon him was one of the acts of Urban at the very Council of Clermont. The crafty and irreligious character of William II. of England (Rufus) also led him rather to minister to his brother's reckless enthusiasm, by purchasing the mortgage of Duke Robert's Norman dominions, than to join himself in the holy war. But the cause rejected by these monarchs was eagerly embraced by the most distinguished feudal princes of the second order: by Godfrey of Bouillon, Duke of the Lower Lorraine or Brabant, with his two brothers, Eustace and Baldwin, and a kinsman also of the latter name; Hugh, styled the Great Count of Vermandois, and Robert, Duke of Normandy, brothers of the French and English kings; Robert, Stephen, and Raymond, Counts of Flanders,

Godfrey of Bouillon.

Chartres, and Thoulouse; and the Norman Boemond, son of the Guiscard, Prince of Tarento, with his cousin Tancred, whom history and romance have equally delighted to exhibit as the brightest examplar of knightly virtue.

In dignity and character, however, in the conduct and the results of the Crusade, the highest place of honour must be conceded to the Duke of Brabant. Godfrey of Bouillon was descended through females from Charlemagne; and ranked, alike by his great possessions and personal qualities, among the most powerful feudatories of the German Empire. His reputation for wisdom in counsel and prowess in arms was deservedly high; and, during the war between the empire and papacy, in which he adhered to Henry

the battle of Merseburg and at the siege of Rome His political importance was increased by the position of his states on the frontiers of France and Germany; and his consequent familiarity with the popular dialects of both countries, as well as his acquisition of the Latin, the customary language of the church, facilitated his intercourse, and promoted his personal influence, among the nations of Europe. But the severe integrity of his character disdained the selfish exercise of these advantages; and, amid the gross and violent disorders of the times, his life was regulated by the strictest principles of morality and religion. His manners were gentle, pure, and benignant; his conduct was just and disinterested; and his piety, though mistaken, was sincere and fervent. These virtues might have qualified him rather for the cloister than the camp, if they had not been associated with energies capable of the loftiest designs: with a head to conceive and a hand to execute the most arduous enterprises which his conscience approved; with resolution, tempered by reflection and judgment, which no difficulties could shake; and with valour, calmed only by moderation, which no perils could deter. Since the siege of Rome his frame had been consumed by a slow fever; his illness dictated the renewal of an early purpose of performing the pilgrimage to Jerusalem: and he no sooner heard of the projected Crusade, than, as if inspired with new

CRUSADE BY KINGS AND NOBLES. 71

Siege of Rome.

sprang with renovated health and youth from a sick-couch to engage in so glorious and meritorious a work.*

The transcendent merits and accomplishments which adorned the principal hero of the first Crusade have demanded an especial portraiture: the few features in the characters of the remaining leaders, which varied their general resemblance in devout zeal and warlike excellence, may be more briefly sketched. In Hugh of France these qualities, though supported by other attributes not unworthy of his royal birth, were destitute of the religious humility and modest demeanour of Godfrey; and the great Count of Ver-

Robert of Normandy and his Father.

mandois was remarkable chiefly for an arrogant and haughty deportment.† Robert of Normandy was generous and merciful, eloquent in debate, and well skilled in military expedients; but profuse in expense, dissolute in morals, and equally rash and unsteady in resolve. His rashness and insubordination had nearly made him a parricide, as he had unhorsed his own father, William the Conqueror, in battle, and had only been prevented from putting him to death, by his father's exclaiming and making himself known. Although, therefore, his conduct during

---

† Anna Comnena, p. 227   Robertus Monachus, p. 84.   Guibert,

the Crusade was thought in some measure to atone for the irregularities of his earlier life, and his exploits often attracted the general admiration, his instability of mind prevented his maintaining the respect of his more illustrious compeers.* His namesake of Flanders resembled him in headlong valour, without sharing any portion even of his abortive talents. The Count of Chartres, one of the wealthiest and most potent feudal princes of France, was also deemed the most learned in all the literate and practical knowledge of the age, experienced and wise in his suggestions, clear and persuasive in discourse. These intellectual acquirements peculiarly fitted him for directing the general design of the war; and he was accordingly chosen to preside in the council of its leaders. In the field, the superiority of his tactical skill was equally recognised; but he was deficient in vigorous enterprise; and in the eyes of the fiery champions of the Cross, his fame was tainted by the questionable quality of his valour.

The veteran and sagacious Count of Thoulouse,† whose youth had been habitually exercised in arms

---

* A well-known instance of Robert's careless spirit was the above-mentioned mortgage of his duchy to his brother William for five years, at the inadequate price of ten thousand marks, to equip himself for the Crusade. *Chron. Sax.* p. 204. Will. Gemeticensis, p. 673.

† The history of this prince is very obscure. His original title was Count of St. Gilles in Languedoc; whence Anna Comnena cor-

against his Saracen neighbours in Spain, had brought from that warfare a deadly hatred of the Mussulman name, and was more fiercely animated than the other crusading princes by the spirit of religious intolerance. His master passion was umitigated fanaticism; and the devotion of his old age, the abandonment of his extensive dominions, and the appropriation of his great riches to the service of the Crusade, might have protected his motives from the suspicion of worldly ambition and avarice, if their sincerity had not been attended by a cold and selfish nature, a proud and vindictive temper, which denied him the friendship of his noble confederates, and alienated the affections of his own native followers. To the purely fanatical zeal which predominated in the character of the Provençal prince, may be opposed the unscrupulous ambition and deep hypocrisy of the Norman Boemond, the Ulysses of the war. To him alone, perhaps, of all the movers and warriors of the Crusade, may be attributed a systematic design of rendering the popular enthusiasm of Europe subservient to views of mere personal interest. If his versatile and unprincipled genius enabled him to feel or to feign* some share in

---

rates his rank, as if he had been the principal personage of the Crusade. In what manner he had acquired the extensive fiefs of Thou.ouse and Provence, and arrogated the title of Duke of Narbonne, which he also bore, seems undetermined. *L'Art de Vérifier les Dates*, vol. ii. p. 289-294, &c.

* Boemond pretended to receive with surprise and admiration the

the prevalent sentiment of his time, the whole recorded tenor of his conduct betrays the settled and absorbing pursuit of temporal aggrandizement. Familiar with all the arts of dissimulation, and no less rapacious than perfidious, he exhibits, among the heroes of the holy war, the singular spectacle of a cool and crafty politician. His vices were odiously contrasted with the generous qualities of his youthful cousin Tancred,* whose frank and courteous bearing, no less than his love of glory and high-minded disdain of wrong and perfidy, rendered him the mirror of European chivalry.†

---

had secretly prompted. At the siege of Amalfi, he embraced the Crusade in an apparent transport of zeal: excited the fanatical ardour of his confederates and followers by an eloquent harangue; and, while their enthusiasm was at its height, rent his own robe into pieces in the shape of crosses for the soldiery. This curious and characteristic anecdote is told by Guibert, p. 485.

* Tancred was the son of Matilda, sister of Robert the Guiscard, and therefore the cousin of Boemond, (Radulphus Cadomensis, *de Gestis Tancredi*, c. 1,) and not either his brother or nephew, as some of the writers in the *Gesta Dei*, less correctly informed than the biographer of the hero, and Gibbon and Muratori after them supposed. The father of Tancred was an Italian marquess, Odo. Ralph of Caen was the personal friend and companion of Tancred in Palestine after the Crusade.

† " O più bel di maniere e di sembianti
   O piu eccelso ed intrepido di core," &c.
                          La Gerusal. Liberata. can. i. 45.

But the poet has here only echoed the praises which the qualities of Tancred extorted even from the Greek princes, never unwilling to detract from the virtues of a Latin, above all a Norman name.—Ann*

Such were the leaders under whom the warlike array of the Western nations was marshalled for the First Crusade. Their confederate powers were collected, according to the local convenience or preference of the chieftains, into four great divisions. The first body, composed of the nobility of the Rhenish provinces and the more northern parts of Germany, ranged themselves under the standard of Godfrey of Bouillon. That prince was accompanied by the two Baldwins, and many other powerful feudal lords, whose forces numbered no less than ten thousand cavalry and eighty thousand foot. In the second division, under the Counts of Vermandois and Chartres, the two Roberts, and Eustace, Count of Boulogne, (brother of Godfrey,) were assembled the chivalry of Central and Northern France, the British Isles, Normandy, and Flanders;* and their formidable muster can be estimated only loosely from the assertion of a contemporary, that the number of lesser barons alone exceeded that of the Grecian warriors at the siege of Troy.† The third host, in the order of departure, was composed of Southern Italians under Boemond and Tancred, and formed an array of ten thousand horse and twenty thousand foot. The last

---

* For "neither surely," says old Fuller, "did the Irishmen's feet stick in their bogs." (*Hist. of Holy War*, lib. i. c. 13.) So also sings Tasso:

"Questi dall' alte selve irsuti manda
La divisa dal mondo ultima Irlanda."

division, which assembled under the Count of Thoulouse in the South of France, was originally formed chiefly of his own vassals and native confederates of Languedoc, Gascony, and Arles, comprehended under the general appellation of Provençals;* with a small admixture of the Christian knighthood of the Pyrenean regions of Spain: but in his route through Lombardy, his army was swollen by so great numbers of Northern Italians, that the combined host which marched under his banners amounted to one hundred thousand persons of all arms and conditions. Besides several feudal chieftains of distinction, Raymond was accompanied by three prelates of high rank: the papal Legate Adhemar of Puy, the Archbishop of Toledo, and the Bishop of Orange.†

Of all the principal leaders of the Crusade, the preparations of Godfrey of Bouillon were earliest completed; and his march from the banks of the Moselle was conducted with admirable prudence and order by the same route which had proved so disastrous to the preceding rabble. When he reached the northern frontiers of Hungary, he demanded of its king by his envoys an explanation of the circumstances which had provoked their destruction. The reply of Carloman exposed the crimes by which the vengeance of his people had been roused; and his just and amicable representations compelled the up-

---

* Raymond des Agiles, p. 144. † Willermus Tyr. p. 660.

right judgment of Godfrey to admit that the wickedness of the crusading mob had merited its fate. He accepted a friendly invitation from the Hungarian king; treated with him for a safe passage through his dominions with supplies of provisions on equitable terms; and left his own brother Baldwin and his family as hostages for the good faith and forbearance which he enforced on all his followers. The noble sincerity of Godfrey won the confidence of the Hungarian monarch, and disarmed the suspicion and hostility of his people. Carloman himself attended the movements of the crusaders with a numerous cavalry, both to observe their behaviour and to protect their march; the whole of his kingdom was traversed without a single act of offence on either side; and, when the Latin host had passed its southern confines, the hostages were courteously dismissed with a friendly adieu. When the crusaders entered the Byzantine provinces, their virtuous and able leader still succeeded in maintaining the same strict discipline; the Emperor Alexius assisted and rewarded his efforts by liberally supplying the wants of his army in its toilsome passage through the desolate forests of Bulgaria; and the first division of the European chivalry peaceably accomplished its entrance into the fertile plains of Thrace.*

---

* Albert. p. 198, 199. Willermus Tyr. p. 652

SECTION V.

THE FIRST CRUSADERS AT CONSTANTINOPLE.

BUT for the friendly succour of the Byzantine monarch, it is acknowledged that the host of Godfrey must have perished in their route through provinces imperfectly cultivated, and already exhausted by the feuds of their barbarous natives. The alacrity with which Alexius at first facilitated the approach of his Latin allies, was succeeded by indications of a more dubious policy; and, in the report of their chroniclers, the conduct of the emperor is branded with the reproach of deliberate perfidy and systematic hostility. In weighing the justice of these charges, some reduction from their truth must be made for the bigoted prejudice of the Latins against a schismatic monarch and nation; and a still larger share of extenuation for the suspicious conduct of the emperor may be claimed for the difficulties and peril of his position. Instead of the reasonable aid which he had solicited from the pope and the temporal sovereigns of the West, he found his dominions overwhelmed, and his throne shaken from its foundations, by the deluge of European fanaticism. His hospitable reception of the first disorderly masses of pilgrims had been requited by the ravage of his territories and the spoliation of his subjects: the very numbers and formidable array of the better-disciplined chivalry of Europe might alone have justified a prudent apprehension of their power and disposition, which their fierce promptitude in resenting was by no means calculated to allay. Of the personal characters and real designs of most of their leaders he was utterly ignorant; and their alliance in the same enterprise with his ancient and dangerous enemy, Boemond, was at least an ominous conjuncture. The plea of delivering the Holy Sepulchre from the hands of the Turks, might easily cover a design of subjugating the whole Eastern world to the spiritual dominion of the Latin Church; the same pretext of fanatical zeal might be readily employed against the infidel Mohammedans and heretical Greeks; and to the confident valour and the envious cupidity of the Western warriors, thus animated by religious hatred and temporal ambition, the rich spoils of Constantinople* and its provinces might offer a more accessible and tempting prey than the distant relief of Jerusalem and plunder of Syria. Moreover, the recent distraction and rapid decay of the Seljukian power had terminated the alarm with which Alexius formerly anticipated the entire ruin of his empire; and the subsiding of the Turkish energies had removed the immediate danger which induced him to implore the approach, and might have

---

* Of the astonishment and envy with which the splendour of Constantinople struck the rude Latins, we may form a lively idea from the burst of admiration which the remembrance of its magnificence recalls to the mind of one of their chroniclers, the chaplain and companion of the Count of Chartres: "O quanta civitas nobilis et decora! quot monasteria quotque palatia in eâ, opere miro fabrefacta! quot etiam plateis vel in vicis opera, ad spectandum mirabilia! Tædium est quidem magnum recitare quanta sit ibi opulentia bonorum omnium, auri et argenti," &c. Fulcherius, p. 386.—(Oh! what a fine and noble city is this! How many palaces and monasteries, constructed with admirable skill, it contains! how many works of art, wonderful to behold, are to be found in its streets and shops! It would be, indeed, a tedious matter to tell how great is its riches in all kinds of goods, of both gold and silver.) The emotions excited by the contemplation of such wealth, however innocent in the breast of the good chaplain, were likely to prompt dangerous wishes and designs to the bold and unscrupulous imaginations of fierce and rapacious warriors.

reconciled him to the presence of auxiliaries, in Greek estimation scarcely more civilized, and only less to be dreaded, than the Mohammedan enemy.

Under these critical circumstances, for the double purpose of averting the ruin with which he was menaced, and of obtaining the advantages which he might yet hope to extract from the oppressive aid of the Western nations, the emperor appears to have had recourse to the timid and tortuous policy habitual in the Byzantine court. While he welcomed the approach of the army of Godfrey, his fleets in the Adriatic were prepared to dispute the passage of the French and Norman crusaders from the Italian to the Grecian ports. That second grand division of the European chivalry, led by Hugh of Vermandois, the two Roberts, and the Count of Chartres, had traversed France and Italy for the purpose of embarkation. At Lucca, where these chiefs, prostrating themselves at the feet of the pope, piously received his benediction, Urban II. committed the standard of St. Peter into the hands of the great Count of France;[*] and here the arrogance of that prince furnished Alexius with a first occasion of offence. Twenty-four knights, in armour gorgeously inlaid with gold, were despatched by Hugh to Durazzo, with a haughty intimation to Alexius himself of the approach, and a command to the imperial lieutenant to make royal preparation for the arrival of

---

[*] Fulcherius, p. 384.   Robertus Monachus, p. 35.

the brother of the King of Kings, and standard-bearer of the pope.* The terms of the letter and the message were resented as an insult; and the Governor of Durazzo, instead of offering the desired reception, stationed his navy to prevent the egress of the great count and his followers from the Italian harbours. The Duke of Normandy, and the Counts of Flanders and Chartres, with their followers, after consuming the autumn in luxurious pleasure, resolved to defer their departure from Italy until the return of spring; but Hugh, regardless alike of the dangers of a wintry passage and the ambiguous disposition of the Greeks, impatiently put to sea. His fleet was dispersed in a storm; his own vessel was wrecked on the hostile shore; and, in lieu of the magnificent descent which he had announced, he entered Durazzo as a suppliant, and found himself a captive. He was, indeed, treated with outward demonstrations of respect; but his person was for some time detained, until the commands of Alexius were received for his removal to Constantinople.†

When the intelligence of the captivity of the Count of Vermandois reached the camp of Godfrey in

---

* Anna Comnena, p. 228. Du Cange, with the true complacent vanity of a Frenchman, has amused himself by proving (*Dissert. sur Joinville*, xxvii., and note *ad Alexiad.* p. 352) that the title of King of Kings thus arrogated by Hugh for his brother, was conceded through the respect of Europe during the Middle Ages *par excellence*

Thrace, it roused the violent anger of the crusaders; and, after an ineffectual demand for his release, the Duke of Brabant was compelled to gratify the eager desire which was felt by his followers to punish the imperial perfidy with the ravage of the fine province in which they were quartered. This severe retaliation speedily produced the submission of Alexius. He had already soothed the captivity, and seduced the pride and vanity of the French prince, by his pompous reception at the imperial court; and Hugh was induced to despatch two of his own attendants to Godfrey with the assurance that, on the duke's arrival at Constantinople, he would find their master not a captive, but a guest. This message produced a cessation of hostilities; but the awakened suspicions of the crusaders prepared them to fly to arms on the slightest provocation;. the Greeks were equally distrustful; and the mutual contempt and hatred of two races, so dissimilar in manners and spirit, inflamed every misunderstanding. On the near approach of Godfrey and his host to the Byzantine capital, the refusal of the duke and his fellow-chieftains to trust their persons unattended with the imperial walls, provoked Alexius to forbid all intercourse between his subjects and the crusaders. The Latin camp was immediately straitened for provisions; and Godfrey was again compelled to indulge the rapine of his followers, and the emperor to arrest the sufferings of his people by conciliatory measures. A third and more dangerous quarrel was produced by the belief of the crusaders in a perfidious design of the emperor to blockade and starve them in their camp, which was enclosed by the waters of the Bosphorus, the Black Sea, and the river Barbyses. To anticipate this suspected treachery, the troops of Godfrey possessed themselves, by an impetuous attack, of the bridge of the Blachernæ, the only outlet and key of their communication with Constantinople and the open country. The hostile seizure of this important post disappointed the intentions of the Greeks; or it more probably excited their apprehension against the ulterior purpose of the crusaders themselves. The imperial troops issued from the gates of Constantinople to dispute the passage of the bridge; after a bloody conflict, they were repulsed and pursued to the city; and the crusaders, inflamed with success and resentment, even attempted a headlong assault upon the walls. But the ramparts of Constantinople were strong and lofty; the Latins were unprovided with any battering engines; and the Greek archers, securely directing an unerring aim, galled them with an incessant flight of arrows. An indecisive contest was maintained until the close of day; but at nightfall the assailants, after setting fire to the suburbs, withdrew from the walls.*

To a state of hostility so inconclusive in its objects,

---

* Albertus Aquensis, p. 200–202. Baldricus Arch. p. 91. Willermus Tyr. p. 653, 654. Anna Comnena, p. 232–234.

and injurious to both parties, a stop was now put by the meditation of the Count of Vermandois. If Alexius had ever really meditated the destruction of the crusaders, experience had shewn the fruitlessness of his efforts; and his desire of an accommodation might be increased by the approach of Boemond and his army. Renouncing, therefore, his earlier designs, or more probably only shifting the jealous expedients of a policy which had prompted him in self-defence to restrict, not to ruin the dreaded power of the crusaders, he proposed to their chiefs, as a condition of his friendship, that they should take an oath of fealty to himself, and swear either to restore to the empire, or to hold in feudal dependence,* such of its ancient provinces as they might recover from the infidels. Upon these terms, he engaged vigorously to support the Crusade with the imperial forces and wealth; and he had prepared the way for their acceptance by inducing the brother of the French king to offer an influential precedent.

---

* Anna Comnena, p. 285. The very circumstance of this proposal being made, is a proof, which perhaps deserves more attention than it has usually attracted, that the idea of the feudal relation, whensoever received, was at this epoch familiar to the Eastern emperor. It is still more observable that the ceremonies with which the Latin princes subsequently took the oaths of fealty to Alexius were also strictly feudal; and though their ready adoption on this occasion in the Byzantine court need not shake our belief in the exclusively barbarian and not Roman origin and existence of the system from which they were borrowed, yet the whole fact is curious.

So overcome was that vain and inconsistent prince by the blandishments and presents of Alexius, that he not only stooped to the performance of the desired homage himself, but undertook to obtain the same submission from his confederates. The proposal was at first received in the Latin camp with the indignation natural to the free and fiery spirit of high-born warriors, who spurned the idea of all allegiance or subjection to a foreign lord. Godfrey himself reproached the baseness of Hugh in having consented to a degradation alike unworthy of his haughty pretensions and real dignity, of his ostentatious bearing and royal birth. But the Count of Vermandois excused his own compliance, and enforced its propriety on Godfrey, by arguments best adapted to the disinterested principles of that single-minded and pious prince: such as the paramount obligation of their sacred vows; the difficulty of reducing Alexius to more becoming terms; the impossibility of prosecuting the holy enterprise without the imperial aid; the probable ruin of the cause by delay and wasting hostility; and the very sinfulness of a contest with a Christian people. The reason of Godfrey was no sooner convinced, than all sentiments of worldly pride and honour yielded to the humbler dictates of religious duty; and no subsequent persuasions, with which he was addressed by the messengers of Boemond and the Count of Thoulouse, to await their

Alexius, could shake the sincerity of his purpose. He declared his resolution to take the required oaths of fealty; and the example of his self-denial secured the acquiescence of his compeers. To remove their lingering suspicions of treachery, Alexius delivered his son as a hostage for their safe return; and Godfrey and his principal companions, repairing to Constantinople, prostrated themselves in homage before the imperial throne. Their humiliation was relieved by a reception of studied honour; and in return for the vows of fidelity which he repeated on his knees with clasped hands, Alexius distinguished the virtue and dignity of Godfrey by the ceremonies of filial adoption, and investiture in imperial robes.* But these empty recognitions faintly concealed the real triumph of Greek pride and policy; and it was no fanciful degradation which converted the brave and chivalric princes and nobles of Western Europe into the vassals and liegemen of a Byzantine despot.†

---

* Anna Comnena, p. 335, 238. Albert. p. 203. Willermus Tyr. p. 656, 657.

† That the humiliation was keenly felt may be inferred from the sullen brevity with which the Latin chroniclers dismiss the transaction; but the daughter of Alexius has related an anecdote, which more plainly marks the struggling emotions of the proud warriors, while it amusingly illustrates the manners of Western Europe. During the ceremony of performing homage, a private French baron, conjectured by Du Cange, with great probability, to have been Robert of Paris, was so little disposed to repress his disgust at the pride of the Greek despot, and the compliance to which religious or

After this ceremony, Alexius urged his adopted son, and his new dependants, to exchange their threatening position near his capital for more eligible and abundant quarters on the Asiatic side of the Bosphorus; and their passage of that strait was apparently hastened, through his dread of their being reinforced, while still under the walls of Constantinople, by the other divisions of the crusading host. Before the departure of Godfrey, the Count of Flanders and his followers had already reached the Byzantine capital from Italy; and their arrival was speedily succeeded, at short intervals, by that of the Duke of Normandy, the Count of Chartres, and the

---

made to submit, that he audaciously seated himself beside Alexius on the imperial throne. When the brother of Duke Godfrey attempted to reprove him for this rude disrespect, he coolly retorted his contempt; and the emperor was so astonished by his insolence, that he could only demand through an interpreter his name and condition. "I am a Frenchman," was the reply, "and of noble birth; and I care only to know that in the neighbourhood from which I come there is a church, whither they who design to prove their valour repair to pray until an adversary be found to answer their defiance. There have I often worshipped, without finding that man who dared to accept my challenge." Alexius, because he well knew, says his daughter, the fierce spirit of the Latins, dissembled his resentment, or rather vented it in an ironical caution, that if the Frenchman still desired to maintain the same boast with safety, in his crusading warfare, he would do well to keep beyond reach of the Turkish arrows, by remaining in the centre of the Christian host. His taunt and his advice were thrown away; and his daughter betrays some satisfaction in proceeding to record that the insolent barbarian fell in the foremost ranks of the Crusaders at the battle of Dorylæum

The Emperor Alexius.

scanty residue of the great army which had originally assembled under Hugh of Vermandois. By the dextrous application of flatteries* and bribes, each of these potent chiefs was persuaded in his turn to perform the same homage as his precursors,† and was then hurried off to join them on the Asiatic

---

* Even the politic Count of Chartres was deluded by the arts of Alexius, who contrived to make each of the Latin princes in turn believe himself preferred to all his confederates. There is extant a curious and apparently authentic epistle from Stephen to his countess, in which he unconsciously shows how completely he was duped by the wily Greek. The emperor had inquired how many were his children; spoken much of the love he bore toward him and his unknown house; pretended that the count must send for one of his sons to be educated at the Byzantine court; and bade him reckon on his imperial favour to provide for the youth: in all which the wise count religiously confided. Mabillon, *Mus. Ital.* vol. i 287.

shore. The embarkation from the Apulian ports of the third grand division, under Boemond and Tancred; their passage of the Adriatic into Greece; and their march through that country, were all regulated by those able leaders with higher martial conduct and discipline. Large bodies of the imperial troops, with dubious intentions, hovered over their route, and sometimes even attempted to obstruct their passage, and cut off their detachments; but the skilful dispositions of Boemond frustrated their attempts; and the impetuous valour of Tancred more than once punished the secret perfidy or open aggression of a pusillanimous enemy. The whole march to the vicinity of Constantinople was triumphantly completed; and here Boemond, being met by Godfrey himself with persuasions to satisfy the imperial demand of fealty, left his army in charge of his gallant kinsman, and with a small train proceeded to the capital of Alexius.*

The belief of that monarch's duplicity in his reception of the other Latin princes is increased by the equal cordiality with which he welcomed this hateful enemy. He alluded to Boemond's earlier invasion of his empire only to extol the valour which he had displayed in that enterprise, and to express his own satisfaction at the pacific union which now effaced every feeling of enmity. With as consummate hypo-

---

* Robertus Monachus, p. 36, 37. Baldricus Archiepiscopus, p. 92.

crisy, Boemond on his part professed his self-reproach at the injustice of his former hostility, and his desire to prove his gratitude for so gracious an oblivion of injuries. But Alexius, as well aware of his ambitious and greedy character as of his habitual faithlessness, designed to secure his allegiance by the only motives of selfish interest which could be binding on a nature so sordid. After causing him to be lodged and entertained in the most magnificent style in one of the imperial palaces, the cunning monarch ordered the door of a chamber filled with heaps of gold and jewels to be left, as if accidently, open when he passed. The Norman was ravished with delight and envy as he gazed at the glittering hoards; and his ruling impulses were betrayed in the involuntary exclamation, that, to the possessor of such treasures, the conquest of a kingdom might be an easy achievement. He was immediately informed that the gift of the emperor made them his own; and, after a slight hesitation, his avarice swallowed the bait. His performance of homage to Alexius was succeeded by dreams of ambition, which perhaps aspired to the imperial throne itself; and his expressions of devotion to its service were accompanied by a proposal that he should be invested with the office of Great Domestic of the East, or General of the Byzantine armies in Asia. A present compliance with this audacious demand, which shocked the pride, and might well

avoided with hollow assurances that the highest dignities of the empire should be the reward of future services; and the baffled or sanguine adventurer was persuaded to join the Asiatic camp of his confederates. The opposite conduct of his high-minded relative had meanwhile excited equal alarm. Disdaining, on his arrival at Constantinople, to imitate the baseness of Boemond, Tancred had quitted the capital unobserved, and crossed the Bosphorus in disguise. By this flight he had only designed to escape the degradation of owning himself the vassal of a foreign prince; but the suspicion and resentment of the emperor were not allayed until Boemond unscrupulously pledged himself by oath for the homage and allegiance of his cousin.*

The arrival of the last army of crusaders under the Count of Thoulouse, exhausted the artifices of the imperial policy. After traversing Northern Italy, that skilful and veteran commander had led his forces into the Byzantine provinces, through the wild passes of Dalmatia. His march, though distressed by the noxious climate and rugged obstacles of that mountainous region, and successively harassed by the savage Dalmatians, and by the no less hostile Greeks, had been prosecuted with so much energy and vigilance, that his host, after exercising a passing vengeance on their treacherous assailants, reached the shores of the Bosphorus in unimpaired strength and discipline; and the news of his formidable approach at the head of one hundred thousand Provençals and Italians, revived the liveliest apprehensions in the imperial court. At some distance from Constantinople, the army was met by messengers both from Alexius and from Godfrey and his associates, with a united request to the Count of Thoulouse to repair to the capital. Raymond complied with the invitation; but, on his arrival, neither the arts of the emperor, nor the solicitations of his confederates, could induce him to kneel before the imperial throne. Once more is the emperor accused, on his failure in this negotiation, of having directed a treacherous surprise of the Provençal camp; and, whatever was its origin, a furious collision ensued between the troops of Raymond and of Alexius. The Greeks were defeated with signal carnage; and, in the first suggestions of vengeance, the Count of Thoulouse was with difficulty restrained from vowing war to the utterance against so perfidious a race. He repelled with contempt the menaces both of Alexius and of Boemond, who now ostentatiously avowing himself the most faithful champion of the empire, proclaimed his resolution to turn his arms in its succour even against his recusant confederate. To the milder expostulations of Godfrey, the aged count so far yielded as to tender an oath that he would abstain from all enterprises against the life and dignity of Alexius; but beyond this concession his cold and stubborn pride was equally impenetrable to threats and entreaties. He declared that he had quitted his native dominions to devote the residue of his life to the service of God alone, not to submit himself to any earthly master; and Alexius, either awed into personal respect by the firmness of his spirit, or desirous of conciliating so powerful a chief, suddenly changed his whole demeanour, loaded him with assiduous attentions, and treated him with such real or affected confidence as to impart his secret hatred and suspicion of Boemond. The old Provençal prince listened with pleasure to these complaints of a rival whose interference had already irritated his jealous and vindictive temper; and his heated passions unguarding the usual wariness of his politic judgment, made him an easy dupe to the superior craft of the wily Greek. Alexius so completely gained the ascendency over his mind, that he lingered at Constantinople after the departure of the other chieftains; and the Count of Thoulouse, who had been loudest in his denunciations against the perfidy of the Byzantine court, was among the last to quit its seductive hospitalities for the Asiatic camp of the crusaders.*

---

* Raymond de Agiles, p. 140, 141. Robert. p. 88. Guibert, p. 490. Willermus Tyr. p. 660–662.- Anna Comnena, p. 241.

THE FIRST CRUSADE.

SECTION VI.

THE SIEGE OF NICE.

EFORE the arrival of the Provençal forces, all the other great divisions of the crusading levies had already completed their junction on the plains of Asia Minor; and their wants rather than their strength had been increased by the wretched remnants of the preceding mob, who, with Peter the Hermit himself, had, in recovered confidence, found their way from various places of refuge to the general muster. The enormous numbers of the congregated hosts of Christendom can be estimated with little hope of precision; either from the tumid metaphors of the Grecian Princes, who has described their desolating course, or from the positive assertions of the

Latin writers, whose ignorance of military affairs might easily mislead their computations, and whose astonishment at the view of so prodigious an array was sure to be vented in exaggeration. If we were to credit some of our usual authorities, six or seven hundred thousand warriors were present in arms; besides an innumerable multitude of ecclesiastics, women, and children.* But the report of the same party in other places,† and every evidence of reason and probability, are alike inconsistent with this conclusion; it may be suspected that the leaders of the war were themselves unable to ascertain the real numbers of a disorderly herd of irregular infantry; and we can rely with safety only on the statement of the most judicious chronicler of the Crusade, that the mailed cavalry, which, according to the rude tactics of the Middle Ages, formed the nerve of armies, amounted to one hundred thousand men.‡ This superb body of heavy horse was composed of the flower of the European chivalry: knights, esquires, and their attendant men-at-arms, completely equipped with the helmet and shield, the coat and boots of chain and scale-armour, the lance and the sword, the battle-axe and the ponderous mace of iron. The crowd of footmen fought principally with the long and cross bow, and were used indifferently as occasion required for archers,

---

* Fulcher. p. 387. Willermus Tyr. p. 664.

scouts, and pioneers; but their half-armed and motley condition formed a miserable contrast to the splendour of the chivalric array, which glittered in the blazonry of embroidered and ermined surcoats, shields and head-pieces inlaid with gems and gold, and banners and pennons distinguishing the princely and noble rank of chieftains and knights.*

From their first camp on the Asiatic shores of the Bosphorus, the advance of the Christian hosts, in bold disregard of minor objects of attack, was immediately directed against Nice, the capital of the Sultan of Roum,† situated in a fertile plain on the direct route to Jerusalem. Resting on the waters of the lake Ascanius, the defensive capabilities of that city had been sedulously improved by art. It was surrounded by a double wall of stupendous height and thickness, provided with a deep ditch, and flanked at intervals by no less than three hundred and seventy towers; its garrison was numerous and brave; and the Sultan Solyman, (or Kilidge Arslan,)‡ who had retired to

---

* Albert. Aquensis, p. 103, 212, 241, 392, &c. This writer fondly dwells on the splendid array of the crusading hosts, and affords us more information than any of the other chroniclers on the armament, composition, &c. of the troops.

† Roum, a corruption of Roma, (Rome,) was the name given to the Mussulman kingdom, founded in Asia Minor by the Seljoukian Turks, about the year 1074, and of which Nicæa, or Nice, the chief city of Bythinia, was the capital. It was against this city, where the first General Council of the Church was assembled under Constantine, A. D. 325, that the crusading army now marched.

‡ De Guignes, vol. i. 245.

the neighbouring mountains with his Turkish cavalry, preserving his communication with the place by the lake, might with equal facility reinforce its defenders, and harass the quarters of the besiegers. Nothing deterred by these difficulties, the crusaders, on their arrival before the city, undertook the siege with an energy suitable to the obstinacy which was anticipated in the defence. Notwithstanding their numbers, the immense circumference of the walls prevented a complete investment; but each independent leader, successively encamping on the first quarter which he found unoccupied, from thence directed and prosecuted his attacks. Contrary to the impressions which later historians have sometimes given, that a chief authority over the crusading hosts was conceded to Duke Godfrey, it is here observable that no traces of such a recognition of supremacy can be discovered in the narrative of contemporary chroniclers. The general plan of operations was sometimes debated and determined in a council of princes; but the details and choice of execution were abandoned to the uncontrollable will of the different chieftains and their respective followers, who were alike too proud of personal rank, and too jealous of national distinctions, to brook any submission to a foreign command. But the same feelings which were repugnant to all subordination and unity of action, in a great degree supplied their want with a generous emulation of glory; and, in the rival valour and industry who should be foremost in urging his approaches to the walls. On the northern side were encamped Duke Godfrey and his Rhenish and German division; eastward extended the quarters of the Counts of Vermandois and Chartres and the two Roberts, with the French, Norman, English, and Flemish crusaders; on the same front, the Provençal and Italian host of the Count of Thoulouse took up a continued alignement; and, toward the south, the city was enclosed by the troops of Boemond and Tancred. Two thousand men who had attended the march of the crusaders, under Taticius, as imperial lieutenant, were the only Byzantine forces in the confederate camp.*

From their respective quarters, each of these divisions pushed forward its attacks, with all the mechanical expedients which the Middle Ages had imperfectly preserved out of the martial science of classical antiquity. Among the principal machines of the besiegers were lofty wooden towers of several stories, termed *belfredi*,† or *belfrois*, which were moved forward on rollers or wheels; protected against conflagration by coverings of boiled hides; filled with archers to dislodge the defenders from the ramparts; and supplied with drawbridges, which, on a nearer approach, being let down upon the walls, afforded a

---

* Robert. Mon. p. 39, 40. Albert. Aquensis, p. 204, 205. Willermus Tyr. p. 666. Anna Comnena, p. 247.

† Du Cange v. *Belfredus*.

passage for the knights and their followers to rush to the assault. The advance of these *belfrois* was sometime preceded, the road levelled, and the ditch of a fortress filled up, by means of a movable gallery or shed of similar materials, but lower structure, called indifferently a fox or cat,* or *chat-chateil* when surmounted also by a tower. Under cover of these galleries, the walls could either be undermined by the slow operation of the sap, or breached by the violent blows of the battering-ram. Balistic engines of various sizes and denominations for hurling masses of rock, beams of timber, stones, and darts, composed the ordinary artillery both of the assailants and besieged; and the most effectual means of defence were afforded by the use of the Greek fire in destroying the hostile machines.†

The mechanical operations of the crusaders were for a while arrested by the gallant efforts of the Sultan of Roum, who, descending from the mountains which overhang the plain of Nice with a swarm of fifty thousand horse, endeavoured by a sudden and impetuous attack, with the assistance of the garrison, to overpower the Eastern camp of the Christians. But his hope of surprising their quarters was frustrated by the capture of the messengers who were intrusted to convey his purpose to the city; he everywhere en-

---

* *Idem, vv. Catus, Vulpes,* &c

countered a determined resistance and a bloody repulse; and his first experience of the valour of the Western Christians compelled him to abandon Nice to its fate. The defence of the city was not the less resolutely maintained; and the attempts of the besiegers to breach the walls were repeatedly foiled, their projectile engines disabled, and their towers and galleries crushed by fragments of rock, or burned by the Greek fire. Some weeks had already been consumed in fruitless labour and slaughter, when the position of the city on the lake Ascanius suggested to the besiegers a more successful expedient. At their desire, Alexius caused a number of small vessels to be prepared in his arsenals, transported over land, and launched upon the lake. This flotilla, manned by seamen and archers in the imperial pay, insured the command of the lake, alarmed the city on that side with desultory attacks, and intercepting all its communication by water with the exterior country, completed the investment of the place.*

Meanwhile the besiegers continued their works with renewed spirit. The veteran Count of Thoulouse, whose approaches had been conducted with most skill and pertinacity, at length succeeded, by the science of a Lombard engineer, in attaching with safety a *chat-chateil*, or castellated gallery, to one of the towers of

---

* Albert. p 205, 206. Willermus Tyr. p. 667. Anna Comnena, p. 245.

the city, which had been injured in a former siege, and was bent forward from its base. The miners of the besiegers propped the superincumbent mass with strong timbers while they loosened the foundations; and the supports being then fired, the whole fell with a tremendous crash, and left a yawning breach. But, instead of seizing the first moment of consternation by which the garrison were paralyzed, the Provençals imprudently delayed the assault until the following morning; and an artful Greek contrived in the interval to rob them of the fruits of success. The wife and sister of the Sultan, whom he had left in the city until this moment, endeavoured on the first alarm to escape over the lake; they were captured by the imperial flotilla; and Butomite, its commander, immediately offered, not only their honourable release, but protection to the people of Nice against the fury of the Latins, if the city were surrendered to his master. The now despairing inhabitants accepted his terms; the troops of the flotilla disembarking were admitted into the city; and when the crusaders, with returning day, were prepared to mount the breach of the fallen tower, the first spectacle which they beheld was the imperial banner floating on its walls. [20th June, 1097.] In their wounded pride and disappointed cupidity at being thus cheated of the honour and spoils of victory, the first impulse of the crusaders was to continue the assault. But a prudential con-

their princes to stifle their own emotions of disgust at the artifice of Alexius or his lieutenant, and to appease the louder resentment of their followers; and, after a few days of repose, the whole crusading host, breaking up from the camp before Nice, pursued the destined route toward Jerusalem.*

---

* Fulcher. Carnot. p. 387. Raymond de Agiles, p. 142. Baldric. Arch. p. 97. Albert. p. 206–208. Guibert, p. 491-493. Willermus Tyr. 668–672. Anna Comnena p. 246–250.

SECTION VII.

DEFEAT OF THE TURKS—SEIZURE OF EDESSA.

IN their passage through Asia Minor, a march of five hundred miles was still to be accomplished before the crusaders could touch the confines of Syria; and the Sultan of Roum, whose spirit had only been roused to increased energy by the loss of his capital and the danger of his kingdom, was already prepared to offer a formidable resistance to their progress. His appeal, both to his own subjects and to the independent chieftains of his kindred race, for assistance in repelling these new invaders, who so unexpectedly menaced their faith and their nation with a common destruction, had been eagerly answered. From all sides the Turkish hordes flocked to his standard; and so innumerable was the force which he collected, that by some of the Latin writers it is supposed to have exceeded three hundred thousand horse. With this immense cloud of cavalry, during the first few days' advance of the crusaders from Nice, while their strength was fresh and their array undivided, he merely hovered on their flanks; but his forbearance ceased when the convenience or the necessities of their march induced them to separate into two distinct columns on different routes. In one division were now Duke Godfrey and the Counts of Vermandois and Thoulouse; in the other, Boemond and Tancred, the Duke of Normandy, and the Counts of Flanders and Chartres.*

Before the latter and less numerous of the two columns had reached Dorylæum—the modern Eskischeker—about fifty miles from Nice, it was suddenly enveloped, while reposing in a valley, by the Turkish swarms. The first astonishment of the surprise, the unearthly yells, and the furious onset of the barbarians, struck dismay and disorder into the Christian ranks; and the fate of the day was held in suspense only by the gallant example, the desperate efforts, and

---

* Albert. Aquensis, p 215 Willermus Tyr. p. 672. Anna

the personal prowess of the three leaders of Norman blood, Boemond, Tancred, and Duke Robert. While the lightly armed and active cavalry of the Asiatics easily evaded a close encounter with the heavy array of the Europeans, their clouds of arrows slew the unbarded horses, and pierced every opening in the body armour of the Christian warriors. Overwhelmed with the dense confusion of the field, oppressed by the ponderous weight of their own equipment, and fainting under the intense heat and burning thirst of the climate, the weary and despairing crusaders with difficulty sustained an equal conflict. To regain some degree of order, their leaders could only cover a retreat and draw off their exhausted squadrons; and the Turks, flushed with success, penetrated into their camp and commenced an indiscriminate massacre of the aged and infirm pilgrims, the women and the children.

In this extremity, the skilful and valorous conduct of Boemond, never elsewhere so nobly contrasted with the baser qualities of his character, saved the whole crusading host from destruction. In the first alarm he had, with cool foresight, despatched notice of the danger to the other division under Godfrey and the Count of Thoulouse; and now reanimating his confederates and followers to rescue or revenge the helpless victims whose shrieks pierced their ears, he rushed again at their head toward the camp, and fell with resistless impetuosity upon the triumphant and sanguinary barbarians. The Duke of Normandy bravely supported his charge; the inspiring shout of "*Deus vult*," which had first been heard at the Council of Clermont, was now the war-cry which rang again through the Christian squadrons; and the fight was renewed with all the courage which a sense of religious duty could add to the stern resolves of vengeance and despair. But the Crusaders were still encountered with equal resolution and superior force; and the tide of Turkish victory was arrested at this juncture only by the opportune approach of Duke Godfrey and the Count of Vermandois, who, at the first summons, had urged their cavalry, forty thousand strong, at the utmost speed to the succour of their confederates. The junction of this formidable reinforcement, in fresh, firm, and ardent array, infused new life into the sinking energy of their brethren, and in the same proportion depressed the confident spirit of the Turks. The quivers of the infidels were already emptied; the length of the struggle had worn down their activity; and in the close combat which they could no longer escape, their inferiority to the warriors of the West in bodily strength and martial equipment was signally displayed. The supple dexterity of the Asiatic was now feebly opposed to the ponderous strokes of the European arm; the curved scimitar and light javelin could neither parry nor return with effect the deadly thrust of the long pointed sword and gigantic lance;

DEFEAT OF THE TURKS.   109

and in a direct charge, the weight and compactness of the Latin chivalry overpowered the loose order and desultory tactics of the Turkish hordes.

While the infidel host bent and wavered before the determined assault of the Christians, the last division of the Crusaders arrived on the field; and Count Raymond directing his Provençals on the flank or rear of the disordered enemy, completed their terror and ruin. [4th July, 1097:] They broke and fled in every direction, were pursued until the close of day with unremitting slaughter, and were compelled to abandon their camp to the possession of the conquerors Of the crusaders, four thousand had fallen; but they were for the most part of humble condition; and the number included persons of both sexes who were massacred when the infidels first burst into the Christian camp. Among the Turkish host, in the battle and the pursuit, thirty thousand had been slain; and no less than three thousand of these were chieftains or warriors of distinction, whose rank was proclaimed by the value of the spoils found on their bodies. The pillage of the Asiatic camp offered a still richer reward to the victors, in immense quantities of gold and silver, arms and apparel, war-horses, camels, and other beasts of burden.*

By the general confession of the Latins themselves, the Turks had displayed a valour and warlike skill

A Turkish Encampment.

which excited their astonishment and deserved their admiration; and the surprise produced by the unexpected discovery of these qualities in an Asiatic nation is evinced in the assertion, that they alone of all Eastern people were worthy of contending in arms with the Christian chivalry, and of sharing with the warriors of the West a common superiority in martial virtues over the despicable Greeks. The conduct of the Sultan of Roum, after the battle of Dorylæum, afforded a more unequivocal testimony of the respect and fear with which the prowess of the Crusaders had impressed the infidels themselves. Abandoning all further hope of successful resistance to the conquerors, Solyman hastily evacuated his kingdom, and the wreck of his army, every where ravaging the land in his flight; and the crusaders were left without opposition to continue their advance through a desolated and deserted country. Their march over the wasted plains of Asia Minor skirted the base of the great mountain range which stretches across that celebrated region from the sea of Marmora to the Syrian gates; and their route may be traced on the modern map by the cities of Kara Hissar, Aksheer, Konich, and Ereckli.

The horrors which attended the passage of so unwieldy a host, undisciplined and unprovisioned by any of the arrangements which are familiar to the military science and economy of our own times, admit but of imperfect description, and may only faintly be imagined. The towns had been swept of their inhabitants and stores, the cultivated districts converted into a scathed and hungry solitude; and the more natural deserts which frequently intervened were parched with sand and destitute of water. Of the poorer and worse provided among the crusaders, hundreds died on every day's march, of want and fatigue, of raging thirst or its fatal gratification; war-horses, baggage-animals, and hounds and hawks—the indispensable incumbrances of a chivalric camp—perished alike from a scarcity of water; and of the splendid cavalry of the princes, nobles, and their followers, which on the field of Nice

Kara Hissar, in Asia Minor.

had mustered one hundred thousand lances, nearly thirty thousand were dismounted before their arrival under the walls of Antioch. In a word, so completely exhausted and disorganized was the whole host before its approach to the Syrian frontiers that, in the tremendous pass of Mount Taurus,.even a small band of resolute men might have successfully maintained the steep and narrow defile against the armed but feebled multitudes who, staggering under the oppression of toil, heat, and intolerable thirst, slowly wound in a lengthened and disorderly train through the mountain chain which here bars the southern route. But the panicstricken Turks, in the precipitation of their flight, neglected the opportunity of defence; the crusading host was suffered, unassailed, to complete the most toilsome and dangerous portion of their march; and every natural obstacle of the country and the climate being gradually surmounted, their straggling divisions were safely reunited in the same encampment on the Syrian soil.*

While the main army of the crusaders prepared to penetrate through the Tauridian pass, two bodies of their cavalry had been separately detached in advance under Tancred, and Baldwin, the brother of Duke Godfrey, to explore the neighbouring regions, and make a diversion against the Turkish power. After both had wandered in some uncertainty among the mountains, the division of Tancred first succeeded in effecting a passage, and continued its southern descent into the coasts of Cilicia. The young chieftains had already arrived before Tarsus, and granted a capitulation to the Turkish garrison, when the troops of Baldwin, who had reached the same vicinity by another route, unexpectedly made their appearance; and the jealous artifice of their leader succeeded, by opening an intrigue with the infidel and Christian inhabitants, in obtaining possession of the city. The generous Italian, repressing his indignation, abandoned the place to his rival; and, turning eastward, pursued a new course of enterprise with so much rapidity, that several important towns submitted to his arms. But his forbearing temper was outraged beyond endurance when he learned that, after his departure from Tarsus, the selfish refusal of Baldwin to receive a party of his followers within the protection of the walls, had exposed them to be massacred by the retreating infidels; and the Rhenish chieftain, leaving a garrison in Tarsus, no sooner came up with his division than Tancred, yielding to the natural impulse of resentment which he shared with his enraged soldiers, led them to a furious assault upon the forces of their treacherous confederate. After a bloody encounter, the Italians were repulsed by a superiority of numbers; but feelings of mutual compunction at so irreligious a fued between brethren of the cross having succeeded to their first emotions of anger, an accommodation was effected; and the two detachments together rejoined the grand army before it reached the Syrian frontier.*

This quarrel of Baldwin and Tancred had one important consequence. The guilt of the original aggression lay so clearly with the former, that, when the circumstances of his conduct became known in the crusading camp, he justly incurred the execrations of the whole host; and respect for the virtues of his brother Godfrey alone saved him from condign punishment. A consciousness of the aversion in which he was held by his confederates, did not tend to lessen his selfish disregard for the general interests of the Crusade; and he gladly availed himself of the first advantageous opening to separate from the main army, and pursue an independent career of ambition. He learned that the Christian cities of Armenia and Mesopotamia endured with impatience the Mussulman yoke; that the Turkish garrisons were few and feeble; and that the inhabitants were ripe for revolt against their oppression. At the instance of a fugitive Armenian noble, and at the head of only two hundred of his own lances, and a more considerable body of infantry, he quitted the crusading camp, boldly directed his march eastward, and victoriously overran the whole country as far as the Euphrates. Encouraged by the sight of the banners of the cross, the Christian population everywhere rose in arms, opened the gates

---

* Albert. Aquensis, p. 214–219. Radulphus Cadomensis, p. 297-801. Willermus Tyr p. 677–680.

of their cities on his approach, and assisted him in expelling the common infidel enemy. After a slight and ineffectual opposition, the Turkish Emirs either fled or submitted to his arms; the fame of his successful exploits soon spread beyond the Euphrates; and the people of Edessa, the most considerable city of Mesopotamia, who, though still governed by a native prince, had long groaned under the exactions of Turkish tribute, obliged their aged duke to implore his aid in delivering them from the infidels. Baldwin eagerly accepted the invitation; he was received with enthusiasm by the Edessenes; and, though his disposable Latin forces were now reduced to eighty horse and a small band of foot, he was so vigorously aided by these new allies, that he found no difficulty in establishing the independence of their state. The means by which he next possessed himself of its government are variously related; but, under their most favourable construction, the event may justify the darkest suspicions of his guilty ambition. Excited by the dread that their deliverer would forsake them, the people of Edessa first compelled their duke to adopt* him as his son and successor; and the old prince was then murdered in a popular insurrection.

---

* For the particulars of the singular ceremony by which this adoption was declared, we are indebted to the lively narrative of Guibert In full assembly of the people, Baldwin was first made to enter in a state of nudity under the same shirt with his new father, who then folded him to his breast and gave him the filial kiss. He was next

If Baldwin was really innocent of his death, he profited not the less by the catastrophe. He received the ducal crown on the following day; and thus became the founder of the first Latin principality in the East. Under his able and vigorous government, his new subjects soon discovered that they had chosen a severe and absolute master, as well as a formidable champion; but he at least completed their emancipation from the hated tyranny of the infidels; extended the limits of their state by his conquests from the Turks of the intermediate territory between their city and Antioch; and rendered the PRINCIPALITY OF EDESSA, by its position beyond the Euphrates, for above fifty years, one of the most important outworks of the Christian power in the East.*

---

wife of the Duke of Edessa. Guibert, p. 496. It is supposed that the Emperor Alexius, in honouring the homage of Godfrey with the filial relation, had also received him between the shirt and the skin. But see Du Cange, *Diss. sur Joinville*, xxii.

* Fulcherius Carnotensis, p. 389, 390. Albert Aquensis, p. 220-222. Guibert, p. 496, 497. Willermus Tyr. p. 682, 683.

ANTIOCH.

SECTION VIII.

SIEGE AND CAPTURE OF ANTIOCH BY THE CRUSADERS

WHILE Baldwin was engaged in establishing his power on the banks of the Euphrates, the main host of the Crusaders had advanced to Antioch, and undertaken the siege of that ancient capital of Syria. The city, which still presented the appearance of pristine grandeur, and contained a numerous Christian population, was possessed by Baghasian, a prince of Seljukian lineage; whose power was maintained by a Turkish garrison of about ten thousand horse, and twice as many infantry, and

whose courage and energy were worthy of his station. After some brave but ineffectual efforts to impede the approach of the invaders, he retired within the walls; and the iron gates of the bridge over the Orontes, which commanded the access to the city from the north, having been forced by the advanced guard of the crusaders under the Duke of Normandy, their whole host passed the river, and overspread the adjacent plain. At this epoch, Antioch, occupying an irregular site of precipice and valley, was embraced within a circumference of about four miles, by a strong wall, which, wherever the natural obstacles of the ground did not afford a sufficient defence, rose to the height of sixty feet. Part of the circuit was covered by the river and a morass which received the torrents from the neighbouring hills, and the remainder by a deep and wide ditch. The formidable aspect of these works at first dispirited the leaders of the Crusade; the lateness of the season—for the summer and autumn had been already consumed in the passage of Asia Minor—was unfavourable for the commencement of an arduous siege; and a proposal to defer the enterprise until the return of spring was only rejected in their council through the energetic remonstrances of the Count of Thoulouse against the dangers of delay and inaction.*

---

* Albert, p. 225, 226. Radulph. Cad. p. 808. Raymond des Agiles, p. 142. Baldric. Arch. p. 101. Guibert, p. 498. Willer-

As soon as the exhortations of that prince renovated the ardour of his confederates, the city was invested, and operations against it were commenced: but, of the five gates in its circumference, three only were blockaded; and by some unexplained negligence or necessity, the communication of the garrison with the exterior country through the other two was left open. From these the resolute and active Baghasian harassed the rear of the besiegers with perpetual sallies, frequently cut off their supplies, and burned the materials which were with difficulty collected for their operations. The want of all warlike stores for the siege, the consequent tardiness of the approaches, and the unskilful attempts to which the crusaders were reduced, all betray the extent of their obligations at the preceding siege of Nice to the aid of Alexius and his Greek engines and artificers. Their few battering and projectile machines were now used without effect; and the single movable tower, which they were enabled to construct with assistance from some Italian vessels lately arrived on the coast, was no sooner advanced to the walls, than the Turks, suddenly issuing from one of the uninvested gates, set it on fire and reduced it to ashes. While this and other partial successes raised the courage of the garrison, and their intercourse with the country secured the constant renewal of their supplies, the besiegers themselves were beginning to suffer the most grievous distresses from want and disease. At first they had found abundant food in the fertile district which was commanded by their camp; and their whole host had rioted in plenty: but the improvident waste and wanton destruction, both of provisions and forage, speedily exhausted the means of support in the vicinity; and when the approach of winter increased the difficulty and expense of transporting distant supplies, the more indigent of the crusading multitude fell a prey to all the horrors of famine. Even the rich were glad to purchase the most disgusting fare at exorbitant prices; and their horses were either starved or killed for food in so great numbers, that of the seventy thousand cavalry with which they commenced the siege, before its third month was completed not more than two thousand remained. The ravages of hunger were, as usual, followed by those of pestilence. The plain of Antioch was deluged with the wintry rains; and the putrifying effect of moisture in an Asiatic climate upon the filthy condition of the Christian camp, produced a contagious disease, which swept off thousands of its squalid population.*

From this scene of accumulated misery, numbers of warriors of inferior rank fled to the establishments of Baldwin in Mesopotamia, and to the delivered

---

* Robertus Monachus, p. 45, 46. Albert. p. 227-233. Radulph Cad. p. 304, 305. Raymond des Agiles, p. 143-145 Baldric.

Christian towns in Cilicia; but the shame of their desertion was exceeded by that of some of the leaders themselves. The Duke of Normandy having withdrawn to the coast, required several citations and a threat of excommunication to induce his return; and the Count of Chartres, at a later period, under the excuse of illness, confirmed the suspicion of his cowardice by retiring from the camp with his division to Alexandretta. But the sacred cause was still more deeply disgraced by the flight of the valiant Viscount of Melun;* together with the great fanatic Peter the Hermit, who, after exciting the warriors of Europe to devote themselves to the imaginary service of Heaven, was foremost in attempting to abscond from the privations of the enterprise. The dangerous effect of this example was prevented by the activity of Tancred, who intercepted the escape both of the Hermit and his companion; and their desertion was only pardoned in the council of the indignant princes, upon their swearing never to abandon the holy expedition. The retreat of Taticius, the imperial lieutenant, with the small body of Greek auxiliaries which he commanded, was permitted with mingled emotions of hope and contempt. He could scarcely obtain full credit for the assertion that his motive

---

* This worthy was surnamed the Carpenter; not because he followed that mechanical occupation; but, as the chroniclers are careful to tell us, by reason of the weighty strokes with which his battle-axe *hammered* the heads of his antagonists. Robert. p. 47.

was to impress Alexius, by his personal influence, with the necessity of forwarding immediate supplies of provisions for the Syrian war, though he offered the pledge of his oath that he would himself return with the convoys; but if the princes were not deluded by this shallow pretext, they prudently dissembled their suspicions, and dismissed him in peace.*

With the return of spring the sufferings of the crusaders were in some degree mitigated by the arrival on the coast of supplies from Europe; but the activity of the Turks in harassing their convoys was undiminished; and the continued freedom of intercourse between the garrison of Antioch and their Syrian confederates, perpetually exposed the besiegers to desultory attacks in front and rear. On one occasion, early in February, an army of twenty thousand men, under the three emirs of Aleppo, Cæsarea, and Ems, was intercepted in an attempt to enter the city, and defeated with signal slaughter by Count Raymond and Boemond. But, in the following month, the same crusading leaders, while escorting a

---

* Robert. p. 47, 48. Raymond, p. 146. Baldric. p. 103 Guibert, p. 501, 502. Willermus Tyr. p. 694. Anna Comnena, p. 252. The Grecian princess, indeed, refers the flight of Taticius to the arts of Boemond, who fearing interruption on the part of the imperial lieutenant in his scheme for acquiring the sovereignty of Antioch, terrified him into a belief that the Latin princes designed to massacre him and his troops on some suspicion that Alexius had betrayed them to the Turks. But all the Latin writers agree in

supply of provisions and military stores from the coast, were suddenly assailed and routed by an ambuscade of the infidels. Godfrey, who had lately risen from a sick couch, was compelled to fly to their succour with the remains of the Latin chivalry; and the ever-enterprising Baghasian, seizing the occasion of this absence of the best troops of the crusaders from the beleaguer, made an impetuous sally from the walls, and forced the Christian lines. The bravery and conduct of the Duke of Brabant were never more vigorously displayed than on this occasion. He retraced his march to the camp with so great celerity, and posted his forces with so much ability, as to intercept the retreat of Baghasian; and a furious conflict ensued under the walls of Antioch. The infidels fought with desperation, but their courage was unequally opposed to the heroic spirit and sinewy force of the Christian knighthood, animated by the individual prowess of its leaders; among whom the two dukes, Godfrey, and Robert of Normandy, and the gallant Tancred, are recorded to have performed the most incredible feats of corporeal strength and valour.*

---

* Thus, we are gravely informed how Godfrey, with a single blow of his falchion, clave a Turk in twain from shoulder to hip. The upper half of the miscreant fell into the Orontes; the legs kept their seat, and were borne by their good steed into the city. Nor was this the only feat of the hero. At one stroke of his sword, he slit an infidel down from the top of the head to the saddle, and even cut through both that and the back-bone of the horse. Again, after the

CAPTURE OF ANTIOCH.

Of the infidels, a son of Baghasian, many other emirs, and two thousand warriors of inferior degree, fell in this sanguinary flight; of the Christians, not more than half that number were slain; and encouraged by their victory, they formed and successfully accomplished the design of barring the egress of the garrison from the two gates which had hitherto been left unblockaded, by the construction of a fortified mound or intrenchment opposite to each. Tancred and the Count of Thoulouse severally undertook the honourable duty of guarding the new posts; the garrison of Antioch was thenceforth effectually confined within the walls; the supplies of provisions which their brethren had hitherto introduced by these gates were cut off and diverted to the refreshment of the Latins; and the whole surrounding country being

---

who had heard of his prowess, by sweeping of the head of a camel with his sword in a trice. The unbeliever still ascribing more virtue to the temper of the blade than to the strength of the arm which wielded it, Godfrey to convince him, borrowed his own weapon, and with that, in like manner, decapitated a second camel. These stories are not related by some one obscure fabler only, but are avouched, the first two with minute particularity, by the monk Robert, (p. 50,) and by Ralph of Caen, (p. 404;) and all confirmed by so dignified an authority as the Archbishop of Tyre, (p. 701, 770.) And Malmsbury, who made a careful collection of the feats of Godfrey, adds to the number (p. 448) the slaying of a lion in single combat near Antioch. The chroniclers are eager in ascribing to Godfrey as great a superiority in bodily strength as in intellectual virtues over the other chieftains of the war. But of some of these leaders, exploits scarcely less astounding are recorded. The Duke

now in unmolested possession of the besiegers, abundance again reigned in their camp.*

Still, little or no impression had been made upon the defences of the city; seven months had already been ineffectually consumed in the siege; and the council of princes was disturbed by intelligence that the Sultan of Persia was collecting a large army for the relief of the garrison. At this dangerous crisis, the alliance of an apostate and a traitor served the cause of the crusaders more beneficially than their arms. Among the Christian population of Antioch, was a man of noble birth, but unprincipled and sordid character, named Phirouz, who, abjuring his religion, had been received into the Turkish ranks, and intrusted with the command of three towers. Stimulated by avarice or disaffection from the service which he had embraced, he opened a secret correspondence with Boemond; and consented, on the promise of a large reward, to betray his post to the besiegers. The Norman made the use of this opening, which was to be expected from his selfish and intriguing spirit. He declared to the council of his compeers his possession of a plan for the surprise of the place; but, before he would reveal its nature, claimed the principality of Antioch for

---

Turk at a blow; and Ralph of Caen was prevented from detailing the stupendous deeds of Tancred only by the silence which the modesty of that hero had imposed on his esquire.

*Robert. p. 49–53. Raymond, p. 147. Baldric. 104–107. Albert. p. 237–243. Guibert, p. 503–506. Willermus Tyr. p 695–703.

himself as the just recompense of his successful merit. The ungenerous preference of his own interest to the common cause of the Crusade, which was apparent through this reservation, disgusted those among his confederates who were actuated by loftier motives of conduct;* but it especially excited less dignified and splenetic feelings in the breast of the Count of Thoulouse, who entertained views similar to his own, and regarded his pretensions with the hatred of a rival. His stipulation was, therefore, at first indignantly rejected; but the increasing urgency of the danger with which the army was menaced by the approach of the

---

* Even the good Godfrey himself, usually so ready to sacrifice his own interests and feelings to the advancement of the sacred cause, could not escape a collision with the selfish meanness of Boemond; nor was his own magnanimity always proof against the sense of a petty injury. This is amusingly shown in a story related by Albert of Aix, (p. 242.) A superb Turkish pavilion, which the Prince of Edessa had captured and sent as a present to his brother Godfrey, was intercepted by an Armenian chieftain, and despatched as his own gift to Boemond. Godfrey, accompanied by his friend, the Count of Flanders, paid an angry visit to the quarters of Boemond to demand the restitution of the tent. The covetous Norman refused compliance; and Godfrey complained to the council of princes. Boemond was at last compelled to deliver up the disputed property; but not before, as Mr. Mills has pithily observed, (*Hist. of the Crusades*, vol. i. 189,) a "piece of silk excited the passions of thousands of men who had despised all worldly regards, and had left Europe in order to die in Asia." The whole scene may recall to the reader's mind some of the squabbles of the Homeric heroes; but the impatience of Godfrey in endangering the harmony of the camp for so frivolous a cause, is at variance with the dignified forbearance of his general conduct.

Turkish succours, and the necessity of either acquiring possession of the city or of suspending the siege before their arrival, prevailed over the reluctance of the council to comply with the extortionate demand. The Count of Thoulouse was compelled by his brother chieftains to stifle his jealousy and abandon his opposition; and Boemond received the solemn pledge of all the princes that, if Antioch were gained by his means, he should be invested with its sovereignty.*

Upon this promise, the crafty Norman disclosed his project, and prepared its accomplishment. In the dead of night, he led his own troops to the base of the towers, where Phirouz held his watch; by the traitor and some associates of his plot, rope-ladders were lowered; and the future Prince of Antioch, to encourage his wavering followers, was himself the first man who ascended the walls. The escalade was effected in safety; the Turkish guards of several neighbouring towers were slain before they could give the alarm; and the gates of the city were opened to the whole crusading host. A horrid and indiscriminate slaughter of the infidel garrison and the Christian inhabitants ensued; until the crusaders had exhausted the first burst of savage fury, roused by the remembrance of their own sufferings in the siege, and the obstinacy

---

* Robert. p. 54. Albert. p. 241. Radulph. p. 308, 309. Baldric. p. 108, 109 Guibert, p. 509, 510. Willermus Tyr. p. 704–707.

of the lengthened defence. [3d of June, 1098.] The remains of the Christian population were then protected from further outrage; but the massacre of the Turks was still pursued with relentless vengeance; and the fugitives who escaped beyond the walls were immediately intercepted and slaughtered by the Latin detachments and Syrian Christians who held the surrounding plains. Such was the fate of the gallant veteran Baghasian himself; but numbers of the garrison effected their retreat into the citadel; and, closing its gates before the victors bethought themselves of completing their success, the refugees there desperately maintained a protracted resistance.*

---

* Robert. p. 55. Albert. p. 245–247. Radulph. p. 308, 309 Baldric. 109–112. Guibert, p. 511. Willermus Tyr. p. 708–712.

SECTION IX.

DEFENCE OF ANTIOCH BY THE CRUSADERS.

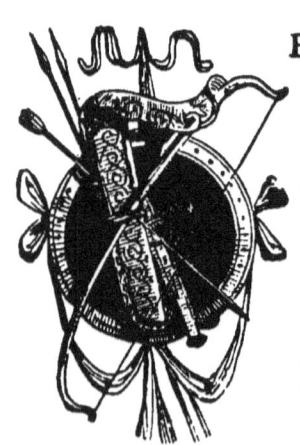

HE divided state of the Mohammedan world had hitherto favoured the progress of the Crusade. The dismemberment of the dominions of Malek Shah had fatally weakened the general power of the Turkish Empire. The monarchs of Persia remained the nominal chiefs of the Seljukian race; but the Sultan of Roum had been unassisted in his struggle to arrest the invasion of the Latins by any succour from that kindred dynasty; the numerous emirs of

among themselves, and agreed only in the effort to throw off their dependence on the court of Ispahan; and the Fatimite or Ommiadan princes of Egypt were the natural enemies of the whole Turkish nation, as the disciples, protectors, and tyrants of their fallen rivals, the Abassidan Khalifs of Bagdad. Before the arrival of the crusaders in Asia, the Khalif of Egypt, availing himself of the distractions of the Seljukian Empire to recover the ancient possessions of his house, had already despatched an army into Palestine, and succeeded in wresting Jerusalem itself and other places from their Turkish conquerors.* When, therefore, the strange rumour reached Cairo of the Christian invasion of Asia, the overthrow of the Sultan of Roum, and the advance of the crusading myriads into Syria, the khalif endeavoured, by sending an embassy to their camp before Antioch, to discover their further designs, to ascertain their force, and, perhaps, to cultivate their alliance against a common enemy. It is not improbable that the news of their previous successes, as tending to precipitate the fall of the Turkish power, was grateful to the Egyptian Prince; and he is said, by one authority, to have encouraged their prosecution of the siege of Antioch, and even to have offered his co-operation. His envoys also expressed his readiness to admit the Christian pilgrims to worship in peace at Jerusalem; but this proposal was haughtily rejected by the leaders of the Crusade, who replied that the Holy Sepulchre was the lawful heritage of Christendom alone, and declared their resolution, by the divine aid, to recover and preserve it from further profanation by infidels of whatever race. So bold and unreserved an avowal of their hostile purpose was not calculated to secure the friendship or to allay the jealousy of the khalif. The negotiations which he had opened were not, indeed, broken off, and he accepted an embassy from the crusaders; but his conduct in the vicissitudes of the siege alternately betrayed his enmity and his fears. When he heard of the destruction with which the besiegers were threatened by famine and pestilence, he imprisoned their envoys: when their princes despatched the heads of the slaughtered Turkish emirs to Cairo as the trophies of victory, he released the ambassadors and loaded them with presents for the principal leaders of the Crusade.*

The report of the danger of Antioch was received with other emotions by the Sultan of Persia; and the alarming progress of the Christian arms had the effect of exciting the Turkish states into a transient union against the invaders. From the banks of the Euphrates and the Tigris, twenty-eight powerful emirs with their swarms of cavalry obeyed the summons of the sultan to range themselves under the standard

---

* Robert. p. 49–52   Albert. p. 236-237.   Raymond. p. 146. Willermus Tyr. p. 696.

of their prophet, and to avenge the cause of their faith and nation. The supreme command was assigned to Kerboga, Prince of Mosul on the Tigris, as the lieutenant of the Persian monarch; he was joined by Kilidge Arslan, the Sultan of Roum, with the remains of his forces; and the whole host, which some of the Latin writers are contented to describe as innumerable,* is estimated by others at two, three, or even four hundred thousand cavalry.† The first operations of this overwhelming multitude were directed against the new Christian Principality beyond the Euphrates; but the undaunted heroism with which Baldwin defended his capital, delayed their advance until the fall of Antioch; and the startling intelligence of that disastrous event roused Kerboga to break up from the unsuccessful siege of Edessa, and hasten his march to the relief of the Syrian citadel.‡

On the approach of his host toward Antioch, the leaders of the Crusade withdrew their diminished forces within the defences of the city; and the Turkish cavalry, filling all the surrounding plains, reinforced the garrison of the citadel, enclosed the Latins in their position, and cut off all their communications with the sea-coast and exterior country.

---

* Robert. p. 56. Fulcher. p. 392. Guibert, p. 512. Willermus Tyr. p. 714.

† Albert. p. 242, and Radulphus, p. 319, give the lowest and highest estimate in the text.

By these measures, the crusaders, now besieged in their turn, were immediately subjected to a second and far more grievous famine than that which they had endured in the preceding winter. A repetition of the same narrative of distress, with many aggravated horrors, would be equally revolting and profitless; and the reader will gladly be spared the shocking and loathsome details of misery which reduced a famishing host to satiate the cravings of hunger with leaves and weeds, with the hides of animals, and the old leather of belts and harness, to devour greedily the vilest offal of slaughter-houses and sewers, and even to prey upon human flesh. For five and twenty days, the ravening and perishing multitudes suffered every frightful extremity of want which language may paint, or imagination conceive; the princely, the noble, and the fair were exposed to privations only less horrid in their intensity than those of the inferior herd of soldiery and camp followers; and the whole host was stricken with one universal sentiment of weakness and despondency. Desertions again became numerous; and the fugitives, who, letting themselves down by ropes at night from the walls, were fortunate enough to escape the cimeters of the Turks, spread their dismal tale of the impending ruin of the crusading cause throughout the few Christian establishments on the sea-coasts and in the interior, in which they could find refuge. Among these apostates to their vows were many persons of distinction, including that Lord of Melun, William the Carpenter, who had lately so publicly renewed his devotional oaths; and the numerous companions of his shame are consigned to indignant oblivion by one historian, only under the conviction that their unworthy names were eternally blotted from the Book of Life.*

The conduct of the fugitives was, indeed, calculated to extinguish the faint gleam of hope which the crusaders might have felt in the knowledge that the Byzantine emperor was now on his march with a large army through Asia Minor to support their operations, and claim the paramount sovereignty of their conquests. The pusillanimous Count of Chartres, who had hitherto lingered at Alexandretta, was so terrified by the wretched aspect and more deplorable report of the deserters who had reached his quarters, that he immediately continued his retreat; and meeting Alexius in Phrygia, communicated the panic to that monarch. Though the emperor had been joined, in addition to his own forces, by numerous squadrons of fresh crusaders from Europe, who were still eager to advance to the relief of their confederates at Antioch, the suggestions of his selfish policy, or the baser influence of fear, made him resolve not to risk his resources or the safety of his person for the deliver-

---

* Robert. p. 57–59.   Albert. p. 248–251.   Raymond, p. 153. Baldric. p. 113–117.   Guibert, p. 512–517.   Willermus Tyr. p. 714–717.

ance of his Latin allies; and, abandoning them to their fate, in despite of the remonstrances and reproaches of their countrymen in his camp, he enforced a general retreat upon Constantinople.* The evil tidings of his retrograde movement were not slow in reaching the crusaders at Antioch; and the first burst of fury at his treacherous or cowardly desertion of his engagements was succeeded by a general apathy of hopeless resignation or sullen despair. Neither the dread of the enemy, nor the threat of punishment, could rouse the soldiery to the requisite exertions for the common defence; they shut themselves up in gloomy expectation of death; and in one quarter of Antioch it was necessary to fire the houses over their heads before they could be driven out to man the ramparts.†

Amid this prostration of mental and corporeal energies, which levelled the proud distinctions of spirit between the gallant chivalry and the meaner multitude of the crusading host, the names of five only of the leaders of the war deserved the honourable record of its chroniclers, by their unshaken constancy and courage: Godfrey of Bouillon, Raymond of Thoulouse, the Papal Legate Adhemar of Puy, Boemond and Tancred. The fortitude of Godfrey was sustained by the purest strength of a religious

---

*Robert. p. 60. Albert. p. 253. Baldric. p. 119 Anna Comnena, p. 255–257. Willermus Tyr. p. 718–720.
†Albert. p. 253. Guibert, p. 517. Willermus Tyr. p. 720.

mind; that of the count and bishop might be inspired by the fiercer confidence of fanatical zeal; the vaulting ambition and cupidity of Boemond were inextinguishable save with life; and in the generous soul of Tancred, the love of glory still shone through the darkest adversity with a steady and unfading light. But the example, the exhortations, and the valorous resolves of these master-spirits of their cause, would have proved alike ineffectual to reanimate the hopes and efforts of their desponding confederates and followers, if they had not invoked the all-powerful aid of superstition. When every prospect of earthly succour had vanished, it required the belief of a special interposition of Heaven in their behalf to rekindle the expiring fanaticism of the multitude; and the character of the Count of Thoulouse, as well as his share in promoting the popular delusion, may indifferently justify the presumption that he was the original mover, or the willing dupe of a pretended revelation.

In the Provençal division of the crusaders, was a priest of Marseilles, Peter Barthelemy by name, who, presenting himself before the council of princes, declared how St. Andrew had shown him in a vision, that the steel head of the very lance which had pierced the side of the crucified Redeemer might be found buried beneath the high altar in the Church of St. Peter at Antioch; that the Count of Thoulouse

infidel enemy; and that its mystic presence in the battle should penetrate the hearts of the unbelievers, and insure a complete victory to the people of God. The minds of the crusaders had been prepared for the reception of this tale, and, perhaps, the expedient itself had been suggested by rumours of several previous apparitions of the saints both to clerical and lay individuals in the army, all leading to the expectation that some visible act of Almighty favour for their deliverance was at hand. If the Count of Thoulouse was not privy to the original imposture, he, at least, eagerly lent his countenance to its success; the policy or conviction of the other chiefs gladly accepted the tale; and Raymond himself, with his chaplain and ten select companions, were appointed to search for the sacred relic. Two days of solemn preparation were spent by the whole army in religious exercises; and early on the third the princes, attended by the clergy and lay multitude, went in procession to the Church of St. Peter. The doors were closed against the impatient crowd; and relays of workmen dug until nightfall to the depth of twelve feet under the high altar, without discovering the promised instrument of victory. But, as soon as the increasing darkness favoured the deception, Peter Barthelemy himself descended into the pit, and, after a plausible delay, exclaimed that he had found the precious object of their search. The steel head of a lance was ther brought up from the excavation, and reverently dis played in a web of cloth of gold to the enraptured gaze of the multitude. All previous incredulity was drowned in a general burst of superstitious enthusiasm ; and the devout and firm assurance of approaching victory succeeded with wonderful rapidity to the abject despair with which the starving host had previously been overwhelmed.*

The first measure by which the leaders of the Crusade showed the sincerity of their renovated hopes, affords a curious picture of fanatical confidence. It was charitably resolved to offer the infidels one opportunity of escape from the destruction to which they were otherwise doomed, in the alternative of withdrawing altogether from the sacred land of Syria, or declaring their conversion to the Christian faith. The ambassador selected to convey these proposals to the camp of Kerboga was Peter the Hermit; and the astonishment, rage, and contempt which their nature provoked, were, if possible, increased by the arrogant deportment and language of the fanatic. The ebullition of furious indignation which prompted the reply of the Emir will excite less of our surprise than the forbearance which enabled a Turkish barbarian to respect the character of an ambassador, and to dismiss in safety the bearer of a message so insulting to his pride and faith. The defiance of the Christians was

---

* Robert. p. 60–62. Albert. p. 253, 254. Raymond, p. 150. 151. Radulphus, p. 316, 317. Baldric. p. 119. Fulcher. p. 391-393 Guibert. p. 517–520. Willermus Tyr. p. 721.

hurled back upon them; and the Hermit was fiercely admonished that there remained for them the choice only between submission to the law of Mohammed, or servitude and death.*

On this reply, the crusaders entertained no further doubt that the vengeance of Heaven had delivered the whole obstinate host of the infidels into their hands. But the Latin chieftains, with that admixture of politic wisdom which generally tempered their fanaticism, spared no exertion to excite the religious ardour, and refresh the physical strength of their followers for the approaching combat. The horses of their cavalry, now reduced from seventy thousand to no more than two hundred in number, were carefully fed on the last remains of their provender; the leaders and soldiery freely shared with each other their last meal; their rusted arms were whetted anew with grim desperation; and the whole army betook themselves to prayer, made confession of their sins, and received the absolution of the sacrament. Thus nerved in body and mind, the host was arrayed, in honour of the apostolic number, in twelve divisions; the dawn of the festival of St. Peter and St. Paul was chosen for the reopening of the gates of Antioch; and, preceded by a body of the clergy chanting a psalm, the army issued from the city and formed in order of battle on the plain.

Adhemar, the Bishop of Puy, headed the fourth division, the most honourable, because it carried the holy lance. He walked at its head, clothed in the robes of a pontiff, and surrounded by the symbols of religion and war. The venerable prelate, pausing before the bridge of the Orontes, addressed a pathetic discourse to the soldiers of the cross, blessing them, and promised the succour and recompense of Heaven. All the army shouted their approbation and assent.

It is singular that the Count of Thoulouse, the destined bearer of the holy lance, was left within the walls with a detachment of the Provençals to watch the citadel; but his place was supplied by the martial Legate who, in complete armour, bore aloft the sacred weapon at the head of one division; and accompanied its display to the eyes of the whole host with the thrilling exhortation to fight that day as became the chosen champions of Heaven. Of the other eleven divisions, one, the vanguard, was led by the Count of Vermandois, as bearer of the papal standard; nine respectively by Godfrey, the two Roberts, Tancred, and the other chieftains of renown; and the reserve was intrusted to Boemond.

The distress and consequent weakness of the Christians had been so well known in the Turkish camp, that Kerboga, notwithstanding their late haughty embassy, was lulled into a delusive security that their necessities must compel them to a speedy submission; and he was so little prepared for their assault, that the foremost corps of his army was cut to pieces before the main body could hasten to support it. But as soon as the Turks recovered from their consternation, they fell impetuously upon the advancing line of Christians; and the brave Sultan of Nice, wheeling round his flank, gained the rear of the reserve under Boemond, and began to inflict a bloody vengeance for the rout of Dorylæum. Thus enveloped in a cloud of Tartar cavalry, the extrication of the crusading army from imminent peril is, as usual, marvellously referred to the personal prowess of its chiefs; and eulogies of their valour supply the place of more intelligible details. In the confused pictures of the chroniclers, and perhaps in the disorderly tactics of the age, it is a hopeless attempt to follow the fluctuating tide of battle, or discern the real causes of victory. Yet, with every allowance for stupendous deeds of heroism in the Europeans, and enormous exaggeration in the reported numbers of the Asiatics, for the desperation of one army and the surprise of the other, the astonishing issue of the struggle can only be explained by the supposition of some gross misconduct or fatal dissension among the Moslem leaders. If we are to believe the narrative of their own chroniclers, two hundred Latin horsemen, supported by the unwieldy array of dismounted knights and men-at-arms, charged, routed, and put to flight the myriads of Turkish cavalry; the pursuit was as sanguinary as the combat had been obstinate; and the whole immense host, which had been permitted for twenty-five days to hold the crusaders besieged in famine and despair within the walls of Antioch, was suddenly destroyed or dissipated in a single morning. While the victory yet hung in suspense, the fanatical ardour of the crusaders was assisted by a new accident or stratagem. Several figures of horsemen in bright armour became visible on the adjacent hills; and the papal legate pointing them out as the holy martyrs St. George, St. Maurice, and St. Theodore, bade the army, with a loud voice, behold the promised succour of Heaven. Responsive shouts of "It is the will of God," burst from the crusading ranks; and the last triumphant charge was inspired by the imaginary presence and aid of these celestial champions.*

---

* Robert. p. 63–66. Albert. p. 254–258. Raymond, p. 154, 155. Baldric. p. 120–122. Fulcher. p. 393–395. Guibert, p. 520–523. Willermus Tyr. p. 723–726.

A belief in the reality of the apparition and aid of the three celestial warriors seems to have been universal among the crusaders. But their credulity with regard to the discovery of the holy lance was less general or lasting. The archbishops Baldric and William of Tyre, indeed, with several of the other chroniclers, betray no distrust of the genuineness both of the vision and the relic; but political jealousy overcame the superstition, and sharpened the intellect of some of the princes and their adherents; and while Raymond des Agiles, the chaplain of the Count of Thoulouse, is loud in maintaining the authenticity of a miracle of which his patron was the appointed instrument, Ralph of Caen, in the opposite interest of Tancred and Boemond, boldly exposes the fraud. Fulk of Chartres also evinces more than one suspicion of the imposture. The sequel of the history is curious

The defeat and dispersion of the host of Kerboga was immediately followed by the capitulation of the citadel of Antioch. By the recovered command of the surrounding territory, the crusaders were enabled for a time to relieve their wants with plentiful supplies of provisions; and the captured horses of the Turks served to remount the cavalry of the victors. The general joy was interrupted only by the obstinate ambition and quarrelsome temper of the Count of Thoulouse, who, still prosecuting his rivalry against the stipulated claims of Boemond to the sovereignty of Antioch, availed himself of the absence of that prince, and the duty with which he had been intrusted of watching the citadel, to hoist his own standard on the walls. He was again compelled by the other confederate chieftains to forego his pretensions; and Boemond was formally installed in his new principality: but the rankling jealousy of the Provençal continued not the less to disturb the harmony of the common cause, and to embarrass the ulterior operations

---

and his Provençals to perpetuate a delusion which conferred a sort of spiritual superiority upon the chosen guardians of the sacred lance, provoked the envious rivalry of Boemond and his friends to proclaim their disbelief. The example of their skepticism shook the faith of the whole army; and to maintain the truth of the revelation, Peter Barthelemy, as its original publisher, was rashly induced to appeal to the judgment of Heaven by the fiery ordeal. Two burning piles being prepared with a narrow path between them, the wretched impostor, or fanatic, rushed through the flames, and was so dreadfully burned on his passage that he expired on the next day.

of the Crusade. In the council of princes, discord, desertion, and the selfish pursuit of private interests, now succeeded to the unity of purpose, which was originally produced by devotional feelings, and had been supported by the pressure of imminent danger. The resentment which the crusaders cherished toward the Greek Emperor for his failure of succour in their hour of need, was vented in an embassy of remonstrance and reproach; and the great Count of Vermandois being selected for this mission, took advantage of the opportunity, on his arrival at Constantinople, to escape the further perils and privations of the Crusade by returning to France.* Baldwin and Boemond were wholly engrossed in securing the establishment and extension of their new states of Edessa and Antioch: the envious ambition of the Count of Thoulouse led him to imitate their example by undertaking the abortive conquest of some Syrian towns; the death of the papal legate, Adhemar, shortly deprived the crusading cause of one of its most popular and zealous supporters, and most skilful and politic counsellors; and even the pious Godfrey himself suffered his ardour for the deliverance of the Holy Sepulchre to be sus-

---

* It is a remarkable proof of the disgrace which, in the chivalric ideas of the age, attended such an abandonment of the crusading vow, that both the Counts of Vermandois and Chartres found in their high rank no exemption from contempt and obloquy; and to redeem their fame they were compelled to undertake a second expedition to Palestine, in which, as we shall hereafter observe, they were

pended by the temptation of gratifying his troops with the more accessible spoils of adjacent districts.*

The delays thus generated by disunion and diversity of objects among the leaders of the Crusade were not without some plausible pretexts: such as the necessity of reposing and refreshing the army after the fatigues and distresses of the siege at Antioch; the difficulty of advancing to Jerusalem through the intervening desert during the drought of a Syrian summer; and the prudence of consolidating the dominion which had already been won, that the arduous conquest of the Holy City itself might be the more surely effected. But the losses and calamities which flowed from division and inaction, far outweighed any attendant advantages. Numbers of the bravest knights and best soldiers were seduced from the general service of the Crusade by the prospect of a profitable establishment in the new Christian States; many gallant lives were consumed in the profitless or unsuccessful assaults of detached corps upon the Turkish garrisons; and the usual improvidence of the crusaders occasioned a third famine and consequent pestilence, the combined effects of which were so terrific that no fewer than one hundred thousand persons are declared to have perished.*

---

*Albert. p. 260–263. Baldric. p. 122, 123. Fulcher. p. 394, 395. Guibert, p. 525. Willermus Tyr. p. 729-732.

† The practices to which the multitude were driven by hunger are almost too horrible for belief; yet the evidence afforded by chroniclers

The ravages of this plague were assisted by the previous excesses in which the whole host had indulged since the victory of Antioch; and in the pages of their chroniclers charges of universal intemperance and debauchery are intermingled with the dreadful picture of their distress. Nor can the feeling be condemned as an irrational superstition which ascribed the calamities of the crusaders to the anger of offended Heaven; for, of all the miseries which they endured throughout the war, the greater portion were only the faithful consequences of their crimes; and the union of fanaticism and profligacy in men who believed themselves the chosen champions of a sacred cause is among the most sacred objects of contemplation in the spirit of the times. At the outset of their enterprise, while the sense of pious duty was fresh and

---

stances, so unanimously attests the prevalence of cannibalism throughout the first Crusade, as to make it impossible to doubt the fact. This loathsome indulgence of hunger was sometimes associated with that of an avarice almost equally disgusting. We are told that the Turks on the eve of battle were used to swallow their money, and that the human savages into whose hands they fell often ripped open the bodies of the slain, or of murdered captives, to search for gold, and afterward devoured their flesh. The cannibalism of the Crusaders was not confined to one season of distress, but had become familiar to the rabble of the camp, and reached its height during the third famine of Antioch, when in their desultory attacks upon the Turkish garrisons, they regularly ate the dead bodies of the infidels, and even of their own slain companions. See Robert. p. 69, 70; Radulphus, p. 315. Baldric. p. 125, and Albert. p. 267, 268: the first three of whom record these brutalities with horror, and the last with indifference.

uncorrupted, the morals of the crusaders were comparatively pure; and, during the siege of Nice, the same authorities which are loudest in reprobating the subsequent disorders of the host, bear testimony to the prevalence of virtue and decorum in their camp. The leaders of the war, in general, presented an edifying spectacle of humility and fraternal concord; the obedient soldiery, emulating their example, were sober, chaste, and vigilant; and from the proudest chieftain to the lowest warrior, all shared alike with undistinguishable zeal and devotion in the labours, privations, watches, and perils of the siege. These sentiments of mutual charity and forbearance did not, indeed, extend to their common enemies; for their fanaticism was fierce and cruel; and mercy to the heathen was an article excluded from their mistaken creed. But among themselves they dwelt in Christian brotherhood, and their conduct was such as became warriors who had devoted their lives to the service of God, and patiently expected the crown of martyrdom which they as firmly believed would be the reward of the slain.* But both the license and the sufferings of the march through Asia Minor first tended to relax the bonds of this voluntary discipline; and the previous self-denial of all ranks degenerated, under the hardening effects of want and danger, into rapacious and selfish brutality. The transition from

---

* See particularly the two Archbishops, Baldric. p. 95; and Wil-

scarcity to luxurious abundance on the arrival of the army before Antioch; the enervating influence of the Syrian climate; the absence of any unity of command or disciplined restraints over a host composed of various and independent nations; and the temptations offered by a rich and fertile district to the riotous indulgence of every sensual passion; all assisted in producing a general corruption of morals. Among great masses of men, the alliance of misery and vice is proverbial; and the subsequent calamities of famine and pestilence gave a frightful completion to the public iniquity. In the hourly contemplation of death, and in the extremity of despair, the multitude, so far from being awed into virtue, became utterly deaf to the voice of religion and conscience; every divine and human law was disregarded and violated; the religious exhortations of the clergy,* and the authority of the princes, were equally despised; and the most licentious and enormous crimes were openly perpetrated. The only hold which their spiritual and temporal rulers could exercise over the minds of the multitude was through their gross and extravagant

---

* As long as ecclesiastical discipline was preserved by the authority of the Legate Adhemar, whose virtues are extolled by all the chroniclers, and whose death, in the third pestilence of Antioch, was lamented by the whole army, the clergy set an edifying example of

superstition; and if pretended revelation were successfully employed to animate the fanatical courage of the soldiery, or served to excite a transient ebullition of remorse,* denunciations of the heavenly wrath always failed to correct the public depravity, and truth and imposture were equally powerless in effecting any permanent reformation of manners in the crusading camp.†

---

* Among other things, a monk was assured in a vision that the anger of God was specially kindled against the crusaders, because Paynim women were the partners of their amours; and the fair infidels were accordingly for a time sent away from the camp. The good Adhemar went further on another occasion: he considered that he was procuring an acceptable sacrifice to Heaven by obliging the warriors to separate not only from the paramours, but from their wives; and all the women, virtuous as well as vicious, were confined in a remote quarter of the camp. Albert. p. 234. Willermus, Tyr. p. 695.

† The dissoluteness of the crusading army before Antioch would surpass belief were it not confirmed by unquestionable testimony. Gibbon has dwelt upon it in his own peculiar way, (xi. 68,) and has transferred to a foot-note an allusion to the "tragic and scandalous fate of an archdeacon of royal birth, who was slain by the Turks as he reposed in an orchard playing at dice with a Syrian concubine." The unfortunate ecclesiastic, who thus suffered himself to be seduced from his vow, and who paid with his life the penalty of his folly, was Alberon, Archdeacon of Metz, son of Conrad, Count of Lunenbourg, and a relation of the Emperor of Germany. The story is told by Albertus Aquensis, *i. e.* Albert of Aix, in Provence, a canon of the church, and who, though not a crusader himself, derived his information from trustworthy sources. He calls the fair partner of Alberon *matrona,*—whence we may infer that she was a married woman, and a person of condition. According to him, her fate was horrible See upon this subject generally, Mailly, *L'Esprit Des Croisades,* iv.

Amidst all the demoralization of the multitude, no decay of fanatical zeal in pursuing the great ultimate object of the war is justly chargeable upon them. They, indeed, were ever clamorous against the delays which the caution, the declining ardour, or the private views of their leaders, opposed to their impatience. After the first burst of enthusiasm had expended itself in the sieges of Nice and Antioch, the latter, with the exception, perhaps, of the single-minded Godfrey, the gallant and disinterested Tancred, and a few congenial spirits, evinced more desire to indulge their love of pleasure and rapine, their mutual enmities and personal ambition, than to complete the purpose of the Crusade. But the people discovered and regarded their selfishness with indignation and disgust; and the soldiery and pilgrims who had survived the third famine and pestilence of Antioch, were loud in their demands to be led without further loss of time to the conquest of Jerusalem. The popular discontent at the continued procrastination of the enterprise was shortly displayed in a temper which it was no longer safe to provoke. The ramparts of the city of Marra, which, together with the Albara on the Orontes, the Count of Thoulouse had captured and intended to retain, were razed to the ground by his own troops, that the place might not, like the possession of Antioch itself, be rendered an object of contention to the chiefs, and of delay to the army. Raymond, finding his prize untenable, was compelled to yield to the wishes of his

152   THE FIRST CRUSADE.

Provençal followers, and declared his readiness to lead them to the deliverance of the Holy Sepulchre; the same tardy resolution was embraced by the other princes; and not until eight months had expired since the final reduction of Antioch, were the crusading forces once more concentrated, and put in combined motion toward Jerusalem.*

---

* Robert. Mon. p. 69, 70.   Albert. p. 267, 268.   Raymond des Agiles, p. 160–164.   Baldric. p. 125, 126.   Guibert. p. 525–527   Willermus Tyr. p. 731–736.

CAPTURE OF JERUSALEM. 153

Jerusalem.

SECTION X.

SIEGE AND CAPTURE OF JERUSALEM BY THE CRUSADERS.

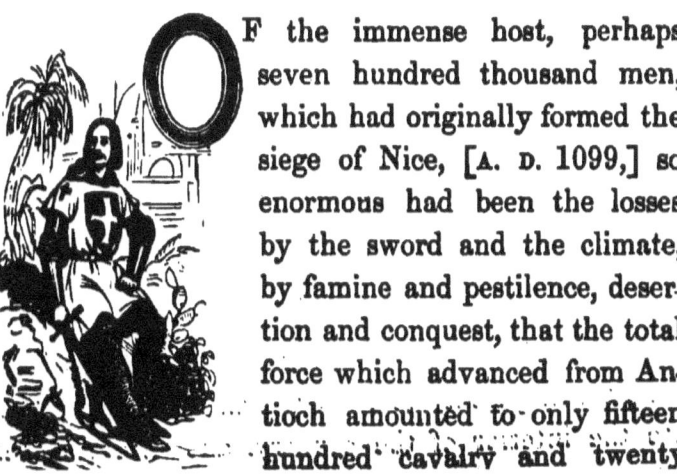

F the immense host, perhaps seven hundred thousand men, which had originally formed the siege of Nice, [A. D. 1099,] so enormous had been the losses by the sword and the climate, by famine and pestilence, desertion and conquest, that the total force which advanced from Antioch amounted to only fifteen hundred cavalry and twenty thousand foot soldiers, with about an equal number of unarmed pilgrims and camp followers. But this remnant of the myriads who had assumed the cross was composed of veteran and devoted warriors, and led by those renowned chieftains and champions of the sacred war, whose zeal and constancy had triumphantly surmounted the fiery trials of peril and temptation: Godfrey of Bouillon, the two Roberts of Normandy and of Flanders, Raymond of Thoulouse, and Tancred. Boemond, pleading the cares of his new principality, did not accompany their march far beyond its confines; but he freely rendered his contributions and support to the success of the common cause; and his confederates, whatever contempt and indignation they might feel at this personal abandonment of his vows, received his excuses and accepted his aid. From Antioch to Jaffa, a distance of about three hundred miles, the crusaders, for the convenience of supplying their wants from the Italian vessels which traded on the coast, chose their route along the seashore. Their advance was easy and unopposed; for the Turkish Emirs of Gabala, Tortosa, Tripoli, Beritus, Tyre, Sidon, Acre, and other intervening places, despairing of successful resistance, either fled from their strongholds, or, deprecating assault, by submission purchased the forbearance of the invaders with large contributions of money and provisions. At Jaffa, turning from the coast, the exulting host struck

march upon Jerusalem itself. With devout and awful curiosity, the rude warriors of Europe now traversed a region filled with places which hourly recalled some sacred association; the clergy successively directed the religious attention of their more ignorant brethren to the memorable scenes of Ramula, Bethlehem, and Emmaus; and at length the holy city burst upon their enraptured gaze. In that glorious sight, the long-cherished object, promise, and reward of their hopes, every toil was forgotten, every suffering repaid. The single mighty passion of a host suddenly broke forth in joyful exclamations and embraces; and these first gladsome emotions, which filled every heart with pious thanksgivings, were as quickly succeeded by feelings of deep humiliation and self-abasement. The proud noble, the fierce soldier, and the lowly pilgrim, confessed their common unworthiness even to look upon the scene which had witnessed the sufferings of the Redeemer of mankind; and the whole armed multitude, as with one impulse, sinking on their knees, prostrated themselves, and poured out their tears over the consecrated soil.*

But the deliverance of the Holy City and Sepulchre from infidel bondage and profanation still remained to be achieved. By the admixture of truth with imposture, the Mussulmans themselves had been

---

* Robert. p. 71. Albert. p. 269-274. Raymond des Agiles, p 165-173. Baldric. p. 127-131. Radulphus Cad. p. 317-319

taught to revere Jerusalem as inferior in sanctity only to Mecca and Medina;* and every motive of religion, honour, and policy, forbade the Khalif of Egypt to yield to the Christians that ancient possession which his arms had recently recovered from the Turks. Finding, therefore, his repeated offers of alliance and peaceful admission into Jerusalem as unarmed pilgrims contemptuously spurned by the haughty warriors of the West, he had prepared for the vigorous defence of the city. No less than forty thousand of the best troops of Egypt, under Istakar, his most distinguished and favourite lieutenant, were assigned for its regular garrison; and this force was swollen by twenty thousand Mussulman citizens and peasantry of the surrounding district, who, on the approach of the Christian invaders, took refuge within the walls. It was abundantly supplied with provisions; and its ancient fortifications, which increased the natural strength of the site, had been diligently restored or repaired. As Mount Sion was no longer embraced within their circuit, the city, including the hills of Acra, Moria, Bezetha, and Golgotha, presented the form of a parallelogram; but, on the southern and eastern faces, the craggy precipices equally defied assault and obstructed any sally; and

---

* D'Herbelot, *Bibliothèque Orientale* v. *Al Cods*, p. 269. A Cods, or the Holy, was the Arabic designation of Jerusalem.

Mount Sion.

the two remaining sides presented the only accessible points of operation.

Before these fronts the besiegers impatiently pitched their camp. The Count of Thoulouse chose his station from Mount Sion along the western side; Eustace of Boulogne extended his troops from the conclusion of the Provençal lines toward the north, until he adjoined the quarters of his brother. Duke Godfrey, whose standard was planted on the northwestern angle at the foot of Mount Calvary; and the two Roberts and Tancred continued the blockade from that point to the verge of the Eastern precipices. In the first confidence of their fanatical valour, the crusaders, fully expecting the miraculous aid of Heaven, rushed, on the fifth morning after the investment, to a furious assault of the walls of Jerusalem, without battering engines, without scaling ladders, without any of the ordinary applications of the besieging art. The astonishing impetuosity of their rash onset, despite of every probability and obstacle, had nearly delivered the city into their hands. Disregarding the superior numbers, the safe position, and the deadly missiles of the garrison, they burst through the barbican, or lower outward gate, and even penetrated to the foot of the main rampart. But here they were arrested, less by any efforts of the panic-stricken infidels, than by the mere inaccessible height of the bulwarks and the absence of all means of escalade. The Mussulmans, perceiving the inability of the assailants to approach them, recovered their courage; hurled down every destructive variety of projectiles on the heads of the exposed and devoted Christians; and finally beat them back with slaughter and confusion to their camp.

The leaders of the Crusade, awakened from their fanatical delusion by this repulse, now prepared to prosecute the siege by the rules of art. They resolved to construct the usual machines for breaching or overtowering the walls; but the immediate vicinity of Jerusalem afforded no timber sufficiently large for these works; and the surrounding country was ex-

plored for materials. It was only at the distance of
thirty miles that, in the grove of Sichem,* trees could
be found of suitable dimensions; and, under the direction of the indefatigable Tancred, these being felled
were transported by the painful but zealous labour of
the soldiery to the camp. Competent artificers were
yet wanting, when the fortunate arrival of some Genoese galleys at Jaffa supplied this deficiency. So
general a superiority in mechanical skill had the
commercial people of Italy attained over the ignorance of the times, that the whole Latin host were
dependent on the fortuitous services of these mariners.
The crews were landed at Jaffa; an escort of troops
was despatched to bring them up from the coast; and,
as soon as they reached the camp, they undertook the
construction of three great movable towers, with proper engines for throwing missiles, undermining the
ramparts, and battering or scaling the walls. The
army awaited the completion of their labours in anxious suspense; for now again were the sufferings of
their former sieges repeated under a new variety of
horror. The country round Jerusalem was destitute
of water; the rocky soil yielded few springs; the

---

* A city of Canaan, and subsequently of Samaria, and the burial
place of the patriarch Jacob, frequently mentioned in Scripture. It
was situated on Mount Ephraim, where afterward stood the Flavia
Neapolis of Herod, now the Nablous of the Arabs. It was one of
the cities of refuge appointed by Joshua, (xx. 7,) and was the
enchanted grove of the poet Tasso. (Gerusal. Liberata. canto xii.)

fountains and reservoirs had been destroyed by the infidels; and the streams of Siloe and Kedron were dried up by the intense heats of summer. The besiegers were agonized by thirst; a scanty supply of water could be procured only at a distance of several miles; and the poorer multitude, who could not pay for its transport in gold, were obliged to wander in quest of the springs, at the hazard of being cut off by the fleet Mussulman hordes which scoured the whole country. Numbers, by abstaining from food, endeavoured to lessen the intolerable thirst which consumed them; and so extreme was the distress, that many gasping wretches were fain to lick up the dews of night from the rocks, and to excavate holes in the earth that they might but press their lips against the moister soil.*

For forty days, amid this horrid drought, had the siege endured, before the readiness of their engines of assault enabled the crusaders to put a triumphant consummation to their labours. When the lofty movable towers, each of three stories, were completed, two, respectively manned and worked by the troops of Godfrey and Raymond, were slowly moved forward toward the walls. The former leader chose his point of attack where the rampart had least elevation, and the great depth of the ditch had rendered the garrison negligent of its defence. Three days were laboriously

---

* These expressive proofs of the height of the people's sufferings are given by Robert the Monk, p. 75.

Godfrey of Bouillon.

consumed in filling up this fosse; and the tower was then successfully rolled over the new level. Meanwhile the Provençals had been less skilful or fortunate; for their tower was repeatedly damaged by the besieged with projectiles and fire. But several approaches were prepared against different fronts of the main ramparts of the place with battering and mining engines; and the eager warriors only awaited the signal of final attack. On the eve of the day appointed for a general assault of the city, the whole host, in full armament, and preceded by the clergy, made a religious procession round the walls to invoke the divine aid. Instead of banners, crucifixes were borne aloft at the head of the troops; every instrument of martial music was hushed; and the only sounds to which the army moved were sacred chants of psalmody. Ascending the Mounts of Olives and of Zion, the crusaders halted on each of those holy places, and knelt in prayer; and when these solemn rites had elevated the devotional and warlike enthusiam of the soldiery to the highest pitch of excitement, the spectacle which was presented from the walls still further inflamed their fanatical feelings with a deadly thirst of revenge against the infidels. The garrison, displaying crucifixes on the ramparts, derided those revered emblems of salvation, and covered them with filth; and the crusaders with shouts of fury vowed to wash out these impious insults in the blood of the perpetrators.

Thus animated by every incentive of natural valour, religious hope, and fanatical vengeance, the crusading host advanced on the following dawn to the assault of Jerusalem. While showers of arrows and stones from the archers and balistic engines were directed against the defenders on the ramparts to cover the principal operations, the battering and mining machines and huge movable towers—all the stages of the latter filled with chosen bodies of knights and men-at-arms—were impelled toward the walls. But the onset was received by the Moslems with a courage guided by skill, and sustained by confidence or despair. From behind the defences, their incessant flights of missiles replied with murderous effect upon the more exposed bodies of the Latin archers; masses of rock were successfully hurled upon the machines of the besiegers; and the dreadful Greek fire was poured in liquid streams against the movable towers. During the day the struggle raged without intermission, and the event still hung in tremendous expense. But, at even, the slaughter among the crusaders far exceeded that of the infidels; the great tower of Count Raymond had been partially burned and disabled; many of the other engines of assault had been destroyed; and the besiegers were reluctantly compelled to desist for the night from further efforts. Yet their heroic spirit was undismayed, their confidence unabated, their labour indefatigable. Though the Provençal tower had been arrested in its advance, that of Duke Godfrey was undamaged, and had been brought into threatening contiguity to the rampart; and on other fronts of attack the walls of the city were shaken, and already imperfectly breached in several places, by the violent strokes of the battering-rams and the more insidious use of the sap. At daylight, the assault and defence were renewed increased with fury; at noon, the desperate conflict was still balanced in appalling indecision; but, at the third hour of the evening, the barbican having been beaten down, the tower of Godfrey was

Capture of Jerusalem.

the iron-nerved chivalry of Europe to close hand to hand for the mastery, with the less vigorous warriors of the East. In that moment, so critical for the suspended cause of Christendom and Islam, the spirit and strength of the Mussulman defenders of Jerusalem, despite of their superior numbers and securer footing, quailed before the personal prowess of the champions of the cross. The frail drawbridge of the tower was let down upon the solid rampart; two brothers, Letoldus and Englebert, of Tournay, in Flanders, were the first and second of the crusading warriors who sprang upon the battlements; and Godfrey of Bouillon, himself the third, planted his banner on the walls.* His victorious example was followed with irresistible energy; in quick succession the Duke of Normandy, the Count of Flanders, and Tancred, burst through the gate of St. Stephen into the city; and at every breach in the works a passage was impetuously forced by their emulous associates and followers. Meanwhile, the Count of Thoulouse, disdaining to enter the place in the train of his more successful confederates, gallantly inspired his Provençals to carry the rampart in their front by escalade; the defenders, appalled by the defeat of their brethren, wavered and fled; and, in all quarters, the ensign of the cross floated over the towers of Jerusalem.

Abandoning all further hope, the fleeing multitude of the Moslems thronged to die under the sacred domes of their Mosques. The victors pursued them with a relentless fury, which consigned men, women, and children to indiscriminate slaughter. The passive and unresisting despair with which the helpless and miserable crowds awaited their fate, neither awakened the pity nor satiated the bloody vengeance

---

* The author of L'Esprit des Croisades arranges the series of the successful assailants somewhat differently, viz. thus:—Godfrey, Eustace, Baldwin de Burgh, Bernard de St. Valier, De Guicher, and De Raimbaud Croton. These took the lead in the order in which they are named, followed closely by D'Amanjeu d'Albret, and Leo-

of their savage destroyers. The outrages which the Infidels had formerly inflicted on the Christian pilgrims, and the insults with which they had recently derided the cross, were sternly remembered and fearfully avenged; the very sight of the sacred places which they had profaned with their false worship served to heighten the fanatical rage of the conquerors against the fugitives who sought shelter in those edifices; and it was the boast of the Latin princes, in a public letter which they addressed to the pope,* that, in the splendid mosque erected by the Khalif Omar on the site of the Temple of Solomon,† they rode up to their horses' knees in the blood of the Infidels. In that principal sanctuary alone, ten thousand persons were massacred; every minor retreat in the city was explored with equally fierce diligence by the swords of the crusaders; and the horrid computation of the total carnage on the battlements, throughout the streets, and in the churches and houses, has been variously extended to an incredible number of both sexes and all ages.‡

---

* Martenne, *Thesaurus Novus*, vol. i. p. 281.

† D'Anville, *Diss. sur l'Ancienne Jerusalem*, p. 42–58.

‡ By the Mussulman writers (De Guiges, vol. ii. p. 99, and Abulfeda, *apud* Reiske, vol. iii. p. 319), the numbers massacred are stated as high as seventy or even one hundred thousand souls: but these were traditional estimates long after the event; and the last probably exceeds the amount of the whole population of Jerusalem at the period. William of Tyre, who alone of the Latin chroniclers

These dreadful scenes of fanatical cruelty, from which reason and humanity equally revolt, were followed by a sudden transition of passion, as strangely but less painfully characteristic of the times; and, the events of the single day on which Jerusalem was stormed, forcibly exemplify the unnatural union of those motives of martial achievement, ferocious intolerance, and fervent piety, which produced the Crusade. The mailed warriors who had sworn and accomplished the deliverance of the Holy Sepulchre in arms, hastened, as humble and repentant pilgrims, to complete their vows of adoration, at that hallowed monument of redemption. Duke Godfrey, after himself staining the example of heroic courage with merciless slaughter, threw aside his reeking sword, washed his bloody hands, exchanged his armour for a white linen tunic, and, with bare head and feet, repaired in pious humiliation to the Church of the Sepulchre. The same religious impulse was quickly communicated to his fellow-warriors; the inhuman fanaticism which had so lately steeled their hearts against every softer emotion, was all at once relaxed into a flood of contrite and tearful devotion; and the whole host in turn, discarding their arms and purifying their persons from the signs of recent slaughter, moved in procession to the Hill of Calvary, and in mingled penitence for their sins, and thanksgiving for their victory, wept over the tomb of the Saviour of the world. After these religious exercises, a loose was given to the general joy both of the Latin conquerors and the native Christians, who had either been retained in the city during the siege, or had gathered in the crusading quarters. Among the latter was the Patriarch of Jerusalem; who, after seeking a retreat from the Mussulman tyranny in Cyprus, had lately arrived in the camp. He instructed his flock to honour, in the person of Peter the Hermit, the faithful missionary whose indignation and piety had been moved by the spectacle of their bondage to the Infidels, and whose holy zeal had roused the nations of the Western World to undertake their deliverance. The grateful multitudes prostrated themselves before the poor Solitary of Amiens, as a revered and chosen servant of God; and, if the sincerity of the fanatic, who, to perform this service, had twice traversed Europe and Asia, may be measured by his indefatigable labours in the imaginary cause of Heaven, the spiritual triumph which rewarded his success must have surpassed the most exquisite enjoyment of temporal ambition.*

Among the conscious offences which humbled the

---

*It is singular that, after his reception of this public homage, the name of the Hermit occurs not again in any contemporary or authentic record; and history has altogether forgotten to notice the subsequent fate of the man who had moved the population of Europe from its foundations.

souls of the crusaders in contrition and prayer before the altar of the Sepulchre, they were so far from numbering their cruelties to the Infidels, that they deemed the late work of slaughter a meritorious offering to the God of Mercies. To every pious and en lightened mind there can be few subjects of contemplation more offensive and painful than this alliance of a devotion, which, though mistaken, was sincere, with so ferocious and dark a superstition. Scenes of bloodshed similar to those which had preceded, also followed the interval of worship; and, on the morning after the capture of Jerusalem, the crusaders deliberately renewed the massacre of the Infidel garrison and inhabitants. The Jews of the city were burned alive in their synagogues; the Mussulman captives who had been spared by the lassitude, and the fugitives who had eluded the first search of the victors, were now dragged from their prisons and hiding-places, and remorselessly butchered. All— even women, children, and infants at the breast— shared the same fate, except a few wretched Mussulmans, who owed their escape from the general slaughter, not to the humanity, but to the covetousness of the Count of Thoulouse, who rescued them for sale as slaves, and incurred the censure of the army by preferring the indulgence of his avarice to that of his fanaticism. With the rest of the crusaders, the former passion was only second to their cruelty; and

that of bloodshed. By previous agreement, the rich plunder of the mosques, which abounded with lamps and vases of gold and silver, was dedicated to the service of the church and the relief of the poor; but each house became the property of the first warrior who burst its door, and suspended his shield from its walls.*

The infidel inhabitants of Jerusalem had been extirpated; and the law of conquest supplied a new and Christian population. When the victorious soldiery had divided the possession of the Holy City, her streets were cleansed from the horrid pollution of recent slaughter by the labour of some Mussulman slaves; the churches and mosques were delivered up to the clergy and dedicated afresh, or now first converted to the purposes of Christian worship; and, tenanted by the various population of her martial citizens from every Western nation, Jerusalem presented the novel aspect of an European settlement. After the occupation of the city, the earliest care of the leaders of the Crusade was given to the duty of

---

*In the Mosque of Omar, no fewer than seventy massive lamps of gold and silver were found by Tancred, and surrendered to the prescribed uses of religion and charity; but not, if we may believe Malmsbury, (p. 443,) before the costliness of the prize had reduced the hero, in a moment of unwonted frailty, to forget the usual purity of his virtue. He attempted to secrete the spoils for his private profit, until he was driven, either by the reproaches of his own conscience, or dread of public censure, to make restitution of his booty

securing their conquest. The establishment of a feudal kingdom in Palestine was obviously suggested by the familiar example of the same form of polity in the Western monarchies, and by the necessity of organizing a martial system of tenures for the defence of the Christian state and the protection of the Holy Sepulchre. On the eighth day, therefore, after the capture of the city, the princely and noble chieftains of the crusading host assembled to confer, by their free voices, the feudal sovereignty of Jerusalem, with its future dependencies, upon one of their body. The accidents of war had diminished the number of those great leaders of the European chivalry who, by their hereditary rank, the strong array of their retainers, or the influence of personal character, were entitled to aspire to this honour. Boemond and Baldwin were already seated in the principalities of Antioch and Edessa, and had withdrawn themselves from immediate participation in the crowning glories of the Holy War; the great Count of Vermandois and the Count of Chartres had, with deeper reproach, altogether deserted the sacred expedition; and although, in chivalric fame, Tancred was at least their equal, the princes of sovereign rank who remained with the army were four only in number; the two Roberts, of Normandy and of Flanders, the Count of Thoulouse, and the Duke of Brabant. Of these princes, if we may believe our Anglo-Norman writers, the crown of Jerusalem was offered first to the brave but prodigal son of the Conqueror, and declined by his modest distrust of his own merits, by his less praiseworthy indolence, or by his preference of his European Duchy. If, on the other hand, we credit the Provençal chroniclers of the Crusade, the same proffer and refusal of the regal dignity must be ascribed to the Count of Thoulouse.* But the tale of Robert's election is entirely discredited by the silence of every immediate chronicler of the Crusade; and the grasping ambition and selfish cupidity ever displayed by the Count of Thoulouse, both before and after the fall of Jerusalem, are not only incompatable with the disinterestedness imputed to him by his adherents, but are expressly stated by a better authority† to have occasioned the rejection of his claims. Between Robert of Flanders and his friend the Duke of Brabant, if there existed any rivalry in pretension, there was at least no equality of merit; and, in opposition to the intrigues of the wily and jealous Provençal, the general voice of the assembly proclaimed Godfrey of Bouillon as the most deserving, both by his prowess and piety, among all the princely champions of the Cross, to receive the crown of Jerusalem and the guardianship of the Holy Sepulchre. The spirit of Godfrey was too magnanimous to shrink from the perilous and unquiet charge which intrusted to him

---

* Raymond des Agiles, p. 179. Albert. Aquensis, p. 288. Guibert, p. 537.
† Willermus Tyr. 763.

rather the sword of the crusader than the sceptre of a feudal king. [July 23, 1090.] He was immediately conducted in solemn procession to the church of the Sepulchre, and there inaugurated in his new office; but, with the pious humility which distinguished his character, he refused to have a regal diadem placed on his brows in that city, wherein his Saviour had worn a crown of thorns; and modestly declining the name with the decoration of a king, he would accept no prouder title than that of Advocate or Defender of the tomb of Christ.*

The estimation in which Godfrey was held by the army, may be known from the universal lamentation which prevailed when he met with a disaster in Asia Minor. When alone in the dense part of a forest, the duke heard the cries of a poor pilgrim, who had been attacked by a bear, while cutting wood. Godfrey hastened to his relief, when the bear quitted his victim to attack his new enemy. He seized the duke by the cloak and dragged him to the ground. His sword being entangled between his legs, Godfrey wounded himself severely in the thigh in attempting to draw it. He continued the fight, however, till the noise brought others to the spot. A knight, named Hascquin, despatched the bear with his sword, and the

---

* The title of Advocate or Defender of a church or monastery was familiar to the age of Godfrey: when, under that term, it was customary for ecclesiastical bodies to purchase the protection of some

almost exhausted duke was borne to the camp, where the loss of a battle would scarcely have spread more consternation than the unhappy spectacle he afforded to the eyes of the Christians.

From the election of Godfrey of Bouillon may be dated the foundation of the LATIN KINGDOM OF JERUSELEM.* By that event, stability was given to the recent conquests of the crusaders; and Jerusalem, which, after a possession of more than four hundred and fifty years since its surrender to Omar, had been wrested out of the hands of the disciples of Mohammed, was converted into the capital of a Christian state. After the worthy choice of a sovereign to defend and govern their conquests, it remained for the crusaders only to secure their maintenance and extension by regulating the martial, civil, and ecclesiastical institutions of the new kingdom. The religious zeal

---

* Robertus Mon. p. 74–77. Albertus Aquensis, p. 275–289. Baldricus Arch. p. 132–134. Raymond des Agiles, p. 175–178. Radulphus Cad. p. 320–324. Fulchrius. Carnot, p. 396–400. Guibert, p. 533–537. Willermus Tyr. p. 746–763, &c.

These references embrace the original authorities for all the details given in the text of the siege and capture of Jerusalem. But, throughout the above narrative, the present compilation is also largely indebted to the labours of our modern English historians of the same events: to the LVIIIth chapter of Gibbon, which, though not exempt from some errors of fact and more obliquities of sentiment, offers a masterly sketch of the spirit and transactions of the First Crusade; and to the more recent and ample work of Mr. Mills, who (*History of the Crusades*, vol. i. c. 1–6) has industriously exhausted the stores of the Latin chroniclers, and executed his design with

and the prudential policy of the conquerors were yet to be exercised in providing for its defence; but their vows were already accomplished; and the great design of the FIRST CRUSADE had been concluded in the triumphant recovery of the Holy Sepulchre.

Ascalon.

CHAPTER II.

The Second Crusade.

SECTION I.—STATE OF THE LATIN KINGDOM.

ITHIN a short month after his election to fill the throne of Jerusalem, the pious and gallant Godfrey of Bouillon was summoned into the field to sustain that arduous office of defender of the Holy Sepulchre, which his modesty had preferred to the regal title. The Khalif of Egypt, roused to equal indignation and alarm by the intelligence of the fall of Jerusalem, had immediately despatched a

great army into Palestine; and the influence of a common religion and cause attracted numerous hordes of Turks and Saracens to the Fatimite standard. The usual exaggeration of the Latin chroniclers has swollen the infidel host into countless myriads: their more authentic record of the Christian force shows that the bands of the crusaders had already dwindled, since the capture of the Holy City, to five thousand horse and fifteen thousand foot-soldiers. But the champions of the cross, however inferior in numbers, were flushed with recent victory, and animated by the unconquerable energy of religious and martial enthusiasm. The armies met at Ascalon; [August 12, 1099 :] and the organized and mail-clad chivalry of Europe once more triumphed over the disorderly multitudes of Egypt, Syria, and Arabia. The Fatimites fled at the first charge of Godfrey and Tancred; and the only resistance which the crusaders encountered was from a band of five thousand black Africans; who, after the discharge of a galling flight of arrows from an ambush, astonished the Latins by a novel mode of close combat with balls of iron fastened to leathern thongs, which they swung with terrific effect. But, after the first moment of surprise, the desperate courage and rude weapons of these barbarians were vainly opposed to the sharp lances and physical weight of the Christian gens-d'armerie; and their destruction or flight completed the easy and merciless victory of the cru saders. Of the infidel host, the incredible numbers of thirty thousand in the battle, and sixty thousand in the pursuit, are declared to have been slaughtered: while of the Latins scarcely a man had been killed. An immense booty, the spoils of the Egyptian camp, fell into the hands of the victors; and the standard and sword of the khalif, being alone reserved from the division of the plunder, were piously suspended by Godfrey over the altar of the Sepulchre at Jerusalem.*

The victory of Ascalon was the last combined exploit of the heroes of the first Crusade. Having accomplished their vow, and bidden a farewell to their magnanimous leader, most of the surviving princes and chieftains of the holy war departed for Europe. Boemond was established at Antioch, and Baldwin at Edessa; but of all his compeers, Godfrey could induce only the devoted Tancred to share his fortunes; and no more than three hundred knights, and as many thousand foot soldiers, remained for the defence of Palestine. But the terror of the Christian arms proved, for a season at least, a sufficient protection to the new state; the Mussulmans were easily expelled from the shores of Lake Genesareth; and the emirs of Ascalon, Cæsarea, and Acre, hastened to deprecate the hostility of the crusading king by submission and tribute. The remainder of Godfrey's brief reign was disturbed only by the intrigues of Daimbert, Archbishop of Pisa, who had been appointed by Pope Pascal II.* to succeed Adhemar of Puy as legate of the holy see, and had now been invested with the patriarchate of Jerusalem. As chief, in this double capacity, of the Latin church in the East, Daimbert audaciously claimed the disposal of those acquisitions which the heroes of the Crusade had carved out with their own good swords; and both Godfrey and Boemond condescended to receive from his hands, as vassals of the church, the feudal investure of the states of Jerusalem and Antioch. But even this submission did not satisfy the pride and cupidity of Daimbert; he claimed the entire possession of Jerusalem and Jaffa; and Godfrey, who shrank with superstitious horror from the idea of a contest with the church, was glad to compound with the demand of the rapacious prelate,† by the surrender of the whole of the

---

* According to the vulgar belief, Pope Urban II. died of joy on learning the conquest of Jerusalem; but, as Mr. Mills has observed, (*Hist. of the Crusades*, vol. i. 268,) the decease of that pontiff occurred only fifteen days after the capture of the city, and therefore too soon to have been produced by the receipt of the glad intelligence in Italy.

† Even the Archbishop of Tyre, despite of the zeal for the supremacy of the church which he may be supposed naturally to have felt, is disgusted by the audacious pretension of the patriarch, and relates the tale with indignant candour. Willermus Tyr. p. 771. The truth is, however, that besides the intense and disinterested devotion of Godfrey to the church, and which was one of the charac-

latter city, and a portion, including the sepulchre itself, of the sacred capital. The patriarch further extorted the monstrous condition, that the unreserved dominion of all Jerusalem should escheat to his see, in case Godfrey died without issue. [July 11, A. D. 1100.] That event occurred too shortly for the happiness of a people whom the good prince governed with paternal benevolence; and to the sorrow not only of the Christian inhabitants of Palestine, but even of their Mussulman tributaries, he breathed his last at the early age of forty years, five days preceding the first anniversary of his reign.*

On the death of Godfrey, the barons of the Latin kingdom of Palestine indignantly refused to ratify the promised cession which the patriarch demanded; and it was resolved that the unimpaired rights of the crown over Jerusalem should be bestowed with its temporal sovereignty. Tancred desired that the election should fall on his relative Boemond, Prince of Antioch; but that prince had, at this critical juncture, been made prisoner by an Armenian chieftain, whose territories he had unjustly invaded; and a general feeling that some preference was due to the claims of the house of Bouillon, decided the choice of

---

venture upon a quarrel with the Holy See, whose emissary the patriarch was. He had no alternative, but to act as he did act, or to abandon his newly acquired kingdom.

* Albert. p. 294–299.   Guibert. p. 537–554.   Will. Tyr. p. 773–

STATE OF THE LATIN KINGDOM.   181

Tancred..

the barons in favour of Baldwin, Prince of Edessa. Resigning his principality to his relative and namesake, Baldwin du Bourg, the brother of Godfrey, hastened to the Holy City; and, after some fruitless opposition, the patriarch solemnly crowned the new King of Jerusalem in the church of Bethlehem. The memory of the wrongs which he had sustained from Baldwin, inspired Tancred with a more excusable and lasting repugnance to his pretensions; and refusing to

retired from Jerusalem to Antioch, of which he assumed the regency during the captivity of Boemond. But an accommodation was effected by the good offices of the barons; and the king and the regent of Antioch were left at leisure to provide for the security of their states against the common Mussulman enemy.* The character of Baldwin rose with his elevation; and, on the throne of Jerusalem, he, who during the Crusade had disgusted his compeers by a selfish and treacherous ambition, displayed a disinterested and magnanimous devotion to his regal duties, which won the respect and love of his people, and proved him no unworthy successor of his brother. During a reign of eighteen years, he not only sustained with zeal and ability the arduous office of defending the Latin state from the assaults of the Infidels, but extended its limits and increased its security.

In these efforts he was much assisted by the remains of several armaments from Europe, which may be regarded as a supplement to the first Crusade. The spirit which had animated that enterprise still burned with undiminished intensity; and, in the course of a few years, Hugh of Vermandois, and Stephen of Chartres—the same leaders who had retired with little honour from their first expedition— the Dukes of Aquitaine and of Bavaria, the Counts of

---

* Albert. p. 300-308. Will. Tyr p. 775, 776.

Burgundy, of Vendôme, of Nevers, and of Parma, and of other princes, severally conducted into Asia whole armies of French, Gascon, Flemish, German, and Italian crusaders, whose aggregate has been computed by a modern writer at the astonishing number of little less than half a million of men.* These successive hosts took the same route, and encountered the same sufferings and disasters, from the dubious faith of the Byzantine court, the incessant attacks of the Turks, and the triple scourge of the sword, famine, and pestilence, which had swept off the myriads of their precursors.† But a very small proportion of those who had reached the Bosphorus, survived the horrors of the passage through Asia Minor: yet the remnant which entered Syria still fed the Christian cause in Palestine with a constant supply of veteran warriors; and by their aid, and more especially by

---

* Mills. *Hist. of Crusades*, vol. i. 290, note.

† Both the Counts of Vermandois and of Chartres, who found themselves compelled by the public contempt of a chivalrous age to return to Palestine, perished in the attempt to redeem the fame which they had lost by the former abandonment of their crusading vows. The great Count of Vermandois died at Tarsus of wounds received in battle with the Turks of Cilicia; and the Count of Chartres only survived his second march into Palestine to be taken prisoner and murdered in the frontier warfare by the Egyptian Mussulmans. He had been driven to engage in the supplementary Crusade by the high-spirited reproaches of his Countess Adela, daughter of the Norman conqueror, who had sworn to allow him no peace until he should repair his dishonour. He was father to Stephen, the English usurper. Orderic Vital. p. 790–793. Will. Tyr. 781–787. Albert. p. 315–325. Anna Comnena, lib. ix. p. 331.

that of some maritime expeditions from the European shores, many Mussulman invasions were repelled, and many conquests achieved. In the third year of his reign, Baldwin I.,* after reducing Azotus, was enabled to form the siege of Acre; and by the opportune arrival of an armament of seventy Genoese galleys, filled with crusaders, in the following spring, that valuable conquest was completed after a protracted resistance. [A. D. 1104.] Beritus and Sarepta were also reduced and converted into Christian lordships; and Sidon became the next object of assault. With an interval of four years, two fleets of Scandinavian

---

* In the preceding year, the King of Jerusalem had narrowly escaped captivity or death, through a rash assault which he ventured upon the Egyptian invaders of Palestine with a vanguard of only a few hundred horse. His followers were overwhelmed by superior numbers, and almost all cut to pieces; and it was on this occasion that the Count of Chartres was taken and murdered. The story of Baldwin's escape presents one of the few gleams of generous sentiment which relieve the dark picture of a fanatical and savage warfare. Upon some former occasion, Baldwin had captured a noble Saracen woman, whose flight was arrested by the pangs of childbirth, and, after humanely rendering her every attention, had released her and her infant in safety. The husband was serving in the Mussulman ranks, when Baldwin, after the slaughter of his followers, with difficulty reached a castle, whither the victors immediately pursued him. The place was surrounded, and the capture of the King would have been inevitable, if the grateful Emir had not secretly approached the walls at midnight, announced his design of delivering the preserver of his wife and child, and, at the hazard of his own life, conveyed him in safety from the castle, which Baldwin had scarcely quitted when it was stormed, and the whole garrison put to the sword. Will. Tyr. p. 787, 788. For the details of this romantic incident, see Michaud,

crusaders, who had performed the long voyage from the Baltic through the Straits of Gibralter to the Syrian shores, [A. D. 1115;] co-operated with the Christian forces of Palestine in the siege of that city; and although the first attempt was repulsed, the second proved successful.*

All these acquisitions were incorporated into the kingdom of Jerusalem. But a more important extension of the Christian territories in Syria had meanwhile been effected, and added to the number of distant principalities. The veteran Count of Thoulouse prevailed upon some of the French princes whom, in the supplemental Crusade, he had guided with the remains of their forces through Asia Minor, to subjugate Tortosa, on the coast of Syria, for his benefit. The nucleus of a new state was thus formed, which Raymond employed his Provençal troops in extending; but he died before he could accomplish the reduction of the city of Tripoli, the object of his ambition, and the destined capital of his Oriental dominions. Some years afterward, that conquest was effected for his eldest son Bertrand, by the King of Jerusalem, seconded by all the Latin princes of the East, and a Pisan and Genoese fleet. Tripoli, with its surrounding district and dependencies, was then erected by Baldwin into a county for the house of Thoulouse; [A. D. 1109;] and this new state, which, although feudally subject to the crown of Jerusalem, partook in extent and dignity rather of the character of a sovereign principality than of a mere fief, contributed much by its position between the territories of Antioch and Palestine to secure and cement the communication and strength of the Christian power.* But the affairs of Antioch were perpetually embroiled by the restless ambition of its prince. During his captivity in Armenia, the government of that state was ably administered by Tancred; but, after obtaining his release, Boemond by his refusal to acknowledge the feudal superiority of the Eastern Emperor Alexius, involved himself in a new war, in which he was assisted by the Pisans. The Byzantine arms prevailing by land, Boemond sailed to Europe to plot a diversion against the Grecian territories of his ancient enemy; and, having succeeded by his martial reputation in assembling a large army of crusaders in France and Italy, he landed at Durazzo. Alexius was then glad to conclude an accommodation with him; and the crusading forces pursuing the usual route through the Byzantine territories to Palestine, the Prince of Antioch returned to Italy, where he died in the following year. After his decease, the noble minded Tancred continued to rule the Syrian principality, until his chivalrous career was appropriately terminated by a mortal wound which he had received in battle; and, after some uninteresting revolutions in the government of Antioch, the eldest son of Boemond, who bore his name, finally arrived in Asia, and successfully claimed the principality as his inheritance.* Meanwhile, the isolated state of Edessa, surrounded on all sides by Armenian and Turkish enemies, was only preserved from destruction by the heroic valour of its count, Baldwin du Bourg, and his relative, Joscelyn de Courtenay, a member of a noble French house, which was rendered more illustrious by his exploits in the East than by the subsequent alliance of a collateral branch with the royal blood of France, and a succession of three emperors to the Latin throne of Constantinople.†

---

* Radulphus Cad. p. 327–330. Fulcher. p. 419, 420. Albert. p. 340–354. Will. Tyr. p. 792–807. Anna Comnena, lib. xiv. p. 329–419.

† The adventure and vicissitudes of fortune which Joscelyn de Courtenay underwent in the East, as well as his chivalrous deeds, might form the groundwork of a tale of romance. He had originally accompanied the Count of Chartres from Europe in the supplementary Crusade, and settled at Edessa with his relation Baldwin, together with whom he was taken prisoner in a defeat which the crusaders sustained from the Emir of Aleppo. After five years' captivity, the friends were released by the stratagem of some Armenian partizans, who, entering the fortress in which they were confined, in the disguise of monks and traders, surprised and slew the Turkish garrison. Baldwin then bestowed a portion of the Edessine territories in sovereignty upon Courtenay. But, upon some jealousy, Joscelyn was treacherously lured to Edessa by his benefactor, put to the torture, and compelled to resign his domains. Indignant at this treatment, Courtenay withdrew to Jerusalem, where his services

By the death of his kinsman, Baldwin I., the Count of Edessa was called to receive the crown of Jerusalem. On the junction of new bands of crusaders from Europe, Baldwin I. had been encouraged to revenge the incessant attacks of the Fatimite khalifs of Egypt, by an invasion of that country; and his career of victory on this expedition was cut short only by the hand of death.* Leaving no issue, he, with his last breath, recommended his cousin Baldwin du Bourg for his successor; [A. D. 1118;] and, after the retreat of the crusading host into Palestine, which was the immediate consequence of the dejection produced by his death, the Latin prelate and barons were induced, by respect for his memory, and the claims of consanguinity, as well as by the advice of Joscelyn de Courtenay, to confirm his choice. Bald-

---

for a fief. Notwithstanding the wrongs by which his patron had cancelled former benefits, Joscelyn generously promoted his elevation to the throne of Jerusalem, and received the county of Edessa from his gratitude. Baldwin a second time falling into the hands of the infidels, after he had become king, Joscelyn obtained his liberation among the consequences of the fall of Tyre. The death of the hero at an advanced age was a worthy termination of his exploits. Being unable to sit on horseback, he was carried in a litter to the field; the Mussulmans fled at the very report of his presence; and he died giving thanks to Heaven that the mere fame of his ancient prowess sufficed to scatter the enemies of God. Will. Tyr. p. 853.

* At El-Arish, supposed to be the ancient Rhinocorura, a frontier town of Syria and Egypt, in the year 1118, on his return from an expedition against the Soldan of Egypt. On his death-bed he requested that his body might be deposited beside that of his brother

win du Bourg was therefore elected without opposition to fill the vacant throne, and immediately recompensed the services of Courtenay by resigning to him the possession of the county of Edessa. The principal event in the reign of Baldwin II. was the reduction of Tyre. The Doge of Venice, Ordelafo Falieri, who had led the navy of his republic on a martial pilgrimage to the coast of Palestine, was induced, after bargaining for the possession and sovereignty of one third of that city,* to co-operate in the undertaking; and by a siege of five months the difficult conquest was achieved. [A. D. 1124.] Tyre was erected into an archbishopric under the patriarchate of Jerusalem; and by the capture of a city, which, though fallen from its ancient grandeur, was still the most opulent port on the Syrian coast, and had formed the last strong-hold of the Mussulmans in Palestine, the Latin power may be

---

* All the maritime republics of Italy, with their characteristic mercantile cupidity, extorted great commercial advantages as the price of their services to the crusaders. At Acre, the Genoese obtained a street and many privileges in return for the aid of their fleet in the siege, (Will. Tyr. p. 791;) the Pisans, by treaty with Tancred, were rewarded in like manner for their services to the state of Antioch, with the property of a street both in that capital and in Laodicea, (Muratori, *Antiq. Ital. Med. Ævi*, Diss. 30;) the Venetians, in addition to their settlement at Tyre, received by stipulation a church and street at Jerusalem; and throughout the Christian possessions in Palestine and Syria generally, the three republics contended, often with bloodshed, for the right of establishing places of exchange, and enjoying the common or exclusive privileges of trade. Sabellicus, *Hist. Venet.* dec. i. lib. vi. Marini, *Storia Civ. e Polit. del. Com*

Ruins of Tyre.

said to have attained its greatest consolidation and security.*

When the kingdom of Jerusalem had thus acquired its utmost extent, it embraced all the country of Palestine between the sea-coast and the deserts of Arabia, from the city of Beritus on the north to the frontiers of Egypt on the south: forming a territory about sixty leagues in length and thirty in breadth; and exclusive of the county of Tripoli, which stretched

---

* Albert. p. 365–377. Fulcher. p. 423–440. Will. Tyr. p. 805–

northward from Beritus to the borders of the Antiochan principality. The whole territory, both of the kingdom and county, was occupied by the warriors of the cross, upon the strictest principles of a feudal settlement, with all the subdivisions and conditions of tenure which belonged to that martial polity. Its adoption was suggested* not more by every feeling and custom of the age which the conquerors had

---

* The institution of the feudal code of Jerusalem dates from the first year of the Latin conquest, and its compilation was directed by Godfrey de Bouillon himself; who, with the advice of the patriarch and barons, appointed several commissioners among the crusaders most learned in the feudal statutes and customs of Europe to frame a body of similar laws for the new kingdom. Their digest was solemnly accepted in a general assembly of prelates and barons; and, under the title of the *Assises de Jérusalem*, became thenceforth the recognized code of the Latin state. The original instrument, which was deposited in the Holy Sepulchre, and revised and considerably enlarged by the legislation of succeeding reigns, is said to have been lost at the capture of Jerusalem by Saladin; but, during the last agony of the expiring state, the provisions of the code, which had been preserved by traditionary and customary authority, were again collected in a written form, A. D. 1250, by Jean d'Ibelin, Count of Jaffa, one of the four great barons of the kingdom; and a second and final revision was prepared in Cyprus, A. D. 1369, by sixteen commissioners, for the use of the Latin kingdom in that island. From a MS. of his Cypriot version, in the Vatican library, was published at Paris, A. D. 1690, by Thaumassière, the edition of the *Assises de Jérusalem*, to which we are indebted for our acquaintance with this " precious monument," as a great writer has justly termed it, "of feudal jurisprudence." But for the history of the code, see *Assises de Jérusalem apud* Thaumassière, *Preface*. Consult also Gibbon, xi. 91–98 for a summary, and L'Esprit des Croisades, iv

brought with them from Europe, than by the obvious necessity of such a state of perpetual preparation for the public defence against the incessant assaults of their infidel enemies; and it is almost needless to repeat, that, under no other form of settlement, probably, could the Latin conquests have been preserved by the scanty array of their resident defenders in so unremitting a warfare with the myriads of Turkish and Egyptian Mussulmans. At its highest computation, indeed, the feudal force of the kingdom of Jerusalem would appear very inadequate to its protection. The four great fiefs of Jaffa, Galilee, Cæsarea, and Tripoli, with the royal cities of Jerusalem, Tyre, Acre, and Naplousa, and the other lordships in chief of inferior extent, which composed the whole kingdom, owed and could furnish the services of no more than two thousand five hundred knights or mounted men-at-arms; and their followers, with the contingent of the ecclesiastical and commercial communities, all of which were bound to render aid to the king on lower feudal tenures than the knights' fees, constituted a militia, for the greater part, probably, of archers on foot, not exceeding twelve thousand in number.* It may be

---

* Gibbon (ch. lviii.) has fallen into an error in estimating the number of knights' fees in the whole kingdom of Jerusalem, exclusive of Tripoli, as six hundred and sixty-six, and appears to have confounded the contingent of the four royal cities, which alone, according to the *Assises*, furnished that number, with the total knightly

STATE OF THE LATIN KINGDOM. 193

inferred that the whole population of martial colonists from Europe could scarcely supply even this provision, scanty as it was, for the public defence; and the policy or the domestic wants of the conquerors encouraged the settlement in Palestine of the native Christians of Syria and Armenia, and even of Mussulman tributaries for the cultivation of the soil and the supply of mechanical labour. From the commingling of blood between the crusaders and all these people in the enfeebling climate of the East, was produced a spurious and effeminate race, contemptuously designated by the writers of their age as *Pullani*, or *Poulains*, who had so utterly degenerated from the valour of their European fathers, as to fill the land without contributing to the strength of the state.*

Crucis, lib. iii.) as stating the number of knights' fees in each of the great baronies of Jaffa, Galilee, and Cæsarea, at one hundred only, but the very superior authority of the *Assises* rates them expressly at five hundred each. *Assises*, c. 324–331.

* Vide Du Cange, *Gloss. v. Pullani.*

SECTION II.

ORIGIN OF THE ORDERS OF RELIGIOUS CHIVALRY.

THE feudal army of the kingdom of Jerusalem, and the casual reinforcement of new crusaders from Europe, formed not the only defences of Palestine. The union of fanatical and martial ardour gave birth to two famous orders of religious chivalry, which were specially enrolled under the banners of the Cross; and the Christian cause in the East was long sustained by the emulous valour, though not unfrequently injured by the less worthy rivalry, of the Knights of the hospital of St. John and of the Temple of Solomon. The origin of both these re-

martial achievement, may be traced to purposes simply of pious and practical benevolence. Long before the era of the Crusades, some Italian merchants purchased a license from the Mussulman rulers of Jerusalem to found in that city an hospital, together with a chapel, which they dedicated to St. John the Eleemosynary—a canonized patriarch of Alexandria— for the relief and wayfaring entertainment of sick and poor pilgrims. By the alms of the wealthier Christian visitants of the Sepulchre, and by charitable contributions which the merchants of Amalfi zealously collected in Italy, and as religiously transmitted to Jerusalem, the establishment was supported; and its duties were performed by a few Benedictine monks, with the aid of such lay brethren among the European pilgrims as were induced to extend their penitential vows to a protracted residence in the Holy Land.* Perhaps through the habitual respect of the Mohammedan mind for charitable foundations, the Hospital of·St. John might escape, but certainly it was suffered to outlive, the storms of Egyptian and Turkish persecution; and when Jerusalem fell into the hands of the crusaders, the house was joyfully opened for the reception and cure of the wounded warriors. The pious Godfrey and his companions were edified by the active and self-denying benevolence of the brethren of the hospital, who not only devoted themselves to the care of the suffering, but were contented with the coarsest fare, while their patients were supplied with bread of the purest flour. By the grateful munificence of Godfrey himself, the hospital was endowed with an estate in Brabant, its first foreign possessions; many of the crusaders, from religious motives, embraced its charitable service; and the society speedily acquired so much respect and importance, that the lay-members, separating from the monks of the Chapel of St. John the Almoner, formed themselves into a distinct community, assumed a religious habit,—a long black mantle with a white cross of eight points on the left breast—and placed their hospital under the higher patronage of St. John the Baptist. [A. D. 1113.] By the patriarch of Jerusalem, their triple monastic vows of obedience, chastity, and poverty, were accepted; and a bull of Pope Paschal II. confirmed the institution, received the fraternity under the special protection of the Holy See, and invested it with many valuable privileges.*

The next transition of the Order to a military character is less accurately recorded; but the change may be referred in general terms to the reign of Baldwin II.: since the services in arms of its brethren under that prince are acknowledged in a papal bull.†

---

* See the Statutes of the Order in Vertot, *Hist. des Chevaliers de St. Jean de Jerusalem. Appendix*
† *Ibid.*

In fact, the constant jeopardy in which the Latin State was placed by the assaults of the Infidels, admitted, as we have seen, of no exemption to any community in the kingdom, whether lay or ecclesiastical, from actively contributing to the public defence; and the martial habits and feelings of the crusaders of knightly rank who had enrolled themselves in the fraternity of the Hospital, would naturally suggest the honourable preference of a personal to a deputed service. The revenues of the Order, by the increase of its endowments, were already far more than sufficient to supply the charitable uses of the Hospital; and it was magnanimously resolved to devote the surplus to the defence of the state. The former soldiers of the Cross resumed their military, without discarding their religious garb and profession; the union of chivalric and religious sentiment, however discordant in modern ideas, was equally congenial to the spirit of the age, and proper to the great cause of the Crusades; and thenceforth the banner and the battle-cry of the knights of St. John were seen and heard foremost and loudest in every encounter with the Paynim enemy. The government of the Order was vested in the grand-master and general council of the knights, all of whom were required to be of noble birth; a distinct body of regular clergy was provided for the offices of religion; and a third and inferior class of sergeants, or serving brethren, both swelled the martial array of the knightly fraternity, and dis-

Grand-Master of the Knights of Malta.

charged the civil duties of the hospital.* The renown which the order acquired in the fields of Palestine soon attracted the nobility from all parts of Europe to its standard; admiration of both its pious and chivalric purposes multiplied, throughout the West, endowments of land and donations of money;

Grand-Marshal of the Knights of Malta.

and the rents of nineteen thousand farms, administered by preceptories or commanderies, as the principal houses were termed, which the knights established in every Christian country, supplied a perpetual revenue to their hospital in Palestine, and served to maintain its regular military force.*

When the Christians were driven from Palestine, the knights of St. John settled on the island of Cyprus, whence they were soon driven by the Turks. They then went to the Island of Rhodes. [1310.] From thence they were driven to Malta, which was given to them by Charles V. in 1530. Their position on this island has been retained to the present day, and they bear the name of Knights of Malta.

The institution of the Order of the Temple of Solomon was of later date than the adoption of a military character by the friars of St. John; [A. ". 1118;] and the Templars in their pristine state of humility and poverty owed more obligations to the Hospitallers, by whom they were originally fed and clothed, than their successors, in the days of their pride and power, cared to acknowledge or strove to repay. The original design of their association differed from that of the Hospital, in having united from the outset the martial with a charitable profession. Even after the conquest of the Holy Land by the crusaders, the roads to Jerusalem from the ports and northern frontiers of Palestine continued to be infested by bands of Turks, who indulged at once their thirst of plunder and their hatred of the Christian name, by the robbery and murder of the numerous defenceless pilgrims from Europe. The dangers which beset these poor votaries to the shrine of the Holy Sepulchre

from the cruelty of the Infidels, roused the pious compassion and chivalric indignation of Geoffroy de St. Aldemar, Hugh de Payens, and other French knights in Palestine, who bound themselves mutually by oath to devote their lives to the relief and safe conduct of all pilgrims. As their association partook of a religious character, they followed the example of the fraternity of the Hospital by assuming the monastic vows and garb; and when Baldwin I. marked his approbation of their purpose by assigning them part of his own palace for a residence at Jerusalem, the title which they adopted of the poor soldiery of Christ and of the Temple of Solomon, was suggested by the contiguity of their quarters to the site of that sacred edifice. The maintenance which they at first received from the charity of the Hospital of St. John was soon more independently provided by the respect which was won for their order throughout Christendom through the grateful report of the pilgrims; with the increase of their means and numbers they aspired to extend their humbler service of guarding the roads of Palestine to the more glorious adventure of offensive warfare against the Infidels; and, thenceforth, in wealth, privileges, and power, and in heroic enterprise, the history of their rise differs little from that of the Hospitallers. The constitution of the two orders was similar; and the number of preceptories and estates possessed by the Templars in every king-

Knight Templar armed and mounted. — Grand-Master of the Knights Templars. — Knight Templar in his domestic dress.

dom of Europe,* were immense sources of influence and opulence, second only in degree to those of the elder fraternity.† But in honourable estimation and martial renown, no superiority could with justice be claimed by either order; and admission into the ranks of both was sought with equal avidity by the flower of the European chivalry. In externals, the knights of the Temple were distinguished from their rivals by their use of a long white cloak or mantle, with a straight red cross on the left breast. The banner and seal of the order in the maturity of its splendour also bore a cross gules in a field argent: for its earlier and well-known device, presenting the singular emblem of two men on one horse, although intended by the pious humility of its founders to commemorate the original poverty of the brotherhood, was not long permitted to survive the condition which it had expressed.‡

---

* In England, both orders early acquired large possessions. The principal preceptory of each was established in London: that of the Hospitallers at Clerkenwell, and of the Templars in Holborn, whence it was removed into Fleet Street. Stow, lib. iv. 62. Dudgale, *Origines Jurid.* c. 57.

† Both Hospitallers and Templars were prohibited from possessing any private property; but their vow of poverty, by a convenient interpretation, was only personal, and did not extend to their enjoying in common the enormous wealth of their orders.

‡ For the rise of the Order of Templars, see *passim*, the twelfth book of William of Tyre. Also Knyghton, p. 2382, Brompton, p 1008, and Matt. Paris (*Hist. Minor.*) p. 419, &c.

SECTION III.

FALL OF EDESSA.—THE PREACHING OF THE SECOND CRUSADE.

URING the reign of Baldwin II. the safety and extension of the kingdom of Palestine were largely indebted to the prowess of the knights of the Hospital and Temple; and before the decease of that monarch, the two orders had

power. As Baldwin II. had no sons, he obtained the consent of his nobles and prelates to nominate, as his successor, Foulques, Count of Anjou, whom he had married to his eldest daughter Melisinda. [A. D. 1131.] In his youth, Foulques had visited Palestine as a crusader, at the head of one hundred knights and men-at-arms, and had left so favourable an opinion of his chivalric qualities on the mind of Baldwin that, nine years afterward, when he had become a widower, the king invited him from France to receive the hand of the princess. Dazzled by the prospect of a royal alliance and a matrimonial crown, the Count abandoned his extensive French fiefs to his son;* and on his arrival in the Holy Land, his nuptials with Melisinda were solemnized, and he was immediately acknowledged as the heir to the throne. The death of Baldwin, which shortly ensued, gave him the undis-

---

* That son was Geoffroy Plantagenet, the husband of the Empress Matilda, and father of Henry II. It is strange that William of Tyre, the eulogist of Foulques, should represent him as sixty years of age when he arrived in Palestine for the second time to celebrate his nuptials with Melisinda; for the learned Benedictine authors of *L'Art de verifier les Dates* (Article, Comtes d'Anjou) prove that he was born only A. D. 1092; and his reign in Palestine commenced A. D. 1131. His family had long been famous for their passion of making pilgrimages to the Holy Land; and one of them, who travelled thither before the era of the Crusades, having bound his servants by oath to do whatsoever he should require, compelled them publicly to scourge his naked back before the altar of the Sepulchre, while in penitential cries he implored the pardon of Heaven for his

puted possession of the crown; and, during a reign of thirteen years, Foulques, without performing any brilliant achievement, sufficiently emulated the courage and virtues of his predecessors in the defence and government of the kingdom. His decease left the state in the hands of his widow Melisinda, and their son Baldwin III., then only thirteen years old, who were crowned together; and it was soon after the martial sceptre of the house of Bouillon had thus devolved upon a woman and a minor, [A. D. 1144,] that the Christian power in the East received the first disastrous shock from the Mussulman arms. Since the death of Joscelyn de Courtenay, the defence of the principality of Edessa had been feebly sustained by his son, who inherited neither his valour nor ability. But its safety was more fatally compromised by the selfish indifference or still more criminal treachery of the princes of Antioch, who coolly witnessed the danger of a state which, by its position beyond the Euphrates, formed the great advanced post of the Latin settlements in Syria; and which, therefore, every motive of honour and policy should have impelled them to succour. Profiting by the disunion of the Christians, Zenghi, the Turkish Emir of Mosul or Aleppo, whose martial activity and skill had already rendered his power formidable during the life of Joscelyn de Courtenay, suddenly entered the State of Edessa with an overwhelming force; laid siege to its capital; and, before the levies of the kingdom of

Jerusalem could march to its relief, took the city by storm.*

The intelligence of the fall of Edessa startled the Christian residents in Palestine from lethargic indifference to an alarming discovery of the renovation of the Turkish power on that frontier; [A. D. 1145;] and the first burst of shame and consternation excited among the guardians of the Holy Land by the disgraceful loss and impending danger, was naturally followed by earnest solicitations for succour from Europe. Throughout every country of Western Christendom, the appeal was received with a general enthusiasm little inferior to that which, half a century before, had stimulated the great design of the first Crusade. The martial and religious feelings of Europe were provoked to indignation by the report of the triumph of the infidels; and this universal spirit was already prepared for a second mighty effort of fanaticism, when it was roused into action by the master mind of the age. [1146.] The report of the calamity which had befallen, and of the increasing perils which threatened, the Christian cause in Palestine, affected his ardent temper with powerful emotions of religious zeal; and his resolution to preach a new Crusade was supported by the private friendship and the public wishes of Pope Eugenius III., as well as by the re-

---

† Will. Tyr. p. 844–893. For the exploits of Zenghi, see also De Guignes, *Hist. Gén. des Huns*, vol. ii. lib. xiii., and the Arabic writers

spect and influence which his virtues and talents had deservedly acquired throughout Europe. Not less than the distinguished part which he had already filled in ecclesiastical affairs, do the nobility of his birth, the uniform sanctity of his life, and the really great attainments of his genius and learning, place him at an immeasurable height of personal dignity above the obscure and ignorant fanatic who had first lighted up the flame which he now rekindled. But St. Bernard could only emulate the successful mission, though he might slight the memory,* of the Hermit Peter; the impassioned oratory of the profound theologian could not produce more astonishing results than the rude eloquence of the Solitary of Amiens; and, in the relation of its effects, the preaching of the second Crusade forms but a copy of that of the first.

Louis VII. of France, by his firmness in repressing the rebellious feuds of his turbulent vassals, had securely established the royal authority; and the tranquil condition of his kingdom left him at liberty to gratify, in a foreign and sacred enterprise, the thirst of glorious adventure natural to a young and success-

---

* In one of his extant epistles, St. Bernard speaks contemptuously of his predecessor the Hermit, as *vir quidam, Petrus nomine, cujus et vos, (ni fallor,) sæpe mentionem audistis, &c.;* (a certain man, by name Peter, of whom, if I mistake not, ye have often heard mention made;) and attributes to his misconduct the destruction of the people in the first Crusade. *Opera Sancti Bernardi, Ep.* 363. Ed

ful monarch. But even the strong desire of chivalrous achievement was secondary in the mind of this religious prince to motives of piety, however mistaken; and feelings of deeply cherished remorse for his involuntary share in the horrible catastrophe at Vitry, and of less reasonable compunction for a long disregard of the papal anathemas, powerfully impelled Louis to offer that atonement, which a false superstition deemed most acceptable to Heaven, by embarking in the great warfare against the infidel assailants of the Holy Land. When, therefore, St. Bernard announced his mission, it was eagerly promoted by the French king; and, in the great assembly of his nobles and people which he convoked at Vezelay, the same spectacle was repeated, which had been witnessed at the Council of Clermont before the first Crusade. From the innumerable multitudes which filled the plain and covered the neighbouring heights of Vezelay to their summit, cries of "The cross, the cross! it is the will of God!" rent the air and interrupted the vehement appeal of the preacher; and, before the assembly broke up, Louis himself, with his queen, the too famous Eleanor of Aquitaine, and a host of the nobility and knighthood of his realm, had been signed with the sacred emblem of their vows. From France, St. Bernard with indefatigable zeal proceeded into Germany; [March 31, 1146;] and his course from the Rhine to the Danube, and from the recesses of the

Queen Eleanor of Aquitaine.

everywhere signalized by the same successful exertions of his fervid zeal and impetuous eloquence. At his soul-stirring exhortations, the great feudatory princes of Bavaria, Bohemia, Carinthia, Piedmont, and Styria, with a crowd of inferior chieftains, assumed the cross; and the conversion of the Emperor Conrad III., after some struggle between the sense of political interest and of religious duty, completed the triumph of the pious orator.*

---

* Udo de Diagolo, *(apud* Bouquet, *Recueil des Hist. François,)* vol. xii. 91-93. Otto Frisingensis, *(apud* Muratori, *Script. Rer. Ital.)* vol. vi. c. 87. These two writers, the first a Frenchman, and the latter a German, who himself accompanied the emperor Conrad

The personal motives of St. Bernard were disinterested, pure, and elevated; his zeal was equally free from all alloy of gross fanaticism, selfish ambition, or worldly vanity; and its mistaken direction was the only error which he shared with the most virtuous and devout of his contemporaries. But the intrinsic greatness of his mind is not the less perceptible through this fatal delusion; and in nothing is his superiority to the spirit of the age in which he lived more conspicuous, than in the wisdom and humanity which tempered his enthusiasm. The first of these qualities was signally displayed in his refusal to accept the command of the intended expedition to the Holy Land, as a station which he felt and confessed his own unfitness to fill from want of martial experience and bodily health. His humane exertions to avert from the Jews in France a repetition of the horrid persecution which their fathers had suffered from the fanaticism of the first crusaders, attest his liberality, and were extended to the protection of that unhappy people, with earnest and consistent benevolence, in Germany and other countries. He sternly silenced, by the exertion of his delegated authority from the pope, the preaching of a fanatical German monk, who had endeavoured to provoke a general massacre of the Jews; and his injunctions in circular

---

Gesta Ludovici Regis VII. (in Duchesne, vol. iv.)—our chief contemporary authorities for the transactions of their respective country.

letters to the crusaders to abstain equally from the murder and spoliation of an unoffending people, breathe the genuine Christian precepts of mercy and justice. The doctrines thus inculcated, indeed, were so new to his age, that fully to appreciate the virtuous and truly pious efforts of St. Bernard in his labour of charity, they must be contrasted with the monstrous opinion then prevalent among all orders of society, that to shed the blood and despoil the wealth of infidels was an allowable vengeance, and even a positive duty, against the enemies of God. The practical application of this inhuman and impious belief to the plunder and slaughter of a rich, usurious, and defenceless race, offered too tempting a prey to the cupidity of the bigoted populace and the yet more malignant instigation of numerous debtors, to be wholly averted even by the eloquent and powerful denunciations of the preacher whose voice had awakened all Europe to arms. Notwithstanding the anathemas of St. Bernard, the Jews were in many places robbed and murdered; and in Germany especially they were saved from extermination only by the imperial protection.*

---

* Pfeffel, *Hist. d'Allemagne,* vol. i. 809.

SECTION IV.

LOUIS VII. AND CONRAD III. IN PALESTINE.

HE presence of Louis VII. and of the Emperor Conrad III.—the first great monarchs of the West who had assumed the cross—seemed to invest the great enterprise in which they had engaged with a dignity superior even to that of the former Crusade. The armies which the two sovereigns prepared to lead to the relief of Palestine comprised the national chivalry of France and Germany, with numerous auxiliaries from England* and Italy; and, if the

---

* The recent cessation of the civil wars of Stephen's reign in-

statements of contemporary writers may be credited, these united forces equalled in number the prodigious hosts of the first holy war. The emperor and the king were each at the head of seventy thousand mailed cavalry; their heavily armed infantry exceeded two hundred and fifty thousand; and the clergy, other defenceless pilgrims, camp-followers, women, and children, might swell the aggregate of the crusading multitudes to nearly a million of souls.* From Ratisbon and Mayence, their places of rendezvous, both the German and French armies successively pursued the same route through Hungary and Bulgaria to Constantinople, which had been traversed by their predecessors in the first Crusade. Manuel Comnenus, grandson of Alexius, was now on the Byzantine throne; but the timid and treacherous policy of that court was unchangeable; and, in the apparent friendship and secret hostility with which the Greek emperor alternately assisted and harassed the march of the crusaders, he faithfully copied the example of his ancestor. He engaged by treaty that they should be received hospitably, and supplied with provisions upon equitable terms; yet, in the bread which his

---

them Roger de Mowbray and William de Warenne. Ricardus Hagulst. p. 275, 276. Huntingdon, p. 394, also says that *multi de gente Anglorum*, (many Englishmen,) accompanied the French host; and his account is curiously confirmed by the Byzantine chronicler Cinnamus, p. 29.

subjects sold to them, poisonous ingredients were frequently mingled; base coin was issued expressly from the imperial mint to defraud the strangers in the interchange of trade; the sick whom the crusading hosts were obliged to leave behind on their march were often murdered; their stragglers were cut off; the bridges on their route were broken down; their columns were galled with flights of arrows from ambush in every forest; and all the impediments of a desultory though unavowed warfare were cowardly opposed to their progress. When, therefore, the German army thus harassed arrived before the walls of Constantinople, Conrad, though he abstained from hostile retaliation, indignantly refused an interview with the Greek emperor, and, crossing the Bosphorus, pursued his march through Asia Minor. But the French king, on his arrival at the Byzantine capital, accepted the apologies and entertainment of Manuel, and suffered himself to be beguiled by the blandishments of his perfidious host, until he was roused from inaction by the appalling intelligence of the destruction of the German army.*

In the march through Asia Minor, the Emperor Conrad was betrayed by his Greek guides into the hands of the Sultan of Iconium, who had assembled immense hordes of Turcomans to oppose his passage. While purposely misled into the most dangerous

---

* Will. Tyr. p. 901-903. Cinnamus, p. 80-32.

Conrad III.

mountain passes of Lycaonia, the Germans were suddenly attacked on all sides; and the heavily armed cavalry were unable either to reach their more lightly equipped assailants on the heights, or to protect the defenceless crowd of footmen from the Turkish arrows. By a desperate effort Conrad succeeded, indeed, with a portion of his horse, in cutting a retreat through the Mussulman hordes: but he was compelled to abandon the infantry and unarmed pilgrims to their fate; and nine-tenths of the whole German host are computed to have been destroyed by the shafts and cimeters of the infidels, or to have perished of hunger and thirst in this calamitous expedition. When Conrad, with the remnant of his followers, had effected his retreat to Nice, where the

blished his camp, no doubt was left of the foul treachery of Manuel, who had not only delayed the advance of Louis by false reports of the success of his German confederates, but was also found to have maintained an intelligence with the Sultan of Iconium. As the Greek emperor is charged with this guilt, not merely by the Latin writers, but on the contemporary testimony of one of his own subjects,* some praise is due to the magnanimous or prudent forbearance which induced the crusading monarchs to sacrifice every natural impulse of vengeance, to the fulfilment of the sacred objects of their enterprise. Now advancing in concert through Asia Minor, but turning aside from the former route of the crusaders to the sea-coast of Lydia, Conrad and Louis reached Ephesus with their forces; but there the destitution of equipments for a longer march, to which his Germans had been reduced by their defeat, obliged Conrad to transport them by sea to Palestine; and the French army alone resumed its route by land. On the banks of the Meander, Louis and his chivalry encountered and overthrew the Turkish hosts with so tremendous a slaughter, that piles of Mussulman bones in the next age still whitened the scene of destruction. But the confidence inspired by this victory served only to lure on the negligent crusaders to their ruin. In their continued march, the vanguard had already passed

LOUIS VII. AND CONRAD III. 219

Louis VII. defending himself against the Turks.

the mountains between Pisidia and Phrygia, when the rereward commanded by Louis in person, while entangled in the defiles, was suddenly assailed by innumerable swarms of Turks, who, covering the surrounding precipices, from thence, with fragments of rock, crushed and hurled whole squadrons of the French gens-d'armerie into the yawning gulfs below The surprise was so complete and dreadful, that the whole rearguard was routed and destroyed before order could be restored; and the king himself, after performing prodigies of valour, was saved only, under favour of the darkness, by climbing a tree, and with difficulty escaped, almost unattended, to the camp of

trating into Syria by land was abandoned; the seacoast was again sought; and the army reached the port of Attalia in Pamphylia. There, after incurring new horrors and losses from famine and disease, the king succeeded in procuring some Greek vessels to transport his bands of nobles and knights to Antioch: but he was relunctantly compelled, by the want of sufficient shipping, to abandon the inferior crowd of infantry and pilgrims on the shore. After his departure, the guard which he had left for their protection, proved insufficient to resist the incessant attacks of the Turks; the people of Attalia not only shut the gates of the city against them, but massacred the defenceless sick and wounded; and the whole wretched multitude perished, either by the swords of the infidels, or the more unnatural cruelty of the perfidious Greeks.*

When the German emperor and the French king had at last reached the shores of Palestine by sea, even the shattered remnants of their hosts supplied so considerable a reinforcement to the Christian power in Palestine, that in a general council at Acre, whither the two monarchs repaired to meet the king of Jerusalem and his barons, it was resolved to undertake some enterprise worthy of the imperial and royal dignity. But though the recovery of the principality of Edessa had formed the original design of the Crusade,

---

* Will. Tyr p. 903–006. *Gesta Ludovici*, p. 395-400 Nicetas, p.

Damascus.

that object was now either abandoned from conviction of the difficulties attending so distant an expedition, or postponed to more pressing considerations of immediate danger or local interest. The vicinity of Damascus rendered the continued possession of that important place by the infidels more perilous to the safety of the Latin kingdom than the loss of the remoter city of Edessa; and the three sovereigns of

Germany, France, and Jerusalem, led their national chivalry and the Knights of St. John and the Temple, to the siege of that great stronghold of the Turkish power in Syria. But Damascus was strongly fortified and skilfully defended; the valour of the Christians was misdirected by ignorance, or paralyzed by discord and treason; and, after a miserable failure, variously attributed to all these causes, the crusading army withdrew from the walls, and retreated in shame and dishonour to Jerusalem. Thence, in despair of the efficacy of further exertions, Conrad and Louis, with an interval of a year between their several departures, both returned to Europe with the broken array of the chivalry; and the Christian cause in Palestine was again deserted, save by the scanty bands but enduring courage of its habitual defenders.*

Such was the abortive issue of the second Crusade. The mightiest efforts of the congregated force of Europe had been exhausted in Asia Minor; [A. D. 1149;] and the presence of the greatest monarchs of Christendom in Palestine had served only to expose the weakness of their vaunted power to the eyes of the triumphant infidels. The sacrifice of the myriads of their followers had absolutely failed to achieve a single advantage for the cause in which two great armies had perished; and, after the fruitless hopes of succour which had been excited by their approach, and, disap-

---

* Will. Tyr. p. 906-914. *Gesta Ludovici*, p. 410-409. Otto Fris

pointed by their failure, the guardians of the Holy Sepulchre were abandoned to sustain the tempest of Mussulman warfare with diminished confidence and increasing danger. Meanwhile, from the distant banks of the Euphrates, the gathering power which had already swept away the Christian bulwark of Edessa, and was destined eventually to overwhelm the Latin kingdom of Palestine, was continually enlarged with portentous vigour. Before the death of Zenghi, the victorious Emir or Atabec of Aleppo, his dominions had already swelled into a considerable empire; and, by its still further extension under his son, the great Noureddin, who added the sovereignty of Damascus to that of Aleppo, and consolidated the Mussulman power in Syria under a single ruler, the frontiers of the Latin states became completely enveloped by the conquests of this formidable enemy.

An Arab Encampment.

CHAPTER III.

The Third Crusade.

SECTION I.—THE RISE OF SALADIN.

NOTWITHSTANDING the failure of the second Crusade, and the increasing power of the Turks, Baldwin III., supported by the feudal array of his kingdom, and the knights of the military orders, continued throughout the remainder of his reign to uphold the Christian cause in Palestine with courage and energy. In order to protect the northern frontiers of the Latin states from the designs of Noureddin, the king stationed himself at Antioch; and, though unable to save the remnant of the Edessene territory, he succeeded in rescuing the Christian garrisons and inhabitants under a safe escort from the impending horrors of Turkish slavery. Being recalled from Antioch to repel a new invasion, in which the troops of Noureddin from Damascus had penetrated to the gates of Jerusalem, he came up with the infidels, who had already been compelled to retreat by the bravery of the military Orders; and inflicted on them, near Jericho, so total a defeat that the whole Turkish host was either slaughtered or drowned in the waters of the Jordan. On the southern frontiers of Palestine, the arms of the Christian prince were subsequently still more successful against the Egyptian Mussulmans; and his reduction of the important city of Ascalon, after an obstinate siege, added a new possession and bulwark to the kingdom of Jerusalem. [A. D. 1153.] By these exploits, and by the generous spirit with which he devoted his last years to the active defence of his people, Baldwin redeemed the reproach of some irregularities of personal conduct which had clouded his youth; without any high degree of ability, his character was graced by many noble and chivalric qualities;* and he died respected even by his infidel enemies, and deeply lamented by his own subjects. As he left no children, he was succeeded by his brother Almeric, whose equal mediocrity of talent was unrelieved by the same virtues and whose temper presented an unpleasing contrast of avarice and overweening ambition. [A. D. 1162.] By these passions, the new king, disregarding the pressure of nearer and more imminent danger from the power of Noureddin, was tempted to engage in repeated projects for the distant conquest of Egypt, which, as fruitlessly exhausting the strength of the Christian kingdom, may be numbered among the accelerating causes of its downfall.

Obeying the usual vicissitudes of the Saracen dynasties, the Fatimite Khalifs of Egypt had for many generations sunken into abject slavery to their own vizirs; and at the period before us, the supreme authority in the seraglio of Cairo was disputed between two powerful rivals, Shawer and Dargham. The latter prevailing, Shawer fled to the court of Noureddin; and that prince, glad of any occasion for extending his influence, openly protected the fugitive, and despatched a body of troops under Shiracouch, the most famous of his Turcoman generals, into Egypt, to reinstate him in the vizirship. The expedition was successful; Dargham was slain in battle; but Shawer, in nominally recovering his power over the helpless Khalif of Egypt, found that he was only himself a

of this new yoke, the Egyptian vizir had recourse to the king of Jerusalem; and Almeric, who had already engaged in hostilities to exact a tribute from Egypt, eagerly received his overtures. The power of Noureddin was far superior to that of the Frankish monarch: but the proximity of Palestine to Egypt enabled the Christian forces to reach Cairo by a direct march from their own frontiers; while from Damascus the interposition of the Latin states would oblige the Turkish cavalry to make a long circuit over the burning deserts of Arabia. This advantage of situation made it easy for the king of Jerusalem, on the invitation of Shawer, to march an army into Egypt, and to besiege Shiracouch in Pelusium, before Noureddin was able to succour his lieutenant. After a long and gallant defence, the Turkish general was compelled to capitulate: but Noureddin meanwhile had made a formidable diversion by pouring his troops into the territory of Antioch; and Almeric, thus prevented from reaping the fruits of his victory, returned by rapid marches to the defence of the Latin state. At his approach, Noureddin made an artful demonstration of retiring: but his retreat was only the prelude to a sudden attack upon the exulting and negligent forces of Almeric; and the Christians, before they could recover from their surprise, were routed near Artesia with immense loss. [A. D. 1163.] After this ominous event, the severest defeat in the open field which the Christian forces in Palestine had sustained since their

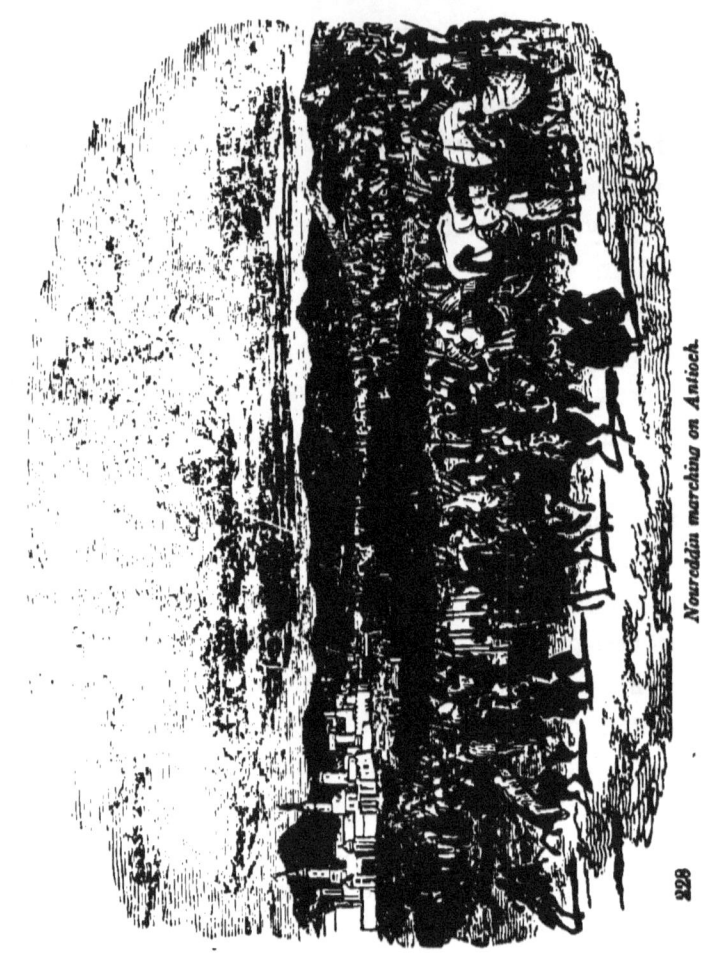

Noureddin marching on Antioch.

conquest of Jerusalem, Noureddin was at leisure to resume his designs upon Egypt; and the veteran Shiracouch was ordered to lead a second and more numerous army into that country. But Almeric, stimulated by ambition and avarice, had made such vigorous efforts to repair the disaster of Artesia, that he again appeared on the Egyptian frontiers with a chosen body of the Christian chivalry, before Shiracouch had reached the banks of the Nile. The Turkish army was exhausted by a calamitous march across the desert; the Christian knights were fresh and vigorous, and their valour and energy, though feebly supported by their Egyptian allies, triumphed over the superior military skill of Shiracouch. After a campaign in which the ability of the Turkish general was admirably displayed, he was a second time obliged to conclude a capitulation with Almeric and the Vizir Shawer, by which he engaged to evacuate Egypt; [A. D. 1167;] and both the Christian and Turkish armies returned to their own states.*

The cupidity of the king of Jerusalem was, however, after so successful an expedition, more than ever attracted by the wealth and defenceless condition of Egypt; and obtaining, through a family alliance which he had at this epoch concluded with the Greek emperor, Manuel Comnenus, the promised aid of the Byzantine navy, he resolved to attempt the total sub-

---

* Will. Tyr. p. 955–974. De Guignes, lib. xiii.

jugation of the country which he had protected from the Turks. A pretence for this aggression was found or framed on the report of a secret negotiation between the Vizir Shawer and Noureddin; and Almeric, drawing together one of the most numerous and best appointed armies which had ever been assembled under the Christian banners in Palestine, suddenly crossed the Egyptian frontiers, attacked Pelusium, sacked that city with horrible cruelty, and from thence advanced to the gates of Cairo. But his perfidy and the ferocious conduct of his followers roused the unwarlike Egyptians to desperation; and while the people of Cairo prepared for a vigorous defence, and implored the distant aid of their ancient Turkish enemies for their deliverance, the Vizir Shawer baited the avarice of the king of Jerusalem by the gift of an hundred thousand pieces of gold, and the promise of nine times that amount as the price of peace. The greedy Almeric suffered himself to be amused by these negotiations, until Shiracouch with a large army appeared on the frontiers, and the crafty vizir, then throwing off the mask, joined the Turks with his troops, and recommenced hostilities. The Christian army was now unable to cope with the united forces of the Egyptian and Syrian Moslems; the Greek emperor had failed in rendering the promised co-operation of his navy; and the king of Jerusalem closed his iniquitous scheme of conquest by a disgraceful retreat into Palestine. But the Egyptian vizir imme-

RISE OF SALADIN.

Shiracouch.

diately fell a victim to his own tortuous policy. For, now jealous of the influence which the victorious Turk had acquired over the feeble mind of the Khalif, he conspired against the life of so dangerous a rival; and Shiracouch, anticipating his treachery, caused him to be seized and put to death, and himself to be invested with the dignity of vizir*.

The new ruler of Egypt survived his elevation only two months; and his death prepared the rise of his nephew, the famous Sallah-u-deen or Saladin. This scourge of the Christian fortunes in Palestine had attended his uncle in all his expeditions into Egypt; and in the second of those campaigns had particularly distinguished himself by a skilful and resolute, though unsuccessful, defence of Alexandria. But the political genius and ambition of the young Curdish chieftain had remained concealed from the world, and, perhaps, from himself, in the pursuit of licentious pleasures; and, on the death of Shiracouch, when the haughty pretensions of elder leaders to the vizirship alarmed the jealousy of the feeble Khalif of Egypt, the apparent weakness of Saladin induced that sovereign to nominate him to the vacant dignity. If the disgust and disaffection of the disappointed emirs at first rendered Saladin the powerless servant of the khalif, his skilful use of the royal treasures soon purchased for him the return, and won the affections of his former rivals; and the new vizir, from the minister, easily became the master of the khalif, and the real lord of Egypt. A single bold measure, favoured by the mortal illness of the Khalif Adhed, was now sufficient to complete the Turkish conquest of that country. One of the followers of Saladin, taking possession of the principal pulpit of Cairo, substituted the name of the Khalif of Bagdad for that of the Egyptian sovereign in the public prayers, as the true commander of the faithful; the people, from indifference or fear, silently acquiesced in the change; and the green emblems of the sect of Ali were everywhere displaced by the black ensigns of the Abassidan tenets. The natural death of Adhed, who expired in ignorance of the event, in a few days completed this great political and religious revolution, by which the Fatimite dynasty of Egypt was extinguished, and that country, after a schism of two centuries, was restored to the orthodox communion of Islamism. The Abassidan Khalif of Bagdad, whose dignity as the spiritual chief of that faith was still revered, and whose nominal functions of temporal sovereignty were dictated by his Turkish masters, was made to sanctify the usurpation of Saladin, as the vizir of the Sultan of Damascus in Egypt; and, as long as Noureddin lived, the youthful conqueror was overawed by his power, and, though not without some symptoms of impatience, affected a duteous submission to his will. But, when the death of the sultan* released him from the necessity of fur-

---

* The character of Noureddin is among the brightest in Mohammedan history; for political ability and valour were the least of his great qualities. A Mussulman writer declares that the catalogue of his virtues would fill a volume; and among these, his justice, clemency, and piety extorted a still stronger testimony even from his Christian foes, who had sufficient reason to fear and detest so powerful and deadly an enemy. Thus William of Tyre, after numbering him among the bitterest persecutors of the Christian name and faith, adds, *princeps tamen justus, vafer, providus, et secundum gentis suæ traditiones religiosus.* (Nevertheless he was a just, crafty, and far-seeing prince, and religious according to the traditions of his race.) A

ther dissimulation, Saladin threw off the mask; gradually extended his influence and dominion over Syria and parts of Arabia and Armenia; and deposing the young and helpless sons of Noureddin, finally united the Mussulman states from the Nile to the Tigris under his single empire.* [A. D. 1173.]

By every motive of religion and policy, the new and puissant lord of Syria and Egypt was urged to attempt the expulsion of the detested enemies of his faith from the intervening territory of Palestine; but he was long obliged to suspend his ultimate designs against the Christians, by the more immediate necessity of consolidating his dominion over his Mussulman opponents. Meanwhile, the Latin kingdom, through its intestine disorders, was fast falling into a state of weakness, which promised to deliver it an easy prey to so vigorous an assailant. On the death of Almeric, which shortly followed that of Noureddin, the crown

---

trait of the frugal and rigid integrity with which he abstained from applying the public treasures to his domestic uses, has often been repeated from the pages of D'Herbelot. To some expensive request from the best beloved of his wives, this absolute lord of the gorgeous East would only reply, "Alas! I fear God, and am no more than the treasurer of his people. Their wealth I cannot appropriate; but three shops in the city of Hems are yet my own, and those you may take, for those alone can I give." *Bibliothèque Orientale*, Art. *Noureddin*.

* Will Tyr. p. 980-995. *Bib. Orient.* Art. *Salaheddin*. Also Bohadin, *Vita Saladini*, (Schultens,) p. 1-10. Abulfeda, (*in Excerpt* Schultens,) p. 1-13. De Guignes, lib. xiii. (vol. ii. p. 201-211)

of Jerusalem devolved on his son, Baldwin IV.; but this prince was afflicted with leprosy, and felt himself so unequal to the toils of government, that he committed the regency of the kingdom to his sister Sybilla and her second husband Guy de Lusignan. [A. D. 1173,] a French knight,* to whom she had given her hand after the death of her first lord, a Count of Montferrat. But Lusignan was destitute both of talent and courage; his despicable character and unmerited elevation provoked the scorn and insulted the pride of the barons of Palestine; their disaffection was fomented by the intrigues of Raymond II., Count of Tripoli, a man himself capable of every perfidy; and the whole kingdom was distracted by the selfish conflict of factions. To terminate their struggle, the royal leper was at length compelled to make a new settlement of his realm, by which, abdicating the crown in favour of his infant nephew, Baldwin V., the son of Sybilla by her first husband, he committed the person of his young successor to the

---

* Lusignan was a native, or at least a subject, of the French domains of Henry II. of England, who banished him for the treacherous murder of the Earl of Salisbury, on which he assumed the cross, the usual resource of malefactors, and came to seek his fortune in Palestine. So contemptible was the estimation in which he was held even by his own kindred, that when his brother heard of his subsequent elevation to the throne of Jerusalem, he ironically exclaimed, "Surely, since the barons of Palestine have made *him* a king, they would have made me a god if they had known me." Hoveden,

Saladin.

protection of his relative, Joscelyn de Courtenay, titular Count of Edessa,* the custody of the fortresses of Palestine to the two military orders, and the general regency of the kingdom to the treacherous Count of Tripoli. Baldwin IV. survived this disposition only three years; his own decease was quickly followed by the suspicious death of his nephew; and Sybilla, supported by the patriarch and the grand-master of the Templars, who hated Raymond of Tripoli, obtained

---

* This Joscelyn de Courtenay was the grandson of the hero, and the last of the three counts of Edessa, who bore the same name After the loss of the Edessene territory, and the marriage of his sister with Almeric, the royal favour had invested him with extensive fiefs in the kingdom of Palestine; but, leaving no son, the male line of the Asiatic branch of the Courtenays became extinct on his death *Lignages d' Outremer,* c. xvi.

the joint coronation of her worthless husband and herself as king and queen of Jerusalem. The proud and contemptuous refusal of many of the barons to acknowledge Lusignan for their sovereign produced a civil war, in which the Count of Tripoli, under pretence of supporting the rival claims of Isabella, sister of Sybilla, to a share in the succession, allied himself with Saladin; and these disorders were scarcely appeased by the address of Sybilla and the submission of most of the insurgent nobles, when the fatal tempest of Mussulman war burst upon the disunited and devoted state.*

---

* Will. Tyr. p. 995, *ad fin.* Plagon, (continuator of William of Tyre, in Martenne, *Vet Scriptorum Coll.* vol. v.,) p. 583–590. Bernardus Thesaurarius, (*apud* Muratori *Scrip. Rer. Ital.* vol. vii.,) c. 140–147.

Alexandria.

SECTION II.

BATTLE OF TIBERIAS AND FALL OF JERUSALEM

AS long as Saladin was occupied in establishing his authority over Egypt and Syria, the peace of the Latin kingdom had not been much disturbed by the incursions of the infidels; and some indecisive hostilities had

But just at the crisis when the Turkish conqueror was prepared to attempt the work of destruction which he had probably long meditated, the Christians themselves were the first to disturb the hollow pacification, which might alone have deferred the hour of their ruin; and a just occasion of war was afforded by the aggressions of a predatory baron, Reginald de Chatillon,* [A. D 1186,] who surprised a frontier castle belonging to the Mussulmans on the borders of the Arabian desert, intercepted and plundered their caravans between Egypt and Mecca, and insolently defied the vengeance of the sultan. Saladin demanded redress of the King of Jerusalem for these outrageous violations of the existing peace; but the government of Lusignan was either too feeble or too corrupt to punish the lawless marauder; and, on a refusal of justice, Saladin invaded Palestine at the head of eighty thousand Turcoman horse and foot. The siege of the castle of

---

* The history of this man constitutes in itself a romance; and its details would be considered incredible if narrated by any modern writer of fiction. He was of obscure birth, and a native of Chatillon-sur-Indre, and, following Louis the Young into Asia, was attached to the troop of Raymond of Poictiers, Prince of Antioch. On the death of Raymond, he was selected by his widow, Constance, as her husband, and thus became Prince of Antioch. This choice filled the Western barons with disgust, and, as his after conduct showed, did no credit to the discrimination of the lady. On the death of Constance, he married the widow of Humphrey of Touron, Lord of Carac; and, possessing no quality of a knight but personal courage, he became in that capacity something like a licensed bandit. His fate

240   THE THIRD CRUSADE.

Mecca.

Tiberias was the first signal operation of the Mussulman host; and, for the relief of so important a fortress, the whole strength of the Christian states was hastily collected. But, including the array of the military orders, the King of Jerusalem could now assemble under his standard no more than twelve hundred knights and twenty thousand foot; and the disproportion of his numerical force was aggravated by his own incapacity and cowardice, as well as by the discord and treason* which prevailed in his camp.

---

* By some of the Latin writers, the destruction of the Christian army is ascribed to the treason of the Count of Tripoli, the enemy both of Lusignan and of the Grand-Master of the Temple.   Mr.

On the plain of Tiberias the hostile armies drew out for a conflict, of which the event was to decide the fate of the Christian kingdom. Few intelligible particulars are related of the sanguinary battle which followed; [A.D.1187;] but those few attest the superior skill of Saladin, who, in the first day's encounter, drove his opponents into a situation destitute of water; by setting fire during the night to some neighbouring woods, increased their intolerable sufferings from the drought and heat of a Syrian summer's night; and on the following morning overwhelmed and massacred their exhausted and fainting host. Not only was the slaughter of the cavaliers and soldiery exterminating, but all the principal leaders of the Christian host were the victims or prizes of this fatal field: the grandmaster of the Hospitallers was mortally wounded and died in his flight; and the chief of the rival order of the Temple, together with the Marquis of Montferrat, Reginald of Chatillon, the worthless Lusignan himself, and many of his nobles and knights, became the captives of Saladin. The scene which ensued is too characteristic of manners to be omitted in this

---

favourable mention of the Count by William of Tyre, and the silence of Ralph Coggeshal, whose chronicle is contained in the fifth volume of Martenne, and who was in Palestine at the time of the battle of Tiberias, as a satisfactory refutation of the charge. But the earlier alliance of the Count of Tripoli with Saladin (Bernardus Thesaur. c. 140) is undisputed; and his sacrifice of the Christian cause to party or personal hatred on that occasion, is surely sufficient to war-

place. When the trembling Lusignan, and Chatillon, the guilty provoker of the war, were conducted to the tent of the conqueror, Saladin generously reassured the craven king of his safety by the proffer of a cup of iced water, the Eastern pledge of hospitality. Lusignan wished to pass the cup to Chatillon; but the sultan sternly declared that the impious marauder, who had so often insulted the prophet of Islam, must now either acknowledge his law, or die the death which his crimes had merited. With more virtue than his life had promised, Chatillon spurned the condition of apostasy; and a blow from the cimeter of the ferocious sultan himself, was the immediate signal for his murder. With less excusable cruelty, while he spared his other noble prisoners, Saladin, in his fanatical hatred of the religious orders, or his dread of their prowess, offered the same alternative of apostasy or death to the knights of St. John and of the Temple who had fallen into his hands. To a man, these devoted champions of the cross, two hundred and thirty in number, proved the sincerity of their faith; and the victory of the Moslems was stained by the cold-blooded murder of the whole body.*

The disastrous effects of the battle of Tiberias were immediately felt throughout the Latin kingdom:

---

* Bernardus Thesaur. c. 147–151. Contin. Will. Tyr. p. 590–600. Jacobus a Vitriaco, *Hist. Hierosol.* p. 1117, 1118, (*in Gestis Dei per Francos.*) Hoveden, p. 636–637. D'Herbelot, Art. *Salaheddin*,

for all the principal fortresses had been drained of their garrisons to swell the ranks of the army; and Tiberias itself, Cæsarea, Acre, Jaffa, and Beritus, rapidly fell before the arms of the conqueror. Tyre was alone preserved through the heroic efforts to which the citizens were inspired by the firmness of a young cavalier, son to the captive Marquis of Montferrat. But Saladin would not suffer any secondary object to arrest his great design upon the Christian capital; and turning aside from the walls of Tyre, he marched to the siege of the Holy City. Jerusalem was already crowded with fugitives from every quarter of Palestine; but the number of warriors within its gates was small, and their commander was a timid woman. Queen Sybilla, herself distracted with sorrow and apprehension, was more solicitous for her own safety and that of her captive consort than for the public defence; and dismay and discord reigned within the place. The first summons of Saladin for its surrender was, indeed, rejected; but when the siege was formed, the resistance was feeble or ineffectual; and in fourteen days, the Turks, despite of the sallies and efforts of the garrison, had advanced their works and engines to the foot of the rampart, and undermined the walls. A desire to capitulate was then expressed; but Saladin, in his fury at the refusal to accept his proffered terms, had sworn to execute a dreadful vengeance

ancestors had shed at the capture of the city in the first Crusade. He now, therefore, received the proposal of a capitulation with bitter contempt; and he only listened to the suggestions of mercy, when his burst of passion was spent, and the suppliant Christians left him to dictate the terms of surrender. He then consented to spare the lives of the inhabitants, and promised a safe-conduct for the queen, her nobles, and soldiery, to Tyre, but declared that the remaining population of Jerusalem should become slaves, unless they were ransomed at the rate of ten crowns of gold for each man, half that sum for each woman, and a single piece for every child.

As soon as these terms had been accepted by the submission of the vanquished, Saladin exhibited traits of a generous humanity which might have been little anticipated from the cruelty with which he had recently stained the victory of Tiberias; and his conduct at Jerusalem well merits the eulogy of an enemy, that he was in nothing but in name a barbarian. He not only performed his promises with a religious fidelity, but exceeded their fulfilment by a full measure of benevolence. When the weeping female train of the queen issued from the gates of Jerusalem, his spirit melted even unto tears at the spectacle of their misery: he advanced to meet the mourners; attempted to console the princess with the courteous sympathy of a warrior of chivalry; released

ransom; and even dismissed them laden with presents. Nor did his generosity end here: for he accepted a price very much beneath the stipulated sum for the freedom of the Christian poor; and even liberated so many of his other captives gratuitously, that the total number who remained in bondage did not much exceed ten thousand, out of a population which is said to have amounted to one hundred thousand. These better feelings of his nature achieved a more difficult triumph over even the fanaticism which was usually his master passion: for learning the humane attentions which the knights of the Hospital bestowed upon the sick, he allowed several brethren of an order which he detested and found ever in arms against him, to remain in the city a sufficient time for the accomplishment of their pious and charitable offices.*

When the queen and her train had been safely dismissed, the magnanimous victor made his entry into Jerusalem in triumphant and splendid procession. The great Mosque of Omar, on the site of Solomon's Temple, which had been converted into a Christian church, was immediately consecrated anew to the worship of Islam, after its pavement and walls had been washed with Damascene rose-water; the golden

---

* Bernadus, c. 151-167. Cont. Will. Tyr. p. 601-613. Hoveden, p. 637-645. D'Herbelot, *ubi suprà*. Bohadin, p. 68-76 Abulfeda,

cross which surmounted the dome of the Church of the Sepulchre was taken down, and for two days dragged through the streets; and after a possession by the Christians of eighty-eight years, Jerusalem was again defiled by the religion and empire of the votaries of Mohammed. Nazareth, Bethlehem, Ascalon, Sidon, quickly followed the fate of the capital; the principality of Antioch was only spared on the ignominious condition of tribute to the Sultan; and of all the possessions of the Christians in Palestine, the seaport of Tyre was almost the only place of importance which was saved from the wreck of their fortunes. But to that city all the Christian garrisons which capitulated had been permitted to retire: the whole remaining strength of the Latin chivalry of Palestine was contained within its walls: and when the Turkish army a second time appeared before the place, it was again so bravely defended under the guidance of Conrad of Montferrat, that the conqueror of Jerusalem was compelled to retire from a fruitless siege. The grateful people resolved to bestow the sovereignty of their city upon their brave leader; and when Guy of Lusignan, having obtained his liberation, attempted to enter the place, they refused to admit him within the walls, or to acknowledge further allegiance to the man on whose incapacity and cowardice they laid the ruin of the Christian cause. Lusignan, indeed, had only obtained his release by a solemn renunciation of his crown to

Saladin; and the sultan, satisfied with this vain confirmation to the title of conquest, had returned to enjoy his glory at Damascus; when he was roused from a brief season of repose by the alarming report that the nations of Europe, burning with ardour to avenge the shame of the Christian defeat, and the loss of the Sepulchre of Christ, were again about to precipitate themselves upon the shores of Palestine.*

---

* Bernardus, c. 167-177. Coggeshal, p. 811, 812. *Hist. Hierosol* (*in Gestis Dei*, &c.) p. 1150-1169

SECTION III.

THE GERMANS UNDERTAKE THE CRUSADE.

THE news of the fall of Jerusalem had filled all Western Christendom with horror and grief. By the superstitious piety of the age, the apathetic indifference which had permitted the hallowed scenes of human redemption again to be profaned with the triumph of the enemies of God, was deeply felt as an offence, which merited and would provoke the wrathful judgments of Heaven.

But after the first shock of the intelligence, the general consternation and despair were at once succeeded by a burst of enthusiasm, equally congenial to the fanatical and martial state of society. All the principal sovereigns of Europe,*—except those of Spain, who found sufficient exercise for their zeal against the Mussulman power in that peninsula—immediately vowed to lead their national forces to the recovery of Jerusalem: but even their earnest preparations were too tardy for the popular impatience; and myriads of their subjects, thronging from every country to the ports of the Mediterranean, took shipping at their private charge, and hastened to the shores of Palestine. The chief means of transport, were, as usual, supplied by the maritime republics of Italy; but numerous bands of pilgrims, embarking from the ports

---

* Henry II. of England and Philippe-Auguste of France met and received the Cross together near Gisors; and the English king appears to have been earnest in his intention of undertaking the Crusade, until prevented by the second rebellion of his sons. At a great council which he assembled at Gidington, in Northamptonshire, it was agreed that a tenth of all rents and movables should be levied from the clergy and laity of the realm for the service of the expedition; and by this means the king obtained seventy thousand pounds from his Christian subjects; while he extorted the enormous sum, for those days, of sixty thousand more from the Jews in his dominions, at the rate of a fourth of all their possessions. Gervase, p. 1529. Hoveden, p. 644. This tax of one-tenth, under the name of the Saladin tithe, was imposed by general consent throughout Europe; and though originally proposed to last only for one year, was perpetuated, by the cupidity of the Papal See, into a claim upon the tenth of all ecclesiastical benefices.

of the Baltic, the North Seas, and the British Channel, from thence accomplished the whole maritime passage to the Asiatic coast.*

By the arrival at Tyre, in quick succession, of all these crusaders, led by many noblemen and prelates of distinction, the imbecile king of Jerusalem soon found himself at the head of a numerous army; and when he was encouraged or impelled by the renovated strength and ardent zeal of his followers to advance from Tyre and lay siege to Acre, the numbers of the Christian host before the walls of that important city rapidly swelled to one hundred thousand men. [A. D. 1189.] The danger of a fortress which, by its position between the sea and the great central valley of Palestine, may be regarded as the maritime key of the whole country, roused Saladin from his inaction; and while the strength of the fortifications and the valour of a numerous Mussulman garrison, defied all the efforts of the crusaders, the Sultan himself, arriving in the adjacent plain at the head of a mighty host, enveloped their beleaguers, and harassed them with perpetual though desultory assaults. The Christians, in their turn, were reduced to the necessity of standing on the defensive; their camp was diligently fortified; and such was the strength and completeness of the works with which they surrounded it, that in the hyperbolical language of the East, the Mussulmans declared not even a bird could penetrate the lines. By sea the contest was maintained with equal obstinacy; for the naval forces of the combatants were so nicely balanced, that, by each successive reinforcement, either party was enabled to relieve the garrison of Acre, or to refresh the wants of the besiegers. The latter, indeed, suffered so dreadfully from famine, disease, and the incessant vicissitudes of combat, that above three hundred thousand crusaders are computed to have perished before the walls and in the plain of Acre; and the losses of the Mussulmans from the same causes were probably inferior only in degree. But, on both sides, this frightful consumption of human life was continually fed by new arrivals; and during nearly two years the strength of Christendom and Islam was concentrated and exhausted in an indecisive conflict before the single city of Acre.*

Meanwhile, the great monarchs of the West were gathering their national powers for the third Crusade. Foremost in preparation, as in dignity among them, was the Emperor Frederic Barbarossa, in whom age had no power either to quench the thirst of glory or to chill the fire of religious enthusiasm. But the chivalrous devotion of Frederic was regulated by those prudential qualities of a great commander, which had been

---

* Bernardus Thesaur, c. 179. *Hist. Hierosol.* p. 1170–1172.

Frederic Barbarossa.

matured in forty years of warfare; and while he boldly resolved to take the same route through the East of Europe and Asia Minor, which had been found so disastrous to former hosts of crusaders, his provident and skilful arrangements showed how attentively he had studied the tremendous lessons of their failure. No individual was permitted to join in the sacred enterprise who was unable to furnish the means of his own support for a whole year; and the march from the confines of Germany to the shores of the Hellespont was conducted with the strictest regularity and discipline. The numbers and composition of the host were worthy of the imperial name and power. Besides his own son, the Duke of Swabia, Frederic was attended by the dukes of Austria and Moravia, by above sixty other princes and great lords of the empire, and by fifteen thousand knights, the flower of the Teutonic chivalry. Their mounted attendants swelled the total array of cavalry to sixty thousand; and the infantry, exclusive of unarmed pilgrims, numbered one hundred thousand men. Throughout their passage over the Greek dominions, the German host encountered a repetition of precisely the same course of treacherous hostility, under the hollow semblance of amity, which the Byzantine court and people had pursued in the previous Crusades; but the vengeance of his troops was generally restrained by the magnanimous or prudent forbearance of Frederic; and though he resented the perfidy of the reigning Emperor of the East, Isaac Angelus, by refusing to visit Constantinople as a guest, he peaceably transported his formidable host across the Hellespont. The subsequent passage through Asia Minor was a yet severer trial of Frederic's patience and ability; but his genius

and the march of the imperial army was effected with far superior order, success, and reputation, to that of any preceding host of crusaders. The sufferings of a route through burning and waterless deserts admitted, indeed, of little mitigation; and thousands of the Germans sank under fatigue, agonizing thirst, and the perpetual assaults of the Turcoman hordes, which hung upon their flanks and rear. But the firmness of the Teutonic array repulsed every attack, and prevented any general disaster; and Frederic not only defeated the Sultan of Iconium, but stormed his capital and compelled him to sue for peace. Having thus overborne all opposition, the aged hero pursued his way in unmolested and triumphant ardour, until he lost his life in the little Cilician stream of the Calycadnus, either by a fall from his horse, or by imprudently bathing in the icy waters of that mountain torrent. [A. D. 1190.] The consequences of this event proved how largely his followers had been indebted for their success to the greatness of his personal qualities. The infidels, recovering from the terror inspired by his name and actions, immediately renewed their hostilities on the report of his death; and thenceforth the German army was incessantly harassed by attacks, and nearly disorganized by famine, sickness, and the efforts of the enemy. Thus, although Frederic's son, the Duke of Swabia, who succeeded to the command, was neither deficient in courage nor ability, so dreadful were the losses of the crusaders that before they reached the Syrian confines, their numbers were reduced to one-tenth of their original force. Their array was still, however, sufficiently formidable, on their arrival at Antioch, to deliver that principality from the oppression of Saladin, whose troops retired at their approach; and from thence the gallant Duke of Swabia, with unbroken spirit, led the remains of the German army to reinforce the crusaders before Acre; but it was only to perish himself of disease, with some thousands of his devoted and way-worn followers, under the walls of that city.*

The arrival of the German chivalry before Acre was followed by the memorable institution of a martial order of religious knighthood, which, emulating the design of the fraternities of St. John and of the Temple, and surviving the original object of its creation for the defence of Palestine, was fated to perform no inconsiderable part in the subsequent history of Northern Europe. Above half a century before the loss of Jerusalem, a German crusader and his lady had founded hospitals in that capital for poor pilgrims of both sexes of their nation; and, when subsequent endowments had enriched these houses, the male brethren were moved by the example of the two great orders, to devote themselves to military as well as charitable services. But their efforts had obtained

---

* *Hist. Hierosol.* p. 1156–1163. Godfridi Monachi *Annales,* p. 848-856. Tageno, p. 407–416. (Both in the second volume of

little distinction, and their fraternity was dissolved by the expulsion of the Christians from Jerusalem. Its purposes were now recalled to the national attention by the private charity of some individuals among the German army, who supplied the want of regular hospitals, by opening their tents before Acre for the reception of their sick and wounded countrymen; and a number of knights joining their benevolent association, the Duke of Swabia seized the occasion to incorporate them, for the national honour, into a regular order of religious chivalry, in avowed imitation of those of the Hospital and Temple. A papal authority approved the design, invested the new order with the same privileges as its elder co-fraternities, and ordained the rule of St. Augustin for its government. A white mantle with a black cross was appointed for the garb of the brotherhood, who were divided into three classes of noble cavaliers, priests and sergeants, all exclusively of German race; and thenceforth, under the title of the Teutonic Knights of St. Mary of Jerusalem, the order worthily aspired to an equality in duties and honour with the two great martial fraternities of Palestine.*

---

* Jacobus a Vit. p. 1083.

RICHARD CŒUR DE LION. 257

SECTION II.

RICHARD CŒUR DE LION IN PALESTINE

WHILE the German army was still threading its toilsome march through the deserts and mountain passes of Asia Minor, the sovereigns of France and

England had availed themselves of the maritime position and resources of their states to escape the same dangers and fatigues by a naval passage to the Syrian shores. Both Philippe-Auguste and Richard Cœur de Lion were in the full pride of youthful ambition, impatient for chivalric distinction, and actuated far more by the thirst of glory than by the religious spirit of the age. Interchanging vows of eternal friendship, which were as passionately broken in the first moment of jealous excitement, they had agreed to combine their forces for the sacred expedition; and on the plain of Vezelay in France, they reviewed a gallant and well-equipped host, which amounted to one hundred thousand men of both nations, and of all arms. Conducting their march in concert as far as Lyons, the two monarchs separated at that city, after naming the port of Messina in Sicily as the place of reunion for their combined armaments: Philippe leading the French forces to embark at Genoa; and Richard proceeding to Marseilles with his army, there to expect the arrival of his fleet* from England.

---

* Before his departure from Normandy, Richard promulgated a code of regulations for the government of his fleet, which, as illustrative of the rude principles of marine jurisprudence adopted in that age, would be worthy of a place in our naval history. A murderer was to be tied to the corpse of his victim and cast with it into the sea; or if the crime were committed on shore, to be buried in the same grave with the dead body. A simple blow was to be punished by the immersion of the offender thrice in the sea; but if blood were drawn, by the loss of his right hand: abusive language by a fine. A

But his impatience would brook no delay; and finding that his own navy had not reached that port, he immediately hired a few vessels for the conveyance of his suite, sailed for the Italian coast, and after rashly exposing himself to several dangerous adventures,* crossed into Sicily. Meanwhile the English fleet, after touching at Lisbon on its way, and successfully assisting in the defence of Santarem against a Mussulman army, reached the Mediterranean in safety, received the land forces on board at Marseilles, and entered the port of Messina some days before the arrival either of Philippe or Richard himself.†

In Sicily both monarchs wintered with their forces; and here several circumstances arose to foment into hatred those feelings of ambitious rivalry which naturally sprang from their conflicting pride and pretensions. Against Tancred, the reigning king of

---

thief was to have his head shaved, tarred and feathered; and in that state to be set on shore at the first opportunity. Hoveden, p. 666.

* On one occasion, when travelling in Southern Italy with a single attendant, he entered a cottage to seize a falcon which he heard was detained there: for it seems that no "base churl" might without offence possess a bird trained for the exclusive sport of the chivalric order. The peasants presumed to resist his violence; and in the broil, as he struck one of them, who had drawn a dagger upon him, with the flat of his sword, the weapon broke; and he was compelled to defend himself with stones until he effected his retreat to a neighbouring monastery. Hoveden, p. 672.

† Hoveden, p. 664–673. Galfridi a Vinesauf, *Itinerarium Regis Anglorum Richardi, &c. in Terram. Hierosol.* (apud Gale. *Scrip-*

Richard Cœur de Lion.

Sicily, Richard had several causes of resentment for the detention in prison of his sister Joan, relict of William II., the late sovereign of the island, and a refusal either to restore her dower, or to pay legacies which her husband had bequeathed to the English crown. To enforce redress for these injuries, Richard had recourse to very violent proceedings: seized a castle, on his sister's release, for her residence, took military possession of other posts, and allowed his troops to commit many excesses. While the French king was interposing as a mediator, the citizens of Messina were provoked to attack the English, and after a bloody engagement, in which the latter prevailed, Richard allowed them to sack the city, and planted his banners on its walls. Philippe was justly offended at an outrage, which in effect, as he resided in Messina, left him a prisoner in the hands of an ally who was also his vassal; and Richard was at last induced to appease him by withdrawing his troops. The submission of Tancred to all the demands of the English monarch restored the general peace; and Richard generously sent Philippe twenty thousand ounces of gold, as the moiety of the sum which he compelled the Sicilian prince to pay in satisfaction of his claims. He also loaded both English and French knights with presents; and on Christmas day feasted the whole chivalry of the two nations, and dismissed every individual with some largess apportioned to his rank. His prodigal dissipation, by such means, of the treasures which had been wrung from his subjects before his departure on the Crusade, exalted his popularity in both armies far above that of his more provident or less wealthy rival; and formed an additional source of jealousy to Philippe. A new ground of quarrel between the two monarchs was soon created by the intelligerce that Richard, disregarding his engagement to marry Alice or Adelia, sister of Philippe, was about to espouse the Princess Berengaria, daughter of Sancho, king of

RHODES.

Navarre, who, in effect, soon after arrived in Sicily, escorted by the queen-mother, Eleanor of England. After much dispute, Philippe at last consented to release Richard from his contract upon his promise to pay ten thousand marks, and to restore Alice with the castles which had been assigned as her dower.*

Their feuds being thus terminated by a hollow reconciliation, Philippe, on the return of spring, was the first to depart with his forces from the Sicilian shores, and arrived without accident at the Christian camp before Acre; but Richard was less fortunate or prudent. Off the coast of Crete, his fleet was dispersed by a storm; and at Rhodes his fiery temper was roused by intelligence that two of his vessels, which had been wrecked on the shores of Cyprus, were plundered, and the crews detained in captivity. To revenge this injury he sailed for Cyprus; and, having in vain demanded reparation of Isaac, a prince of Comnenian race, who had revolted against the Byzantine throne and seized the government of the island, the English monarch disembarked his troops, took Lymesol, the tyrant's capital, by storm, and, being assisted by the defection of the islanders, compelled him to surrender at discretion. The English prince made an ungenerous use of his victory; for he threw the fallen usurper into chains, which, with a mockery of respect, were forged of silver; grievously taxed the Cypriots, who had welcomed him as their deliverer; and asserted the title of conquest to the lordship of their island. After celebrating at Lymesol his nuptials with Berengaria, which had been deferred in Sicily on account of the season of Lent, Richard finally sailed for Acre. The numbers of his land forces have not been recorded; but the magnitude of the whole armament may be estimated by the enumeration of his fleet, which consisted of fifty galleys of war, thirteen large store-vessels, and above one hundred other transports filled with horses and men. On the short voyage from Cyprus to the Syrian shore, the English navy intercepted an enormous troop-ship of Saladin, having on board, according to the Latin chroniclers, for the reinforcement of the garrison of Acre, the incredible number of fifteen hundred men, and well supplied with stores of the Greek fire. The great bulk and lofty sides of this vessel long defied the attacks of the light galleys of the Christians; but she was at length carried by boarding; her hull being either scuttled, during the conflict, by the desperation of her own crew, or pierced by the beaks of the English galleys, she sank with all her stores; and every soul of the infidels, except thirty-five, was either massacred or drowned.*

Siege of Acre.

A few days afterward Richard disembarked his army before Acre; and his arrival was greeted in the Christian camp with enthusiastic rejoicings. Notwithstanding the previous junction of the King of France and his forces, the operations of the long-protracted siege had continued to languish; but the English monarch had no sooner landed his battering engines than, despite of an illness under which he was labouring, he caused the attack to be pressed with the utmost vigour; and as well by his personal example as by prodigal rewards, animated the whole crusading host

---

* Hoveden, p. 688–692. Vinesauf, p. 316–329. Bohadin, p. 166. But the Mussulman historian rates the troops on board this great store-ship at only six hundred and fifty, still indicating in the

Movable Towers used in Sieges.

with a new spirit. Every effort of Saladin to rout the besiegers or relieve the place was repulsed; and at length, after an heroic resistence, finding their defences shattered on every side and their numbers daily diminished, the exhausted and despairing garrison obtained the reluctant permission of the sultan to capitulate. Upon condition that Saladin should restore the wood of the true cross which he had taken in Jerusalem, release fifteen hundred chosen Christian captives, deliver up Acre, and ransom the garrison by

Tower and Battering-ram.

the monarchs of France and England agreed to spare the lives of all the Mussulmans in the place. Upon these terms the city was surrendered; and the banner of the cross was again planted on its ruined walls. The garrison and inhabitants, with the exception of some thousand hostages, were permitted to depart unmolested; and the sultan immediately broke up his camp and withdrew from the vicinity of the captured fortress. His subsequent failure, from reluctance, or more probably from inability, to pay the ransom of the prisoners within the stipulated period, was the signal for a tragedy horribly characteristic of the barbarous and fanatical spirit of crusading warfare. The Mussulman hostages, to the number of above five thousand, being led out from the city to the French and English camps, were slaughtered in cold blood; and Richard himself, in a letter still extant, boasted of the massacre as an acceptable service to Heaven. The sultan

Richard Cœur de Lion at Acre.

his Christian captives; and on both sides repeated butcheries continued to darken the mutual hatred of the combatants.*

---

* Hoveden, p. 692–698. Vinesauf, p. 329–346. Bohadin, p 180–188. Hoveden, indeed, declares that the massacre of the Christian captives by Saladin preceded that of the Turkish hostages by Richard; but Bohaden says otherwise; and it is not probable that the sultan would thus have provoked the destruction of his people, whom he had wished to save. The expressions in Richard's letter, as given in Hoveden, (p. 698,) are (Thus, as in duty bound, we put them to death,) *Sic ut decuit, fecimus expiare;* and no writer in that fanatical age seems to have imagined that even the cold-blooded slaughter of infidels could be otherwise than meritorious and acceptable to Heaven. The old romance of *Richard Cœur de Lion* goes

The capture of Acre was hailed by the Christians as a glad omen of the recovery of the Holy Sepulchre. But these sanguine anticipations were shortly chilled by the retirement of the King of France from the Crusade. The causes of this secession, for which severe illness afforded some plea, have been sought in feelings of jealousy at the superior glory won during the siege of Acre by the liberality and prowess of his royal associate. The eminent political abilities of Philippe-Auguste, indeed, though they placed him in sober estimation at an immeasurable distance above his irrational and fiery rival, were of little weight in the fields of Palestine; the martial qualities by which he was himself distinguished would sustain no comparison with the transcendent personal heroism of the "Lion-hearted" Plantagenet; and he who, in the annals of Europe, figures as the ablest monarch and most renowned conqueror of his age, is discerned only through the wild romance of the Crusades as the envious or recreant deserter from a holy war. But the withdrawal of Philippe was produced less by any in-

---

ject deserved to be associated with pleasurable emotions, thus prefaces the tale of the butchery with a poetical descant on the charms of the vernal season :—

> " Merry is, in time of May
> When fowlis sing in her lay
> Flowcres on apple-trees and perry
> Small fowles sing merry
> Ladies strew her bowers
> With red roses and lily flowers," &c.

consistency in his own character than by the intemperate conduct of Richard. The reckless spirit with which the English king had already wasted so much of the season for action in Sicily and Cyprus, and the intolerable arrogance of pretensions that would brook no control, alike foreboded any but a happy issue to the confederacy of which he was so puissant a member; and, unless the King of France had been prepared to submit unconditionally to his capricious and haughty dictation, their separation might alone avert an open rupture, and the total ruin of the Crusade. The real disgrace of Philip was his subsequent perfidy in attacking the dominions of his absent rival, contrary to the solemn oath which Richard exacted from him on his departure; but the interests of the Crusade itself were promoted by his abandoning to his rival the undivided possession of the supreme command; and, as an evidence of his sincerity in the cause, he left with Richard ten thousand of his best troops under the conduct of the Duke of Burgundy.*

After the retirement of the French king, Richard prepared to resume the design of the war,† and still

---

* Hoveden, p. 697. Vinesauf, p. 844. That Richard, however, was greatly incensed at his rival's desertion, is evident from the intemperate expressions of his letter.

† He had some difficulty in inducing his army to quit the licentious pleasures of Acre: a city so abounding, according to Vinesauf, *vino peroptimo et puellis pulcherrimis,* (in choicest wines and fairest damsels,) that by deep potations the countenances of the gravest

found himself able to muster nearly thirty thousand English, French, and German warriors under the standard of the cross. He conducted the advance of this combined force from Acre in a southerly direction upon Jaffa, along the sea-shore; and in the order of his march no inconsiderable share of military skill and discipline is observable. Nearest to the coast, and in communication with the English fleet, which attended the expedition with supplies of provisions and stores, were the camp-train and followers; while the army itself, covering these accessories, moved in five divisions: the Templars in the van, the Hospitallers closing up the rear; and the archers and other light-armed foot on the left or outward flank to check with their missiles the desultory but galling onsets of the Turkish cavalry. By day, clouds of these horsemen hovered around the front, flank, and rear of the Christians, and harassed their march with incessant assaults: by night, Saladin encamped in their vicinity, and broke the repose of the wearied soldiery with frequent alarms. But the firm array, the unshaken valour, and the patient* determination of the Europeans, exhausted all the artifices of Asiatic warfare. The daily march was accomplished in compact array,

---

* The heroic fortitude of the crusaders is attested by the unsuspicious evidence of an enemy and an eye-witness. Many of them who had received several Turkish arrows at a time in their chainmail, the thick cloth lining of which alone protected them from wounds, marched on, while these shafts bristled on their backs, with

and with a slow but resolute advance; at sunset the army regularly halted; and thrice during the night the loud voices of the heralds, breaking the deep silence of the camp with solemn injunction to remember the Holy Sepulchre, roused the slumbering sentinels of the religious host to watchfulness and prayer. At length Saladin, reinforced by new swarms of the Moslems from all parts of his empire, and finding every desultory attempt to arrest the progress of the Christians unavailing, resolved upon one mighty effort to accomplish their total destruction. On the morning of the sixteenth* day after the advance of the crusaders from Acre, when near Azotus, the brazen kettle-drum of the sultan sounded the attack; and the whole infidel host was suddenly precipitated, in one tremendous charge, upon the Christian array. So rapid and furious was the onset, so vastly superior were the numbers of the assailants, and so overwhelming the force and weight of the shock, that the small squadrons of the crusaders, enclosed within their own infantry, were for a time crushed together from all sides by the pressure. Galled by the Turkish arrows, the chivalry impatiently demanded permission to extricate themselves by a charge; but the fiery Plantagenet, now alone calm, cool, and collected, and

---

* Not the eleventh, as the exact Gibbon (c. lix.) with unusual inaccuracy has stated; for Richard commenced his march from Acre on the 22d of August, and the battle of Azotus was fought on the 7th of September. Hoveden and Vinesauf, *in locis*.

Richard I. at Azotus.

foreseeing a decisive victory, restrained the impetuosity of his knights, until he observed that the quivers of the infidels were emptied and their strength exhausted. Then, causing the infantry to open out, he led and let loose the Christian chivalry in all directions upon the wavering enemy. The whole Turkish host, unable to resist the vigour and strength of these steel-clad squadrons, broke and fled to the adjacent hills. So successful and sanguinary were the charge and pursuit, that above twenty emirs and seven thousand of the flower of the Turkish cavalry were slain on the field; and the result justified the boast of Richard, that, in forty campaigns, the veteran sultan had never sustained so severe a defeat.*

After this signal victory, the crusaders, without further molestation by the infidels, pursued their triumphant march to Jaffa; and, Saladin having wisely destroyed the works of fortresses which he was hopeless of preserving, they took possession both of that city and Cæsarea, with other dismantled castles in their vicinity. It is said that Richard desired at once

---

* Hoveden, p. 698.   Vinesauf, p. 846–860.

to have followed up his success by advancing against Jerusalem, but was prevented by the factious opposition of the French barons, who, seconded by the wish of the army to repose from their fatigues, insisted upon the necessity of first rebuilding the fortifications of Jaffa and its dependencies.* However this might have been, two months were consumed in restoring these works, and in vain negotiations with Saladin,† before the crusaders again moved forward toward Jerusalem. They penetrated without serious opposi-

---

* During this cessation of active hostilities, Richard, while pursuing the sport of falconry with his usual imprudence, beyond the precints of the Christian lines, was attacked by a party of Saracens, and only escaped captivity or death through the generous devotion of a Provençal knight named Guillaume de Pratelles, who drew off the attention of the enemy by feigning to be the king, and as such surrendered himself. Richard proved not ungrateful; for his last care in Palestine was to ransom his preserver. Vinesauf, p. 372.

† In the course of these negotiations, which were more than once interrupted and resumed, Richard and Saladin seem to have seriously entertained a singular project for an accommodation of the Christian and Moslem interests by means of a marriage between Saphadin, or Malec-al-Adel, the brother of the Sultan, and the widowed queen of Sicily, sister of the English king, who had accompanied him to Palestine. With his Christian bride, the Mussulman prince was to receive from his brother the sovereignty of Jerusalem; but the whole design, according to Bohadin, though agreeable to both Saladin and Richard, was frustrated by the repugnance of both Asiatics and Europeans to so unnatural an alliance. Bohadin, p. 209. During the negotiations, the two armies mingled in constant and amicable intercourse; and frequent kindnesses were interchanged between their sovereigns. When Richard was ill, Saladin sent him the choicest fruits, and the yet greater refreshment of snow during the burning heats of summer. Hoveden, p. 693.

tion to Ramula within a short distance of the Holy City. But here the inclemency of the season, want of provisions, and the consequent and alarming increase of sickness, arrested their march; and Richard himself admitted the present hopelessness of success. The army, therefore, fell back to the coast; and the winter was spent by the soldiery in repairing the walls of several of the conquered fortresses, and by their leaders in treacherous intrigues or violent dissensions At length, on the return of spring, Richard so far succeeded in restoring unanimity as to assemble all the Christian forces in Palestine under his standard; and at their head again he advanced toward Jerusalem. The general enthusiasm of the army was kindled by the renovated hope of success; the chieftains and soldiery joined in a solemn oath that they would not quit Palestine until the Sepulchre of Christ should be redeemed; and when the army reached the valley of Hebron, and arrived even in sight of the Holy City, the accomplishment of their vows seemed at hand. The Moslems were filled with consternation; numbers fled from Jerusalem; and even Saladin despaired of preserving his proudest conquest.*

But, at this critical juncture, the sultan was delivered from his apprehensions by the unexpected retreat of the crusading host. [A. D. 1192.] The causes of this failure are variously ascribed by the

---

* Hoveden, p. 698-714. Vinesauf, p. 360-409. Bohadin, p

Hebron.

Christian chronicles to the contemplated difficulties of a siege, to the envious or treasonable defection of the Duke of Burgundy and his French followers, and to the indecision of Richard himself. But the best attested account is that which refers the abandonment of the enterprise to the act of the king.* Whether he was swayed by his usual impulses of caprice, urged to hasten his return to Europe by repeated intelligence of the dangerous machinations of his faithless brother and rival, or secretly conscious that the resources of the Crusade were unequal to the capture of Jerusalem, it is vain to inquire. But he suddenly paused in his operations; and, when its walls were within his view, proposed the appointment of a council, selected from among the barons of Palestine and the chiefs of the military orders, to decide upon oath if it were preferable to engage in the siege of the Holy City, or to make a diversion against Damascus or Cairo. To the general surprise and disappointment, the council decided upon the expediency of deferring the enterprise before them; and Richard, amid the discontent of the whole army, commenced a second and final retreat to the sea-coast. Yet whatever were the motives of necessity or inconstancy which dictated this resolve, he poignant'y felt the mortification or shame of his failure; and, when one of his followers led him to a height from whence he might take his last view of Jerusalem, he hid his face in his shield, exclaiming that he who was unable to rescue, was unworthy to look upon the Sepulchre of Christ.*

Saladin was not slow to reap his advantage on the retreat of the crusaders; and, finding that Richard had continued his march from Jaffa to Acre, he poured

---

* Hoveden, p. 715. Vinesauf, *ubi suprà*.

down from the hills with his troops on the former
city, and assaulted the place so unexpectedly, that
numbers of the Christian garrison and inhabitants
were slain in the streets, and the remainder only saved
their lives by shutting themselves up in some of the
towers. They had already been reduced to sue for a
capitulation, when Richard arrived off the port to
their succour. He had prepared to embark for Europe before he heard of their danger; but fired with
indignation that Saladin should have renewed the
offensive while his foot was still on the strand of Palestine, he threw himself into a galley, and, followed
only by a few knights and archers in six other vessels,
sailed for Jaffa, leaving his army to retrace their
march after him along the coast. When his small
squadron had approached the shore, finding that some
of the garrison still held out, he plunged into the sea;
his attendants inspired by his heroic example, quickly
followed, and the opposing Moslems on the beach were
so dismayed by the fury of the attack, that they fled
before this handful of assailants, and abandoned Jaffa
to its deliverers. Though Richard, including the rescued garrison, had with him only fifty-five knights,
of whom but ten were mounted, and two thousand
foot-soldiers, he displayed his contempt for the infidels
by encamping without the gates; and in this situation, on the morrow of his arrival, the Turkish
cavalry, recovering from their surprise, and ascer-

Richard Cœur de Lion at the battle of Jaffa.

overwhelming numbers. He not only sustained their repeated charges, but each time rushed into the thickest of their squadrons at the head of his ten knights, and everywhere carried death and confusion into their ranks. Never had even he performed such prodigies of valour and personal strength; whole squadrons of the quailing infidels fled before his single arm; and the Mussulman writers themselves are the most admiring witnesses and warmest eulogists of these incredible exploits.* Night put an end to the unequal

---

* This concurrent testimony of Christian and Mohammedan writers compels history to ascribe to Richard feats of personal he-

combat; but so hopeless was Saladin of prevailing against the hero, that he raised the siege of Jaffa without any further attempt.*

This was the last and most brilliant achievement of the lion-hearted king on the shores of Palestine; and with it ended the third Crusade. The exertions of Richard brought on a fever which increased his longing desire to return to Europe; and the awe inspired by his prowess and victory facilitated his overtures for a renewal of former negotiations. Saladin himself was weary of fruitless hostilities, and languishing under a bodily decline, which in a few months bowed him to the grave. Richard consented to dismantle the fortifications of Ascalon, which, as the key of Egypt from the Syrian frontiers, was in the hands of the Christians an object of jealous dis-

---

Such was the admiration which he extorted from his enemies, that Saphadin, during his last action before Jaffa, observing him dismounted, sent him two Arabian horses, on one of which he continued the conflict until nightfall. Some time before, the same Turkish prince had solicited and obtained, at the hands of the Christian hero, the honour of knighthood for his son. But the most striking proof of the reality of his astonishing prowess, is the enduring terror in which his very memory was held by the Moslems; for, above half a century after his fiery spirit had been quenched in the grave, "his tremendous name was employed by Syrian mothers to silence their infants; and if a horse suddenly started from his way, his rider was wont to exclaim, 'Dost thou think King Richard is in the bush?' *Cuides tu que ce soit le Roi Richart?*" Gibbon, ch. lix. from Joinville.

* Vinesauf, p. 412–421. Bohadin, p. 288–249. Abulfeda,

quietude to the Sultan; and the latter on his part agreed to leave them in unmolested possession of Tyre, Acre, and Jaffa, with all the maritime territory between the first and last of those cities; to abstain also from attacking the territories of the Prince of Antioch and Count of Tripoli, and to grant all Christian pilgrims free access to the holy places of Jerusalem. Upon these terms the two monarchs concluded a truce between the nations of their respective faiths for three years and three months; and Richard, embarking at Acre, bade a last adieu to the scene of his glory, and commenced that homeward voyage, of which we are in another place to relate the calamitous issue.*

Such was the termination of the third Crusade. Its grand object in the recapture of Jerusalem had not been accomplished; but the total ruin with which the affairs of the Latin kingdom were threatened by the fatal defeat at Tiberias had been averted; the tide of Mussulman conquest was arrested; and a great part of the sea-coast of Palestine, with its chain of fortresses, remained in the hands of the Christians. The recovery or preservation of this territory, which for eighty years deferred the final triumph of the Moslems, was chiefly attributable to the heroic achievements of the English king; and, but for his intemperance and caprice, even greater advantages might have been reaped from his splendid exploits. Yet it may be doubted whether his want of complete success was not full as much produced by the political vices of the Latin states, as by the errors of his own conduct. The factions nursed in Palestine during the feeble reign of the leper Baldwin IV. had grown into uncontrollable strength and violence; their quarrels were embraced by the crusaders from Europe; and even while the victories of Saladin threatened to involve all parties in a common ruin, the dissensions of the Christians were more dangerous to the general cause than the arms of their infidel enemies. The conflicting pretensions of aspirants to the Latin throne of Palestine supplied a constant subject of disunion. By the death of his consort Sybilla and her children, during the siege of Acre, the worthless Lusignan had lost his only title to a matrimonial crown; and he found a formidable competitor in Conrad, the gallant prince of Tyre, who had espoused Isabella, or Melicent, sister of the late queen. From their personal enmity, the King of England supported the cause of Lusignan, and the French monarch that of Conrad and his consort. After the departure of Philippe, Richard, to suppress a civil war, found it necessary to recognise the royal title of Conrad, and consoled Lusignan with the crown of Cyprus; but this accommodation was scarcely concluded, when Conrad was murdered in the streets of Tyre by two of the Hassassins.

whose systematic employment of the dagger against their enemies introduced a new term into the languages of Europe. By the partisans of Conrad, his murder was imputed to the instigation of Richard; and this charge was made the plea for new dissensions; but all evidence of the open and fearless impetuosity of Plantagenet's temper is opposed to the belief that, if he had sought the life of Conrad, he would not have stooped to so perfidious and dastardly a mode of gratifying his enmity.* The widow of Conrad accepted the hand of Henry, Count of Champagne, who in right of this marriage was recognised, both by the public voice and the assent of Richard, as King of Jerusalem;† and his undisputed assumption of the visionary title at length removed one of the

---

* Bohadin, indeed, (p. 225,) asserts that the murderers, who were taken and put to the torture, confessed that they were employed by the King of England; but both Vinesauf (p. 377) and Hoveden (p. 717) agree in reporting the declaration of the Hassassins, that they had killed Conrad in revenge for an injury which he had offered to their chief; and this version of the tale has great internal probability. Richard, in fact, since his reconciliation, had nothing to gain by the crime; and Conrad himself so little suspected him as, on his death-bed, to desire his widow to commit the fortress of Tyre to the keeping of the English prince. No conclusion, either of the innocence or guilt of Richard, is fairly to be drawn from the exculpatory letter from the chief of the Hassassins, an evident forgery subsequently produced at his trial before the Imperial German Diet Fœdera, vol. i. 71.

means by which the factions of Palestine had aggravated the disasters of the Christian cause.

But the Christians in Palestine were indebted for their safety, after the third Crusade, far less to any union among themselves than to the death of their formidable enemy. Saladin* only survived his treaty with Richard a few months; and on his decease the great empire which he had consolidated was almost immediately dissolved. In its division, three of his numerous sons erected distinct thrones at Cairo, Damascus, and Aleppo; but most of his veteran soldiery preferred to range themselves under the standard of his brother Saphadin; and at their head that prince carved out for himself, at the expense of his nephews, a considerable sovereignty in Syria. [A. D. 1193.]

---

* The really great qualities of Saladin have sometimes been too absolutely lauded; for, as Mr. Mills has well observed, (*Hist. of Crusades*, vol. ii. 82,) his character was but a "compound of dignity and baseness." He had established his throne over the Moslems by treachery and bloodshed; and his first successes against the Christians had been stained by atrocious cruelty. But his government of his own people, after his power was secure, was mild and equitable; as a Mussulman, in his latter years, he was eminently pious, just, and charitable; and we have seen that, even toward enemies, he was sometimes capable of the most magnanimous and generous conduct. He is, perhaps, the brightest exemplar in history of an Asiatic hero; and his virtues, like the dark traits which obscured them, exhibit the genuine lineaments of his clime and race.

General View of Jerusalem.

CHAPTER IV.

The Fourth Crusade.

SECTION I.—THE FRENCH, GERMANS, AND ITALIANS UNITE IN THE CRUSADE.

T this stage of the narrative considerable difficulty is felt by the historian in arranging chronologically the series of events that crowd so rapidly upon him, and it

the opening sentences of this chapter relate to incidents that preceded by years what it is customary to call the FOURTH CRUSADE.

At the expiration of the three years' truce which the English king had negotiated, the dissensions of the infidels revived in the Christians the fond hope of reconquering Jerusalem; and at the instigation of the military orders, a new Crusade* was proclaimed by Pope Celestin III. Throughout France and England, from whatever causes, the appeal was heard with indifference; but in Germany the design was promoted by some momentary schemes of ambition which the emperor—the execrable Henry VI.—appears to have cherished of aggrandizing himself in the East; and, supported by his influence, the preaching of the clergy in that country was so successful, that the Cross was enthusiastically taken by many princes and prelates of the empire, and by vast numbers of nobles and persons of inferior rank. Thus composed, three great armaments, all from Germany, successively reached the port of Acre, and raised the most

---

* As the exhortation of the pope to the nations of Europe to engage in this design was general, some writers have dignified the abortive result with the title of the Fourth Crusade; and numbered the subsequent expedition, which was directed against the Byzantine Empire, as the Fifth of Nine. But the more usual, which seems also the more convenient division, restricts the term of distinct Crusades to Seven, or at most Eight, great efforts, which were either produced by some signal occasion, such as the loss of Edessa or Jerusalem, or else productive of some considerable event.

Henry VI. Emperor of Germany.

confident anticipations among the Latins in the East of a decisive triumph over their infidel enemies. But the Mussulmans both of Egypt and Syria, forgetting their civil feuds in the common danger of their religion and empire, rallied around the standard of Saphadin; and though the combined chivalry of Germany and Palestine gained some victories in the field, these successes were always either marred by their dissensions, or counterbalanced by the elastic spirit of Turkish hostility, which started into new and vigorous action, as often as misconduct or exhaustion relaxed the efforts of the Christians. By the death of the emperor, the German princes and prelates were recalled through political interests to Europe; and at their departure they left the Latin possessions in Palestine only slightly enlarged by their aid. The general superiority, however, which their arms had asserted over the Mussulman power was useful in sustaining the dignity and safety of the Christian state; and though the nominal capital of the kingdom was still unrecovered, the German victories had given security to the throne of Henry of Champagne, whose real sovereignty extended over great part of the seacoast of Syria. To these considerable fragments of the Latin monarchy of Palestine, Cyprus was soon after added, on the death of Henry, by the union of his queen, thus widowed for the third time, with Almeric of Lusignan, the successor of Guy in the sovereignty of that island; and on the solemnization of this marriage at Acre, Almeric and Isabella assumed, in 1197, the joint title of King and Queen of Jerusalem and Cyprus.*

The exhortations of Pope Celestin III. had failed to reanimate the religious zeal of the chivalry of France: but a fresh impulse was given to their fanaticism when Innocent III., three years afterward, ascended the papal throne. The convenient precedent of the Saladin tithe might suggest to that celebrated Pontiff a tempting occasion for again taxing the clergy of Europe under the pretext of a new Crusade; but perhaps the single motive of filling the papal coffers by

---

* For all these transactions in Palestine, see Bernardus Thesaur p. 813–818. *Chron. Sclavorum*, lib. iv. v. vi. (in Freher, *Rerum Script. German.* vol. ii.) Cont. Will. Tyr. lib. ii. Abulfeda, lib. iv &c.

this disgraceful expedient has been too confidently attributed to Innocent, in whom the ambitious desire of extending the spiritual and temporal dominion of the Holy See was at least as strong as any mere cupidity of gold. But whatever were his objects, he entered on the design of again arming Europe against the infidels with all the energy which distinguished his character. He wrote himself to the sovereigns of Christendom, exhorting them severally either to take the cross in person, or at least to contribute their forces and treasures to the sacred enterprise; and his legates were despatched throughout the kingdoms of the West to levy on all ecclesiastical bodies the fortieth part of their revenues, and to obtain the pecuniary subscription and personal services of the laity by the promises of indulgences and pardon for their sins.

So productive were these efforts, that the free offerings of the princes and people exceeded the total amount imposed on the clergy; but the most powerful auxiliary of the papal design was a fanatical priest named Foulques, of Neuilly, near Paris, who professed to atone for a life of sin by dedicating its remains to the service of heaven; and who, without the rude originality of the Hermit Peter, or the learning and dignified virtues of St. Bernard, yet with a success little inferior to that of either, by the vehemence of his exhortations, and by his pretended revelations of the divine will, now kindled the flame of religious enthusiasm throughout Flanders and France.*

When the fame of his preaching and his miracles had already prepared the public mind of those countries for the sacred enterprise, the martial and fanatical zeal of the French nobility was roused into action by the example which was offered to them at a great tournament in Champagne. There Thibaut, the youthful count of that province, and his cousin Louis, Earl of Blois, both of them nephews, by a common relationship, to the monarchs of France and England, and the former brother to the late King Henry of Jerusalem, resolved to exchange the martial sports for the sterner duties of chivalry, and solemnly devoted themselves and their fortunes to the service of the cross [1200.] Their spirit was enthusiastically caught by the assembled knighthood; their vows were embraced on the spot by Simon de Montfort, Lord of Mante, and a numerous band of the noblest chevaliers of France; and, when intelligence of the inspiring design reached

---

* Foulques did not live to contemplate the full consequences of his preaching. He died before the crusading armament sailed from Venice. Du Cange on Villehardouin, No. xxxvii. His denunciations were of the usual kind, and such as custom had made familiar to the ears of that generation; and his oratory is described by contemporaries as plain, but impressive. Addressing Cœur de Lion, he said, "You have three daughters to dispose of in marriage, Avarice, Pride, and Luxury." "Well," replied Richard, "I give my pride to the Templars, my avarice to the monks of Citeaux, and my luxury to the bishops."—Rigord, Hisotriographer to Philippe Auguste.

the court of Baldwin, Count of Flanders, brother-in-law of Thibaut, that prince, with a great body of Flemish knights, hastened to enrol himself in the holy cause. Meanwhile, in Italy and in Germany, the papal exhortations and promises of spiritual rewards had not been without their desired effect. In the former country, Boniface, Marquis of Montferrat, brother of the murdered Conrad of Tyre, and in the latter, the Bishop of Halberstadt, both seconded by great numbers of knightly and plebeian warriors, assumed the cross; and the King of Hungary, with his subjects, sealed the sincerity of their faith by the same test.*

The French nobles did not suffer the ardour of their followers to cool by inaction. To forward the enterprise and arrange its details, the three Counts of Champagne, Blois, and Flanders, with their principal associates, met twice in deliberation at Soissons and at Compeigne; and the result of their councils was a resolution to avoid the disasters which the fatal experience of former Crusades had shown were the inevitable attendants of a land expedition to Palestine, and to imitate the maritime passage of Philippe-Auguste and Richard Plantagenet. But, as the barons of the inland province of Champagne could not command the same means of naval transport as those sovereigns, they determined upon attempting to pur-

---

* *Vita Innocent. III.* (*apud* Muratori, *Script. Rer. Ital.* vol. iii.) p. 506–526. *Histoire de la Prise de Constantinople, par* Geoffroy

chase the aid of one of the maritime republics of Italy, who, throughout the Crusades, had been wont to hire out their services both as the common carriers and allies of the Western pilgrims. Among these states, Venice had already attained a preponderance of power and resources; and to that city, with full powers to negotiate on their behalf, the French barons despatched six chosen deputies, and in the number Geoffroy de Villehardouin, marshal of Champagne, to whose pen or dictation we are indebted for a simple and expressive narration of the whole Crusade.

The ducal crown of Venice was at this time worn by Enrico Dandolo, who, at the extraordinary age of ninety-three years, and in almost total blindness, still preserved the vigorous talents, the active heroism, and the ambitious or patriotic spirit of his youth. He received the noble envoys with honour; and, after the purport of their embassy had been regularly submitted to the councils of the state, invited them to meet the assembled citizens in the Place of St. Mark. There, before a multitude of more than ten thousand persons, the haughty barons of France threw themselves upon their knees to implore the assistance of the commercial republicans in recovering the Sepulchre of Christ. Their tears* and eloquence pre-

---

* These doughty champions of chivalry were, as Gibbon has observed, by habit great weepers. *Mult plorant,* &)., is the phrase of Villehardouin on almost every occasion of excitement. This name, which afterward became so conspicuous in the annals of the East.

Piazza of St. Mark, Venice.

vailed; the price of the desired aid had been left by the envoys to the assessment of the doge and his immediate council; and for the sum of eighty-five thousand silver marks—less than £200,000 of our modern English money, and therefore not an unreasonable demand—the republic engaged to transport four thousand five hundred knights, nine thousand esquires and men-at-arms, with their horses and equipments, and twenty thousand foot-soldiers, to any part of the coasts of the East which the service of God might require, to provision them for nine months, and to escort and aid them with a fleet of fifty galleys; but only on condition that the money should be paid before embarkation, and that whatever conquests might be made should be equally divided between the barons and the Venetian state.*

On the return of the envoys to France, these terms received a joyful approval from their associates; but several untoward circumstances arose to obstruct the performance of the treaty. The young Count of Champagne, the ardent promoter and destined chief of the enterprise, was already stretched on a death-

---

took its rise from a village, or castle, in the diocese of Troye, between Bar and Arcy. The elder branch of the family, to which the marshal belonged, expired in 1400, and the younger, which acquired the principality of Achaia, merged in the family of Savoy. Michaud, ii. 46.

* Andreæ Danduli, *Chron. Venet.* (in *Script. Rer. Ital.* vol. xii.) p. 320–323, in which the original treaty is given. Villehardouin, No. xiii. xiv.

bed; and on his decease some time was lost before the mutual jealousy of the French barons, which prevented their electing one of their own body to succeed him, was reconciled by the choice of a foreign leader in the person of the Marquis of Montferrat. Many of the nobles and their followers had, meanwhile, in inconstancy or impatience, wholly deserted their engagements, or found their own passage to Acre: so that when at length, nearly two years after the tournament in Champagne, the Marquis Boniface mustered the French, Italian, and Flemish confederates at Venice, their numbers fell short of expectation, notwithstanding the junction of some German crusaders; and they were utterly unable to subscribe the stipulated cost of the enterprise. [1202.] Though the Marquis and the Counts of Blois and Flanders made a generous sacrifice of all their valuables, above thirty thousand marks were yet wanting to complete the full payment; and as the republic, with true mercantile caution, refused to permit the sailing of the fleet until the whole amount of the deficiency should be lodged in her treasury, the enterprise must have been abandoned, if the Doge had not suggested an equivalent. He proposed that, upon condition of the crusaders assisting in the reduction of the strong city of Zara, on the Dalmatian coast, which had revolted from the republic, their payment of the remaining sum should be postponed until the conclusion of the

he engaged, on their assent, himself to take the Cross, and to lead the naval forces of his republic.*

The confederate barons gladly acceded to this expedient, when another obstacle was opposed to its adoption, which had nearly frustrated the whole enterprise: the people of Zara had placed themselves under the sovereignty of the King of Hungary; and the pope, through his legate, positively forbade the crusaders to turn their arms against the subjects of a prince who had himself taken the Cross. But the Venetians, who entertained little reverence for the authority of the Holy See, succeeded in persuading their more scrupulous allies to disregard the prohibition of Innocent; the desire of honourably discharging their obligations prevailed with the French barons over their fear of the papal displeasure; and, although the Marquis of Montferrat, their leader, abstained from accompanying them, they sailed to Zara with their followers in the Venetian fleet, which was commanded by the venerable doge, as he had promised, in person. Zara was deemed in that age one of the strongest cities in Europe: but the inhabitants, after a siege of only five days, were terrified or compelled into a surrender; and though their lives were spared,

---

* Notwithstanding the expression of Villehardouin, that the venerable Doge had lost his sight by a wound, it may be doubted whether he was totally blind; for the statement of his descendant and chronicler, much more probable in itself, is only that he was *visu debilis*

the city was pillaged with great cruelty, and both its houses and defences razed to the ground. In his first burst of indignation at their disobedience, Innocent excommunicated both the crusaders and Venetians; and when the French barons sent a deputation of their number to Rome to express their penitence, he assured them of pardon for their sins, only upon condition of their making restoration of their booty to the people of Zara, and withdrawing from all alliance with the more stubborn republicans, who still set his spiritual censures at defiance. The fanatic De Montfort, alone, whose subsequent share in the Crusade against the Albigenses has given a horrible celebrity to his name, showed full obedience to the papal mandate by wholly abandoning his associates; but the rest of the French nobles and their troops continued to winter with the Venetians at Zara, where, after its surrender, the Marquis of Montferrat joined them; and it was during this season of repose that an entirely new destination was given to the combined armament.*

---

* Danduli, *Chron. ubi suprà; Vita Innocent III.* p 529–531.
Villehardouin, No. xx. liv

Street in Constantinople.

SECTION III.

AFFAIRS OF THE EASTERN EMPIRE.

TO explain the occasion of a change of purpose in the crusaders, which produced one of the most singular and memorable enterprises in history, it is now necessary to revert to the state of the Byzantine empire; the annals of which, during the thirteenth cen-

rapid notice in this place. Our retrospect will ascend to the reign of the first Alexius: the crisis of whose fortunes was involved and has been described in the transactions of the earliest Crusade. Following closely on the triumphant career of the Latins through the Lesser Asia, Alexius richly gathered the fruits of victories, which they were impatient to abandon for the ulterior objects of their great enterprise; and, as the Turkish forces were successively withdrawn from the shores of the Propontis and Ægean sea to the defence of the interior, the emperor restored to the Byzantine dominion the whole circuit of the sea-coast from Nice to Tarsus, or from the Bosphorus to the Syrian gates. Even in the interior of Asia Minor, the Sultan of Nice, after the loss of that capital, had been compelled to remove the seat of his throne from thence to Iconium, above three hundred miles from Constantinople; and, amid the exhaustion of the Turkish power in its struggle with the crusading invaders, Alexius, by policy and arms, so diligently improved his advantage, that, before his decease, the Greek Empire, which, at the outset of his reign, was straitened and shaken on all sides by hostile pressure, and seemed to rock to its foundations, had not only assumed an aspect of renovated strength, but expanded with offensive force against its former assailants.*

In the succeeding reign of his son John, termed in derision the handsome, or Calo Johannes, a prince more honourably distinguished both for his pacific virtues and warlike qualities, [1118,] internal concord and happiness were preserved by a mild and vigorous administration; while the dignity of the empire was asserted, and its security increased, by twenty-five years of victorious contest with the Turks. From the Latin princes of Syria, the Greek emperor won equal respect by the powerful assistance which, in the interval between the first and second Crusades, he rendered them in repelling the infidels, and by the vigour with which he obliged Raymond, the reigning Prince of Antioch, to do homage to him for his possessions. Manuel, the second surviving son of John, who was preferred in the succession to an elder brother both by parental and popular favour, inherited his father's martial spirit with his throne; but did not emulate the worth of his private life and civil government. [1143.] During an active reign of thirty-seven years, the ambition of Manuel, rather than the necessity of his position, involved his empire in continual wars, not only with the Turks and Hungarians, its natural enemies on the Asiatic and European frontiers, but also with the ancient foes of his house, the Normans of the two Sicilies. In the hostilities, indeed, which kindled anew the quarrel of the preceding century, Manuel was not the first aggressor.

for the subjugation of the Byzantine empire, Roger, King of Sicily, upon pretext of some slight shown to his ambassadors at Constantinople, despatched a great armament into the Ionian and Ægean seas; and the Normans, disembarking from their ships, reduced Corfu and other islands, and overran the continent of Greece. Manuel was at the time absent from his capital; but his return and revengeful activity soon terminated the triumph of the invaders. With the powerful co-operation of the Venetians, his navy outnumbered that of the Normans, and swept the seas of their galleys; his troops, which he led in person, overpowered the garrisons which they had left in Greece; and a single campaign sufficed to clear the empire of its audacious assailants. It was then that the ambitious hopes of Manuel rose with his success; and the glorious issue of a just and defensive war suggested dreams of aggrandizement, which embraced the sovereignty of Italy, and the reunion on his brows of the imperial crowns of the East and West.*

With the plea of punishing the Norman invaders of his states, a Byzantine army, under the command of Palæologus, a leader of noble birth and approved valour, was landed upon the shores of southern Italy; and favoured by the declining health and death of

---

* Johannis Cinnami *Historia*, lib. ii. iii. Nicetas Choniates, *in Manuel Comnen.* lib. i. iii. *ad.* c. 6. (Both in *Scriptor Byzant.*)

the Sicilian king, and by the affection of the people for the ancient community of language and faith which had bound them to the Greek empire, the whole of Apulia and Calabria was rapidly reannexed to the Byzantine dominion. From this epoch, throughout the subsequent contests between the Western emperor, Frederic Barbarossa, on the one side, and the papacy and Lombard republics on the other, the intrigues, the blandishments, and the gold of Manuel, were unsparingly employed to extend his influence in Italy, and to promote his visionary scheme of wresting the sovereignty of the whole Peninsula from the German usurper of the Roman title. To the pope he threw out the lure of terminating the schism of the Latin and Greek churches; to the Lombard cities he was prodigal both of money and promises; but the intrinsic weakness of the Greek empire was unequal to the prosecution of his ambitious design; its weight was severely felt in the balance of Italian politics; and when the pope and the Lombard republics had terminated their great struggle with Barbarossa, the subsidies and the negotiations of Manuel were alike disregarded. In Southern Italy fortune was equally capricious to the Eastern empire; the death of his brave lieutenant Palæologus was followed by the loss of his transient conquests; and, in a truce concluded with William the Bad, the successor of Roger on the Sicilian throne, in which that prince acknowledged himself the vassal of the

Byzantine throne, the dignity and pretensions of Manuel were only saved by his abandonment of the Italian soil. [1156.] In other quarters the warlike reign of Manuel was signalized by victories both over the Hungarians and Turks, though in his last years its splendour was clouded by a severe defeat which he sustained from the infidels in the Pisidian mountains. To his own subjects, even his more successful wars were productive of heavy burdens; his private life was licentious, and his political character was stained, as we have seen, with the reproach of pretended friendship and treacherous hostility to the Latins in the Second Crusade.*

With the death of Manuel ended the greatness of the Comnenian race. His infant son and successor, Alexius II., was oppressed by a perfidious guardian and daring usurper of his own blood, Andronicus, himself a grandson of the first Alexius, who, after deposing and murdering his imperial ward, himself terminated a tyrannical and bloody reign of less than three years by an ignominious and cruel death. The popular insurrection in which he fell was headed by Isaac Angelus, another member, by descent in the female line, of the Comnenian family. The leader or tool of the insurgents was raised to the throne, and under his feeble reign of ten years, the empire crumbled into ruin. A revolt of the Bulgarians was

---

* Cinnamus, lib. iv.–vi. Nicetas, *ad fin Manuel.*

Isaac Angelus.

provoked by his tyranny in seizing their flocks and herds to supply the wasteful pomp of his nuptials: and his tame acquiescence in their assertion of independence severed their country from the Byzantine crown, after a possession of nearly two centuries, and established the second kingdom of Bulgaria under a race of their ancient princes. The inglorious and indolent reign of Isaac was frequently, and perhaps justly, threatened by abortive conspiracies; but his worst and successful enemy was his own ungrateful brother Alexius, whom he had redeemed from a Turkish prison, and who repaid the obligation by surprising his security, depriving him of his eyes, consigning him to a dungeon, and seating himself on his throne. The son of the deposed prince, who was named also Alexius, a boy only twelve years of age, was spared by the pity or contempt of his uncle; and he had subsequently contrived to escape into Italy, when the news of the assembly of a great crusading armament at Venice, inspired his youthful hopes that its leaders might be induced, by adequate offers, to defer the ultimate object of their enterprise for a season, and to direct their powerful arms to the restoration of his father. The entreaties of the young prince for their aid were supported at Venice by ambassadors from his protector, the Duke of Swabia, who had married his sister: but it was at Zara, during the inaction of winter, that the friends of Alexius were permitted more successfully to negotiate a treaty with the Latin barons and Venetian republic, which was eventually to deliver the imperial inheritance of his house into the detested hands of foreign and barbarous spoilers.*

To induce the Venetians to accept the overtures of the young Greek prince, there were not wanting many motives both of passion and policy. The

---

* Nicetas, *in Adron. Comnen.*, *in Isaac Angel.*, *in Alex. Angel.*, ad lib iii. &c.

alliance between their state and the Emperor Manuel Comnenus in the last age, had been converted, by his protection of Ancona, the commercial rival of the republic, into deadly enmity; in revenge for a general confiscation of the property of the Venetians in his ports, to which Manuel was provoked by their insolence, their fleets had ravaged the Byzantine islands and coasts; and though the emperor, by a final submission to their demands, had appeased the haughty republic, the hatred of the people of Constantinople, during the license of subsequent revolutions, had repeatedly exposed the Venetian merchants in that capital to spoliation and massacre.* The arms of the republic, or the dread of her vengeance, generally, indeed, obtained indemnification for these outrages; but repeated broils cherished mutual national antipathy; and when the Pisans availed themselves of the temper of the Greeks to supplant the Venetians in their commercial relations with the empire, the exasperation of the latter people had reached its height. By assisting young Alexius, their republic would therefore both revenge her wrongs and regain her commercial advantages in the East. The politic Dandolo was not slow to anticipate the benefits which would accrue to his country from such an alliance; and he eagerly employed all his influence

---

* Cinnamus, lib. vi. c. 10. Nicetas, *in Manuel.* lib. ii. c. 5; *in Alex. Man Filio*, c. 11; *in Isaac.* lib. ii. c. 10.

with the confederate barons to engage them in the design.*

For its adoption even as a means of advancing the ultimate object of the Crusade, some plausible arguments might be adduced. As the possession of Egypt was supposed to form the principal support of the Turkish arms in Palestine, the original design of the crusaders had been to attack the infidels at that source of their power. But it was now contended by the Venetians, that any loss of time in deferring the projected invasion of Egypt would be richly repaid to the profit of the Crusade, by the advantages likely to arise from the command of the Byzantine resources, which young Alexius offered as the price of his father's restoration. The proposals, indeed, of the imperial exile, were of the most tempting nature; for he engaged not only to pay two hundred thousand marks among the crusaders as soon as his parent. should be re-established on the throne; but also to put an end to the schism of the Greek and Latin churches by submitting his empire to the spiritual dominion of the Roman See; and either to combine personally with the crusaders, at the head of the Byzantine forces, in the subsequent expedition against Egypt, or in default of his own presence, to send ten thousand men at his charge for one year, and to

---

* Nicetas, *in Alex.* lib. iii. c. 9, expressly accuses the Doge and Venetians as the instigators of the French crusaders.

maintain five hundred knights during his life for the defence of Palestine.* These promised benefits to the cause of the church and the Crusade might at first have a powerful influence in winning assent even among the more devout leaders of the war; but it must be doubted whether the motives of their subsequent conduct were equally pure and disinterested; and since the diversion of their arms against Zara had familiarized the minds of the crusading host to the postponement of their vows, it may be suspected that the successful siege and sack of that city had but awakened their appetite for a more splendid achievement and a richer booty.

The influence of such feelings is detected in their second and more deliberate contempt of the prohibition, which Innocent III. now fulminated against their design. The Byzantine usurper, anticipating the proposal of young Alexius, had, by a solemn embassy to Rome, offered to place the religious affairs of his empire under the government of the Latin papacy, and requested the presence of a legate from Rome; and the ambitious Innocent, hoping thus to secure the submission of the Greek Church, as the price of keeping the reigning tyrant on the Byzantine throne, promised him protection against his enemies.

The pontiff, therefore, proceeded positively to

interdict the crusaders from espousing the cause of the imperial exile, or arrogating to themselves any authority for the redress of wrongs among Christians, or the suppression of schism, for which it was the province of the Holy See alone to provide.

But, by the Venetians, the commands of the pope were immediately treated with such open disregard, that the cardinal legates, whom he had despatched to Zara to enforce them, hopelessly quitted the place and sailed direct for Palestine; and their example was followed by a number of barons and other crusaders, including many most renowned for their devout and warlike spirit, who conscientiously dreaded to incur the papal censures, by turning their arms against the Eastern Empire; while not a few disguised, under the same pretext, their secret dread to engage in an enterprise so perilous and disproportioned to the assembled force of the confederates.

Since, indeed, submission to the papal authority was identified with every pious sentiment of the age, it is impossible not to conclude that, in the minds of the remaining leaders and soldiery, the temptations of glorious or gainful adventure had triumphed over religious considerations; and chiefly through the personal persuasions, as it is said, of the Venetian Doge, the proposals of young Alexius, despite of the impending thunders of the Vatican, wer finally accepted by the marquis of Montferrat, the Counts of Flanders, Blois, and St. Paul, with eight other great French barons, and the majority of their followers.*

---

* Villehardouin, No. xlv. xlvii. lii. *Vita Innocent III.* p. 583 *Ejusdem Epistolæ*, No. lxvii &c.

Dandolo, Doge of Venice.

SECTION III.

EXPEDITION AGAINST CONSTANTINOPLE.

HOWEVER apparently inadequate for the conquest of an ancient empire, the armament wherewith the Doge of Venice and the confederate barons now sailed for Constantinople, was of its kind the most complete and formidable which the world had yet witnessed. The fleet was composed of fifty great galleys of war, one hundred and twenty flat-bottomed horse-transports, called *palanders* or *huissners,** two hundred and forty vessels filled with troops and warlike engines, and seventy store-ships laden with provisions. On board this navy of nearly five hundred sail—of which the enumeration conveys so magnificent an idea of the wealth and power of the great republic—there were embarked, under the confederate barons of the Crusade, six thousand cavalry, composed of two thousand knights with their esquires and sergeants, or mounted attendants, and ten thousand foot: besides the Venetian sea and land forces, of which the numbers might be loosely estimated at twenty thousand more.† Although the Byzantine usurper was early apprized of the destination and force of this hostile armament, he made not a single effort to oppose its course; the crusaders were permitted successively, during a tardy navigation, to refresh themselves and their horses, and to replenish their provisions on the coasts and islands of Greece; and they finally approached the port of Constanti-

---

* The origin of the former term for such a description of naval transport has been lost; the latter is derived from the *huis,* or door in the side of the vessel, which was let down as a drawbridge for the purpose of shipping and landing the horses. Du Cange, on Villehardouin, No. xiv.

† According to Sanuto, *Vite de Duchi de Venezia,* (in *Script. Rer. Ital.* vol. xxii.) p. 528, the land forces of the republic in the expedition were four hundred and fifty cavalry and eight thousand foot. But after the first siege of Constantinople, Villehardouin (No. clii.) estimates the total combined army of French and Venetians at only

nople itself without having encountered an enemy. The Byzantine navy, which, it is said, had but lately numbered sixteen hundred vessels of war, might have sufficed to harass, and even to destroy, on its passage, an armament, so encumbered with horses and stores: but the Greek admiral, Michael Struphnos, brother-in-law of the usurper, had, in the baseness of his avarice, broken up the hulls of the shipping, that he might sell, for his private profit, the masts, rigging, and iron work; and the port of Constantinople now contained only twenty galleys. The shores of the Propontis might have furnished abundant timber for the construction of a new navy: but the eunuchs of the palace, to whom the charge of the imperial forests was intrusted for the purpose of the chase, would not suffer a tree to be felled for the public defence. To this and every other object of patriotism, the whole nation indeed was alike insensible: for the unwarlike and degenerate Greeks, as a race in whom the despotism of centuries had extinguished every spark of generous shame, beheld in cowering apathy the approach of a detested enemy; and without favouring the cause of the younger Alexius, the people both of the capital and provinces were equally indifferent to the danger of the tyrant who filled their throne.*

If that usurper himself, or his adherents, had been

---

* Villehardouin. No. lvi. lvii. Rhamnusius, *De Bello Constanti-*

capable of exerting even the passive courage of a defence, the natural strength and resources of the capital might have defied the efforts of assailants, whom the able-bodied inhabitants outnumbered at the lowest estimate as ten to one. When the Venetian navy arrived before the walls of Constantinople, and the gorgeous city, which the admiration of the crusaders deemed well worthy of being the mistress and queen of the world, burst in all her magnitude and splendour upon their astonished gaze, there was no heart so stout, is the simple and emphatic confession of the noble companion and chronicler of the adventure, but recoiled with dread at the spectacle of her massive ramparts and gigantic towers; for never surely had so great an enterprise been essayed.* But with the awe which the bravest might not feel ashamed to confess, was not the less mingled a magnanimous spirit which rose with the danger; and each warrior, looking upon his arms, reflected with unshaken resolution that the hour was at hand in which these must serve the need, and would suffice to insure the event, of glorious achievement. As a strong wind swept the armament past the walls of the majestic capital toward the opposite shore, the fleet was there brought to anchor;

---

* *Et sachiez que il ne ot si hardi cui te cœur ne fremist, et ce me fut merveil, car onques si grande affaire ne fat enterpris*—(and know that no one was so bold that his heart did not tremble; and no wonder, for never was so great an enterprise undertaken.) Villehar-

and the chivalry disembarking, took possession of the Asiatic suburb of Chrysopolis, the modern Scutari and during nine days reposed in an imperial palace and gardens. This interval of inaction was marked by some negotiations, in which the Byzantine usurper offered to expedite their march through Asia Minor against the infidels, but menaced them with destruction if their purpose was hostile to his state; while the Doge and barons sternly replied, that they had entered the empire in the cause of Heaven to avenge the wrongs which he had committed, and boldly admonished him that if he hoped for mercy he must descend from the throne which he had unjustly seized.*

After this declaration, they prepared to cross the Bosphorus to the European shore,—the whole body of the chivalry being divided into six corps or battles, two composed of Flemish knights with their attendant archers under Count Baldwin and his brother, three of French crusaders led respectively by the Counts of Blois and St. Paul, and the Lord of Montmorency, and the sixth or reserve of Italians and Germans under the marquis of Montferrat. The knights and sergeants embarked in the palanders, with their horses ready saddled and caparisoned; the Venetian galleys took them in tow; and, in this order, they stood across the strait toward the European suburb of

Galata, which commands the entrance of the port The Greek cavalry were drawn out on the beach in far superior force to oppose their landing: but when the knights, as soon as the water reached only to their girdle, leaped from the vessels, lance in hand, the enemy immediately fled; and the horses being brought on shore, the cavaliers mounted, pursued the flying squadrons, and captured the imperial camp without striking a blow. On the following morning, after a faint sally by the Greeks, the assailants entered the town of Galata with the fugitives; the chain which from thence secured the mouth of the harbour was broken; and the whole Venetian fleet entering the port of Constantinople in triumph, the remains of the imperial navy either fell into their hands, or were driven on shore and burned.*

Though the port was thus captured, the gigantic works, by which the city itself was completely enclosed and separated from the suburbs, might still bid defiance to the efforts of the crusaders: but their courage and confidence were unbounded. Though their numbers were insufficient to observe more than a single front of the walls, they determined to commence a regular siege; and this magnanimous resolution presents the singular and amazing example of the investment of the largest and strongest capital in the world by a few thousand men. The perils and

the hardihood of this extraordinary enterprise were
enhanced by the privations under which it was prose
cuted. Of flour and salt provisions, the confederates
had a supply but for three weeks left; clouds of Greek
cavalry confined their few foragers to the camp; and
their only fresh meat was obtained by the slaughter
of their own horses. Delay was therefore far more to
be dreaded than the resistance of the enemy; and the
preparatory operations of the siege were urged with
superhuman exertions. The possession of the harbour determined the point of attack; and against the
walls on that side two hundred and fifty great projectile and battering engines were planted. When
by incredible labour the ditch had been filled up, and
some impression made upon the defences, the French
and Venetians agreed to attempt a simultaneous
assault: the former from their approaches against the
land faces; the latter from their galleys upon the
fronts which overlooked the port. Standing upon
the raised deck of his vessel, with the gonfalon, or
great banner of St. Mark, floating over his head, the
venerable Doge himself led the naval attack; and
such was the ardour excited by his presence, his
voice, and his example, that the line of galleys was
boldly rowed to the beach under the walls; by
ladders from the foot of the ramparts, and by drawbridges let down upon their battlements from the
masts of the loftier vessels, the defences were sur-

on one of the twenty-five towers which were carried by the assailants.

But meanwhile the attack on the land side had been less successful; every gallant effort of the French chivalry to scale the walls through the imperfect breaches had been repulsed by the assistance of some Pisan colonists and the valour of the Varangian, or Anglo-Saxon and Danish guards, ever the firmest support of the Byzantine throne;* and the numerous cavalry of the Greeks, pouring from the gates, threatened to surround and overwhelm the scanty array of the exhausted crusaders. The Doge learning their danger, after setting fire to the quarter of the city which he had entered, and which was thus reduced to ashes, drew off his triumphant forces to the succour of his fainting allies; and the pusillanimous Greeks, without daring a closer or prolonged encounter, disgracefully retired within the shelter of their walls. The confederates passed the succeeding night in eager rather than anxious suspense: but such

---

* On the subject of the Anglo-Saxon emigrations which filled the ranks of the Varangian guards of the Byzantine throne, there is some difference of opinion. Du Cange, indeed, (Notes on Villehardouin, No lxxxix. &c.,) labours to prove that these Varangians came from .he northern continent of Europe only: but the words of Villehardouin are explicit, *Anglois et Danois.* It is not probable that a French knight could have confounded their race; and his statement is in agreement with the fact, that impatience of the Norman tyranny had, ever since the epoch of the Conquest, driven multitudes of the bolder spirits among the oppressed English to seek a more honourable

was the terror with which the usurper Alexius was seized at the balanced success of the conflict, that, under cover of the darkness, he basely fled from his capital with a part of the imperial treasures. On the discovery of his absence, the trembling nobles of the palace drew his blind and captive brother Isaac from the dungeon to the throne; and, when morning dawned, the leaders of the crusaders were astonished by an embassy from the restored emperor, announcing the revolution, desiring the presence of his son, and inviting them also to receive his grateful acknowledgments.*

The first proceeding of the confederates, on the receipt of this message, was to depute two barons and two Venetians to wait upon the emperor with their felicitations, and with a less welcome demand for the fulfilment of the engagements which his son had contracted in his name. While he admitted that their services were entitled to the highest recompense which was his to bestow, Isaac heard with consternation the extent of the conditions which he was required to ratify: the payment of two hundred thousand marks of silver, the employment of the imperial forces in the service of the Crusade, and the submission of the Greek Church to the spiritual authority of the pope. But the immediate subscription of the

---

* Villehardouin, No. lxxxii.-xcix. Danduli, *Chron.* p. 821, 822 Nicetas, (*in Alexio*), lib. iii. *ad fin. Vitæ Innocent. III* c. 91, p

emperor to these onerous terms was peremptorily insisted upon, and, however reluctantly, obtained. On the return of the envoys to the camp, young Alexius was permitted to make his triumphant entry into the city, attended by the Latin chiefs; and the joint coronation of the aged emperor and his son, which was joyfully celebrated, seemed to announce a peaceful conclusion to the recent struggle. This fallacious promise of concord between two nations so mutually obnoxious as the Latins and Greeks, was of short duration. To satisfy the rapacious demands of their deliverers, the emperors, in the low state of the Byzantine treasury, were compelled to make many grievous exactions from their subjects: the warlike Franks cared not to conceal their insolent disdain for a pusillanimous people: and, above all, the veneration of the Greeks for the peculiar forms and doctrines of their faith—the only symptoms of virtuous feeling which, discernible as it is throughout the long annals of their degradation, may command some share of our respect—was outraged by the undisguised design of subjugating their church to the papal yoke. From the very altar of the Cathedral of St. Sophia, the Patriarch of Constantinople was compelled, at the dictation of the crusaders, to proclaim the spiritual supremacy of the Roman Pontiff; and the people were required to subject their consciences to the doctrines and discipline of a church which they had ever been taught to regard with horror as schismatic and heretical. By these measures, their political and religious antipathy was extended to the young emperor, as the ally and creature of the detested foreigners; and the conduct of Alexius himself did not tend to win the favour, or to command the respect, of his offended subjects. While the boisterous orgies and rude freedoms, which marked the social intercourse of the Western Nations, shocked the superior refinement or ceremonial pride of the Greeks, the young emperor, regardless alike of the difference in national manners, and of his own dignity, continued to visit the quarters, and to share in the debaucheries and gaming of the Franks. In one of these carousals, he suffered the diadem to be snatched in sportive or contemptuous familiarity from his head, and exchanged for the coarse woollen cap of some low reveller; and the contempt, as well as the aversion of his subjects, was not unjustly provoked against the unfeeling or thoughtless boy, who could thus basely, in the eyes of insolent barbarians, sully the lustre and dishonour the majesty of his imperial crown.*

Through all these causes, Alexius soon found that he had become so odious to his countrymen as to render the continued presence of his Latin allies indispensable to the security of his throne; and he endeavoured, by the promise of further rewards, to

---

* Nicetas, *in Isaacum et Alexin Angelos*, c. 1-3. Villehardouin, No. xcix.-ci.

induce them to postpone their departure, and the prosecution of their crusading vows, until the following spring. He found them little loth to accede to his terms. On the first restoration of Isaac, indeed, the Latin barons had given some signs of pursuing the original purpose of their confederacy, had sent a defiance to the Sultan of Egypt, and had deprecated the anger of the pope at their repeated disobedience by entreaties for pardon, and by assurances that thenceforth their arms should be devoted exclusively to the sacred service of Palestine. The Venetians also had condescended to solicit a reconciliation with the Holy See; and Innocent was so well satisfied with the prospect of bringing the Greek Church under his dominion, and so rejoiced to recognise the slightest symptoms of penitence in those stubborn republicans, that he extended absolution to them, as well as to their more submissive baronial confederates. But, in truth, both the Doge and his noble allies were by this time almost equally ready to disregard the papal displeasure and the objects of the Crusade for their personal profit; and Alexius seems to have experienced little difficulty in purchasing their continued services until the spring, as soon as he had quieted their consciences by repeating the condition, that he would then accompany them to Egypt with the recruited forces of his empire.*

EXPEDITION AGAINST CONSTANTINOPLE. 323

To occupy the interval, and enforce the recognition of his disputed authority over the imperial territories, the Marquis of Montferrat, with a body of the cònfederate chivalry, successfully conducted the young prince in an expedition through the Thracian provinces; but, during this absence, the hatred of the people of the capital was fatally aggravated by the misconduct of the Latins. Though, for the prevention of feuds, a separate quarter had been assigned to the strangers in the suburb of Galata or Pera, some Flemings and Venetians, during a visit to the city attacked a commercial colony of Mussulmans, which had long enjoyed the protection of the Byzantine emperors. The infidels, though surprised, defended themselves bravely: the Greek inhabitants assisted them, while some Latin residents aided the aggressors; and, during the conflict, the latter set fire to a building, from whence the flames spread with such frightful rapidity, that, before they could be extinguished, a third part of the magnificent city was reduced to ashes. During eight days, the conflagration raged over above a league in extent from the port to the Propontis: immense quantities of merchandise and other valuable property were destroyed, and thousands of families were reduced to beggary. The Latin chiefs expressed their vain sorrow for a calamity which, as produced by the unbridled license of their followers, it should rather have been their care to pre-

little disposed to credit their sincerity. Moreover, as some of the Italian settlers in the capital had instigated or shared the outrage, the vengeance of the sufferers was specially directed against the ingratitude of these foreigners who had long been naturalized among them; and to the number of fifteen thousand persons, the whole body were compelled to abandon their dwellings, and to consult their safety by flight to the suburban quarters of the crusaders.*

From this epoch, the national animosity of the Greeks and Latins mutually increased to a deadly height; and, when the young emperor returned to his capital, he found the rupture incurable, and his own position such, that he was scarcely permitted to choose between the party of his subjects and that of his allies. By the Greeks, he was more than ever abhorred as the tool of their oppressors; by the Latin chiefs, without consideration for the difficulties which oppressed his government, his hesitation in fulfilling the pecuniary conditions of the alliance was resented with suspicion and menaces. Not deigning to admit the public distresses which the late conflagration had grievously aggravated, as any excuse for delay in the collection and payment of their promised reward, the confederate leaders suddenly adopted the most violent counsels; and an embassy was sent, in the name of

---

* Nicetas *in Isaac. et Alex.* p 272–274. Villehardouin, No.

the Doge of Venice, and of the barons of the army, tc defy the two emperors in their own palace. After fearlessly delivering their haughty message, the envoys mounted their horses, and returned to the quarters of the confederates; and hostilities, to which the two emperors were the only reluctant parties, as they were also the first victims, immediately commenced on both sides.*

Such was the unhappy condition of the nation and the times, that the only man among the Greeks who had courage and ability to undertake the defence of his country, was placed in the odious light of a traitor and an usurper. Alexius Angelus Ducas, surnamed Mourzoufle, from his shaggy eyebrows, a prince allied by blood to the imperial house, had been the chief instrument in urging the vacillating young emperor to resist the haughty demands of the Latins; and in the war of skirmishes which now ensued, his personal valour and energy were invidiously contrasted with the weakness or reluctance of his sovereign. The seditious populace of Constantinople demanded the deposition of Isaac and his son, whom they stigmatized as the secret friends of the invaders; and after the prudence of several members of the nobility had induced them to decline the proffered dignity of the purple, a young patrician, named Nicholas Canabus, was tempted by his vanity to accept the Byzantine crown. But the valour of Ducas had meanwhile gained the suffrages of the Varangian guards; the imperial puppet of the hour was displaced without resistance; Isaac and his son were persuaded to seek safety in flight, and were betrayed into a dungeon, in which the former soon expired with grief and terror; and the more deserving patriot or successful conspirator was unanimously called to the throne. [A.D. 1204.] From the hour in which Ducas assumed the insignia of empire, a new impulse was given to the Byzantine counsels: the walls of the capital were guarded with active discipline; many sallies were at least boldly directed; two attempts, frustrated only by the intrepidity and skill of the Venetian sailors, were made to burn the Latin fleet; and if it had been possible to nerve the hearts of the Greeks in the national cause, its ruin might yet have been averted by the spirit of their leader. But in every encounter before the walls and in the adjacent country, Ducas was deserted by the cowardice of his new subjects; he found it necessary to negotiate with the invaders; and when they insisted on the restoration of the deposed emperor, he attempted to remove that obstacle to an accommodation, since Isaac was already dead, by the murder of his remaining prisoner Alexius.*

---

* Villehardouin, No. cxiii.–cxix. *Vita Innocent. III.* p. 534, 535 Nicetas, *in Isaac. et Alex.* c. 4, 5, *in Mourzuflum*, c. 1.

SECOND SIEGE OF CONSTANTINOPLE. 327

Theodore Lascaris.

SECTION IV.

SECOND SIEGE OF CONSTANTINOPLE

HEN the intelligence of this event reached the camp of the crusaders, the causes of resentment which had separated them from the young ally and

miseration and horror at his untimely and cruel fate. They passionately swore to revenge his death upon a perfidious usurper and nation;* and the crime of Ducas served only to exasperate the enmity, while it inflamed the ambition of these formidable assailants. Conceiving themselves now released from all obligations of forbearance toward a race so inhuman and treacherous as the Greeks, and easily adopting the convenient doctrine that it was a religious duty to punish their murder of a prince by the conquest and dismemberment of his empire, the Doge and confederate barons proceeded to sign a treaty of partition by which, in the hardy confidence of valour, and undaunted by the disparity of their force to the perilous magnitude of the enterprise, they anticipated the result of their astonishing achievements. It was agreed that, after liquidating, out of the booty to be captured, the pecuniary claims of Venice for the expenses of the armament, the remainder should be equally shared between the troops of the crusaders and the republic; that the existence of the empire should be preserved, and one of the confederate barons raised to its throne, but with only a fourth of its present territories for the support of his title; and that, of the remaining three-

---

* Yet if Nicetas (p. 280) may be credited, in preference to the Latin authorities who do not notice such a transaction, the crusading barons, by the advice of the Doge of Venice, were still willing to have granted peace to the usurper for fifty thousand pounds of gold:

fourths, one moiety should be surrendered in full sovereignty to Venice, and the other divided into imperial fiefs among the nobles of the Crusade.*

The winter had been consumed in desultory conflicts or in necessary preparation; but, with the return of spring, the confederates having completed the arrangement of their daring project, proceeded to put it into execution. To prevent a repetition of the failure in the last attack upon the walls from the separation of their forces, it was determined that the assault of the capital should be attempted from the port alone; and the Venetian fleet being distributed into six divisions, to correspond with the former arrangement of the chivalry into as many *battles*, one body of knights embarked in the palanders of each squadron with their horses and followers. In this order the whole armament crossed the harbour, and assaulted the same line of defences, against which the Venetians had before successfully exerted their efforts. But, though the depth of water permitted the vessels to approach near enough to the walls for the combatants on the ramparts and on the drawbridges and ropeladders, which were let down from the upper works of the galleys, to fight hand to hand; the insecure footing of the assailants on these frail and floating machines, and the firm vantage-ground and superior

---

* *Epistola Balduini, in Vita Innocent. III.* p. 526. Danduli.

numbers of the besieged, rendered the combat so unequal, that the former, after astonishing feats of valour, were finally repulsed at every point. Instructed but not intimidated by this failure, the Venetians now undertook to supply their allies with the means of approaching the walls in steadier array; the large vessels were strongly lashed together in pairs, to increase their stability and impulsive force; and three days having been spent in preparation and refreshment, the assault was again given with resistless vigour and happier fortune.

From sunrise to noon, the slow advance of the heavy line of vessels was retarded by volleys of missiles which were showered from the walls; [April 12;] the recent success of the Greeks had animated their spirit into a courageous resistance; and the issue of the conflict still hung in dangerous suspense: when a strong breeze, suddenly springing up from the north, all at once drove the double galleys with propitious violence against the walls. The names of the two linked vessels—the Pilgrim and Paradise—having on board the martial Bishops of Soissons and Troyes, which first touched the walls, were repeated with loud shouts as an omen of divine aid; the panic-stricken Greeks fled from their posts; four towers, with a long line of rampart, were escaladed and carried; and three gates being burst open, the knights led their horses on shore from the palanders, mounted, and swept through

mazes of a vast capital, indeed, their cavalry might have been useless, their feeble numbers might have been lost and overpowered; in the hands of a brave people, every house might have been defended, every church and palace and massive building converted into an impregnable fortress. So conscious were the victors of their danger, that they immediately began to fortify the first quarters which they had seized; passed the night under arms; and setting fire to the streets in their front, produced a new conflagration, which in a few hours consumed another portion of the city equal in extent, according to the confession of their chronicler, to any three towns in France. But these precautions were needless against an enemy whom neither patriotism nor despair, neither the ruin of their country and fortunes, nor the violence with which the licentious passions of a ferocious soldiery menaced their own lives and the honour of their women, could rouse to one generous or manly effort. The Emperor Ducas, finding it impossible to animate his craven subjects with any portion of his own spirit, abandoned them to their fate, and retired from the city with his family. After his flight, the brave efforts of two other illustrious Greeks, Theodore Ducas and Theodore Lascaris—the latter of whom was destined subsequently to re-establish and sustain the fortunes of his country—proved for the time equally ineffectual; a suppliant train bearing crosses

Desecration of the Churches.

of the crusaders for the fallen capital; and when morning dawned, the Latin chiefs, who had anticipated that the reduction of the whole city would still cost them at least the labour of a month, found themselves masters of the Eastern empire.*

But while they gladly accepted the submission, they were deaf to the abject prayers of the Greeks. Constantinople was abandoned to a general pillage, during which the miserable inhabitants witnessed and endured every extremity of horror. Yet even the brutal and licentious soldiery were surpassed in

---

* Villehardouin, No. cxx.–cxxx. *Epistola Balduini in Vita Innocent. III.* p. 585, 586. Nicetas, *in Murzuflum* c. 2.

cruelty by the Latin residents who had been recently expelled from the city, and chiefly by whose revengeful malice two thousand of the unresisting Greeks were wantonly murdered in cold blood. Insult and sacrilege were added to rapine and debauchery; the churches and national worship of the Greeks were defiled and profaned; and by the followers of a crusading army was strangely enacted at Constantinople the same impious scene, which another European capital was to exhibit to modern times, of enthroning a painted strumpet in a Christian cathedral.* The worst vices were freely perpetrated by the rabble of the camp and Latin suburbs; but attempts were made to control the privilege of rapine for the general benefit of the victors; on pain of excommunication and death, all individuals were commanded to bring their booty to appointed stations for a public division; and though some incurred the penalty of disobedience, and many more successfully secreted their spoils, the quantities of treasure which were collected exceeded the most greedy or sanguine expectation. After satisfying the claims of the Venetians, the value of the share which fell to the French crusaders is estimated, by their chronicler, at four or five hundred thousand marks, besides ten thousand horses; and

---

* This " Goddess of Reason" of the thirteenth century was seated on the throne to represent the office and person of the patriarch, while drunken revellers in ribaldrous songs and dances mocked the

another eye-witness declares that, by the division of the booty, the poorest of the host were rendered wealthy.*

But the gain of the adventurers, however enormous, bore a small proportion to the destruction and waste of property by which their victory was attended. It would be vain to estimate the wealth of ages which had been consumed in three conflagrations, or spoiled in the wantonness of a sack. But every scholar and lover of the arts must deplore the irreparable loss of those relics of the literature and sculpture of classical antiquity, which perished in the fall of Constantinople. Her libraries, still containing many precious remains of the best ages of Greece and Rome, which have not been preserved to our times, were now abandoned to the flames by the ignorant indifference of the barbarian conquerors; but their malevolence or cupidity was more actively exercised in the destruction of those beauteous monuments of which Constantine had robbed the ancient seat of empire to enrich his new capital. In the furious violence of conquest, or in mere wanton love of destruction, the statues of marble were mutilated or thrown down from their pedestals: but those of bronze were melted, with insensible and sordid avarice, to afford a base coin for the payment of the soldiery. This barbarous abuse

---

* Villehardouin, No. cxxx.–cxxxv. *Vita Innocent. III* p. 586–588.

SECOND SIEGE OF CONSTANTINOPLE. 335

Tower of St. Mark's, Venice.

of the right of conquest was probably the work of the rude barons of France: for the more refined Venetians, with better taste, if not with less injustice, converted a portion of their spoil into a national trophy; and removed to St. Mark's Place in their capital those four celebrated horses* of bronze which, at the distance

---

* Before St. Mark still glow his steeds of brass,

of six centuries, still present the most striking memorial of the glory and ruin of the once mighty republic.

After the division of their booty, the leaders of the confederate host assembled to consummate the more important work of partitioning an empire. For the preliminary business of nominating one of their number to fill the spoliated throne of the Cæsars, six persons of each nation, French and Venetian, were appointed under one of the provisions of the existing treaty; and this council now balanced the claims of the Marquis of Montferrat, hitherto the chosen leader of the Crusade, and of the Count of Flanders: for though the superior merits of the Doge to either were generously suggested by the French electors, his own countrymen, with the patriotic jealousy of republican freedom, declared the imperial dignity incompatible with the office of the first magistrate of their commonwealth. The final choice of the council fell upon the Count of Flanders, determined, perhaps, by his descent from Charlemagne, his alliance by blood to the King of France, and the anticipated repugnance of the French barons to obey an Italian sovereign. As soon as this decision of the electors was announced, Baldwin was raised upon a buckler, according to the Byzantine custom, by his brother barons and knights, borne on their shoulders to the church of St. Sophia, invested with the purple, and exhibited to the Greeks as their new emperor. His rival, and

SECOND SIEGE OF CONSTANTINOPLE. 337

Ceremony of raising an elected King on a Buckler.

now his vassal, the Marquis of Montferrat, was consoled by the possession of Macedonia and great part of proper Greece, with the regal title; and the remaining barons shared, by lot or precedence of rank, the various provinces of the empire in Europe and Asia, which remained at their choice, after the stipulated appropriation of three-eighths of the whole to the Venetian republic. Besides that proportion of the capital itself, Venice thus obtained the sovereignty of

seas, and of a long chain of maritime ports on the continent from the capes of the Adriatic to the Bosphorus. While the republic, in virtue of this partition, arrogated to her venerable Doge and his successors the proud and accurate title of lords of one fourth and one-eighth of the empire of Romania, to the new sovereign of Constantinople had been reserved in immediate sovereignty only one-fourth of the Byzantine dominions; and on all sides the narrow and inadequate limits of his throne were surrounded by vassals, who only nominally acknowledged, and by enemies who wholly denied the legality of his reign.*

The eagerness of the Latin adventurers to occupy their several allotments of the territorial spoil, discovered the total insufficiency of their divided strength to secure the work of conquest, which they had so daringly achieved. The dispersion of the French barons, each attended by no more than a few score of lances, over the vast provinces of the empire, betrayed to the subjugated nation the weakness of their conquerors, while the impolitic contempt by which the Greeks of all ranks found themselves excluded from employments and honours in the Latin court, increased their impatience to escape from a yoke, which they still wanted courage or concert to break. By degrees, therefore, from the capital and

---

* Villehardouin, No. cxxxvi.–cxl. Danduli *Chron.* lib. x. c. 8. Du Cange, *Hist. de Constantinople sous les Empereurs Français*, lib 1.

its neighbouring provinces on the European shores, the noblest born and the bravest of the Greeks withdrew into less accessible quarters of the dismembered empire to range themselves under the standards of native leaders. In Europe, for a moment after the fall of Constantinople, the imperial title was still arrogated by the two fugitive usurpers, the elder Alexius Angelus and Ducas Mourzoufle; and between them an apparent reconciliation was effected. During his short reign, Ducas had endeavoured to strengthen his pretensions to the imperial dignity by seizing the hand of a daughter of Alexius; and being now driven out of Adrianople on the advance of the Latins, he obtained, through the tender of allegiance to his father-in-law, a promise of such protection as his camp could afford. But he had no sooner placed himself in the power of Alexius, than that tyrant, even more perfidious than impotent, caused him to be deprived of his eyes and thrust from the camp. In this sightless and horrid condition, as he was endeavouring to escape across the Hellespont into Asia, Mourzoufle was arrested by the Latins; brought to trial for his own worst crime, the murder of young Alexius; and condemned to be cast, alive and headlong, from the lofty summit of the Theodosian pillar at Constantinople upon the marble pavement beneath.* The execution of this dreadful sentence on him was soon followed by the captivity of his betrayer Alexius, who was surprised by Boniface of Montferrat, and transported to an Italian dungeon. By the fate of these two usurpers, the principal support of the national cause of the Greeks devolved upon a young hero, who might maintain, in right of his wife, the hereditary claims, while he spurned the base qualities of the Angeli; and in whom the valour of Ducas was unsullied by the guilt of treason and murder. This was Theodore Lascaris, who had also married a daughter of Alexius Angelus; and whose gallant devotion to his country had already been signalized in the two sieges of Constantinople. Retiring, after the fall of the capital, across the Bosphorus into the recesses of Bithynia, and being joined by the most generous and congenial spirits of his nation, he there organized a resistance against the Latin adventurers, which not only prevented them from ever gaining a secure establishment in the Asiatic provinces of the empire, but prepared their expulsion from their European conquests. But the fate both of the Latin and Greek dynasties, which for sixty years were to dispute the sceptre of the Eastern empire, will reclaim our attention hereafter; and the connection of the History of the Crusades with the revolutions of Constantinople closes at the period before us.

In the division and enjoyment of a conquered empire, the confederate barons who had embraced the

forgotten the original object of their expedition, as if it had never been undertaken for the deliverance of the Holy Sepulchre; and the vain trophies of a victory, not over Paynim but Christian enemies—the gates and chain of the harbour of Constantinople—sent by the new emperor of the East to Palestine,* were the only fruits of the Fourth Crusade which ever reached the Syrian shores.

---

* Nicetas, *in Balduin*, p. 888.

Gethsemane.

Baldwin I., Emperor of the East.

CHAPTER V.

The Last Four Crusades.

SECTION 1.—HISTORY OF THE LATIN EMPIRE OF THE EAST.

FROM the first hour of its establishment, the LATIN EMPIRE OF THE EAST was foredoomed to a hopeless condition of weakness and decay. The appropriation of three-eighths of the conquered provinces to the Venetian republic; the division of an equal portion among feudal chieftains, who acknowledged only a nominal supremacy in the imperial possessor of the remaining fourth; the escape of the bravest of the Greeks into Epirus and Asia, and the common and deep detestation with which the whole race of their subjugated countrymen regarded the government of the Western barbarians and the supremacy of a heretical church, all conspired to promote the rapid dissolution of that splendid but unreal fabric of conquest, which a few thousand adventurers had suddenly founded amid the ruins of the Byzantine throne.

The mutual jealousies and dissensions of the conquerors would alone have been fatal to the stability of their dominion; and the contempt in which they held the pusillanimous character of the Greeks, blinded them to the imprudence of outraging the national feelings of an acute and subtle people, who eagerly watched every symptom of their weakness and disunion, and silently awaited the season of reaction and revenge.

So insensible were the Latins to the insecurity and danger of their position, that, only a few months after the conquest of Constantinople, as if no better occupation could be found against the common enemy, their two principal potentates, the emperor Baldwin and Boniface of Montferrat, the new king of Macedonia, engaged in an open civil war, which was

Doge of Venice, and of the sovereign peers of the dismembered empire.*

This quarrel was scarcely composed when the titular reign of Baldwin was suddenly disturbed by a more formidable opponent, [A. D. 1204,] whose hostility was provoked by the Latin pride, and assisted by Greek disaffection. This was Calo Johannes, or Joannice, king of Bulgaria, the ancient enemy of the Greek empire, who, on its subversion, had welcomed the Latins as natural allies, and invited their friendship by a congratulatory embassy. But Baldwin, who pretended to have succeeded to all the rights of the deposed dynasty, repulsed the Bulgarian envoys with disdain; treated their master as a revolted rebel against the Byzantine throne; and instead of accepting his alliance, demanded his allegiance. Joannice smothered this insult only until his emissaries had prepared the Greek provincials of Thrace to become the ready instruments of his vengeance. An extensive conspiracy was quickly and secretly organized; and the signal for its explosion was the departure from Constantinople of Henry, the brother of Baldwin, with the flower of the Latin chivalry, to attempt the reduction of the Asiatic provinces. Throughout Thrace, the Greek population rose simultaneously and

---

* Geoffroy de Villehardouin, *Histoire de la Prise de Constantinople*, Ed. Du Cange, fol. Paris, 1657. Paragraphs No. cxl.–clx. Du Cange, *Hirtoire de Constantinople sous les Empereurs François*,

suddenly against their oppressors; the Latins in the open country, unarmed and surprised, were everywhere mercilessly slaughtered; [A. D. 1205;] the feeble garrisons of the towns, for the most part, were either overpowered by the first shock of the revolt and massacred, or escaped in dismay by a gathering retreat upon the capital; and the loss of Adrianople, the second city of the empire, where the Venetians had established their chief post, and whence their forces were driven in disorder by the insurgent populace, completed the sum of disaster. To aggravate its effects, Joannice himself, at the head of his Bulgarians, and of a yet more fierce and savage horde of Comans,* or Turcoman auxiliaries, poured into Thrace, and discovered

---

* In the Memoirs of Joinville (Johnes's Translation, p. 204) is a curious passage illustrative of a custom of this wild horde of the Comans. Louis IX. of France was joined in Palestine by "a most noble knight" of Constantinople, who informed the king that, when the Comans had once concluded an alliance with the Latins, their chief had insisted on the contracting parties "being blooded, and drinking alternately of each other's blood in sign of brotherhood." Joinville adds that, when this Byzantine knight and his companions took service with the French, they required the like pledge of himself and his countrymen; "and our blood being mixed with wine, was drunk by each party as constituting us all brothers of the same blood." The mention of this barbarous rite, thus borrowed by the Latins from the pagan Comans, furnishes the indefatigable Du Cange with an occasion to discuss the whole subject of brotherly adoption in arms. *Diss.* xxi. The Comans were a Tartar, or Turcoman horde, who encamped in the 12th and 13th centuries on the verge of Moldavia. They were mostly pagans, but some were Mohammedans, and the whole tribe was converted to Christianity in 1370

to the Latins the extent of the combination against them.

At this perilous juncture, Baldwin and his gallant compeers, who had rallied the broken remains of their chivalry round the capital, evinced the same high and dauntless spirit, and the same untempered disdain of all prudential considerations, which had already achieved and endangered the possession of an empire. Instead of awaiting the arrival of Henry of Flanders and his more numerous bands, who had been recalled from the Asiatic war on the first alarm, the emperor resolved to take the field at the head of his scanty array, and to advance for the immediate recovery of Adrianople from the insurgents. The march was accomplished, and that city had already been invested, when the Latin chivalry was enveloped in a plain by a cloud of Bulgarian and Turcoman horse, who, according to their usual mode of combat, fled before every charge; lured their enemies into a precipitate and disorderly pursuit; and when the heavily armed French cavaliers had utterly exhausted their own strength and that of their steeds, turned suddenly upon them, surrounded, and cut them to pieces. The Count of Blois, whose rash contempt of a salutary caution had involved the Latin army in their destruction, paid the penalty of his presumption, and was slain on the spot; the emperor Baldwin, whose impetuosity had been carried away by the example, fell

nant of the Latin host was saved from destruction only by the presence of mind, the skill, and the patient courage of the aged Doge of Venice and of the Marshal Villehardouin, the historian of the war.*

While the venerable Dandolo assumed the general direction of a retreat, his noble compeer rallied a rearguard, and at its head firmly sustained the furious assaults of the pursuers; and in such order was safely accomplished an arduous march of three days, from the walls of Adrianople to the shores of the Hellespont. There, the exhausted forces of the Latins were met by the troops under Henry of Flanders, who had landed from the Asiatic coast; whose junction restored the balance of strength; and whose arrival, if it had been awaited before the late expedition, might have averted its disastrous issue. In the first ignorance of the Latins of the fate of their captive emperor, the regency of his dominions was intrusted to his brother Henry; but, after the lapse of a year, the king of Bulgaria, who had formerly obtained the papal friendship and patronage by professing his conversion to the Latin church, replied to the solicitations of Innocent III. for the release of Baldwin, that his imperial prisoner had expired in his dungeon. The manner of his death was never ascertained; but the fact (although twenty years later it was strongly

* Villehardouin, No. clxv.-cxciii. Nicetæ Acominati Choniatæ, *Historia*, (*in Script. Byzant.*), p. 883-416. Du Cange, *Hist. Con-*

brought into doubt) was firmly believed by his Eastern subjects; and after an affectionate delay, until all hope of his existence had been lost, his brother Henry consented to assume the imperial title.*

In the brief and calamitous annals of the Latin Empire of the East, the reign of the virtuous and prudent Henry presents the sole interval of comparative prosperity. By the death of his original compeers in the Fourth Crusade, he was gradually left to sustain with his single energy the arduous duties of defending the Latin States against the hostility, both of the Bulgarians in Europe, and of the Greek refugees of Asia. The King of Macedonia, after a zealous and gallant co-operation against the common enemy, which was cemented by a family alliance with the emperor, was slain in an unfortunate skirmish by the Bulgarian troops; the valiant marshal and faithful historian, Geoffroy of Villehardouin did not long survive him; and the decease of both had been preceded by that of

---

* Villehardouin, Nicetas, Du Cange, *ubi suprà ad fin. Gesta Innocentii III.* (in Muratori, *Script. Rer. Ital.* vol. iii.) c. 109. The balance of evidence is certainly on the whole against the identity with the captive emperor, of the claimant who appeared in Flanders about twenty years afterward, but his story was not improbable, and scarcely justifies the confidence with which Gibbon (ch. lxi. notes 29, 30) has pronounced it an imposture, chiefly, perhaps, for the purpose of ridiculing the "fables which were believed by the monks of St Alban's." He was hanged as an impostor in the great square of Lisle, by order of Jane, Countess of Flanders, the daughter of the lost Baldwin.

the brave old Doge.* But, though deprived of these pillars of the Latin glory and fortune, Henry, by his courage and wisdom, nobly upheld and repaired the shattered edifice of dominion. By rescinding the impolitic exclusion of his Greek subjects from the public service, he conciliated their affections; and his jud`· cious measures were assisted by the treacherous cruelty and tyranny with which the Bulgarian king repaid the Byzantine provincials for their seasonable revolt and alliance. That barbarian had already commenced a project for the depopulation of Thrace, and for the forcible withdrawal of the inhabitants beyond the Danube, when his measures were arrested by the approach of Henry; who, moved by the entreaties of the Greeks, hastened to the deliverance of the repentant rebels at the head of only a few hundred knights and their attendants. The inhabitants, on his approach, welcomed him with open arms; Bulgarian hosts of immense numerical superiority were repeatedly defeated by the skill of Henry and the well-directed valour of the Latin chivalry; and Joannice was ignominiously expelled from the Thracian

---

* Dandolo was buried in the Church of St. Sophia at Constantinople, and his mausoleum existed till the destruction of the Greek empire; but it was demolished when that church was converted into a Turkish mosque. A Venetian painter, who worked for several years at the court of Mohammed II., obtained from the Sultan, on his return to his own country, the cuirass, the helmet, the spurs, and the cloak of the Doge, which he presented to the family of that illus

provinces. The murder of the Bulgarian tyrant by his own subjects shortly afterward relieved the Latin empire from his hostility; and his successor gladly accepted an honourable peace from his conqueror.

The moderation of Henry induced him to seize the first opportunity of concluding with the Greek sovereigns of Nice and Epirus similar pacifications; [A. D. 1216;] which defined the limits of their respective states, and enabled him to close in tranquil glory a reign of ten years, which was too short for the happiness of his subjects.*

The mention of the Greek empire of Nice may momentarily divert our attention to the Asiatic shores of the Bosphorus. [A. D. 1204.] When Theodore Lascaris withdrew from servitude at the capture of Constantinople, to sustain the cause of personal and national freedom in the fastnesses of Bithynia, his authority was acknowledged by only three cities and two thousand armed followers; but his service was soon embraced by all his fugitive countrymen from the capital, who shared his disdain of a foreign yoke; and his martial efforts were favoured by the calamities of the Bulgarian war, which compelled the Latins to withdraw their forces from the prosecution of their Asiatic conquests. On the twofold claim of his own

---

* Villehardouin, No. cxcii. *ad fin.* *Gesta Innocent. III* c. 106 107. Du Cange, *Hist. Constant.* lib. ii. c. 1–22.

merit, and of his union with the daughter of Alexius Angelus, the right of Lascaris to the imperial dignity was universally acknowledged by his adherents; and establishing the seat of his government at Nice, he made that city the capital of a state, which he quickly extended by his arms from the Hellespont to the Meander. His reign of eighteen years was terminated by death, in the meridian of his age; but his place was filled by a noble Greek of congenial virtue, John Ducas Vataces, who had married his daughter, and succeeded to his throne; [A. D. 1222;] and whose glorious career of thirty-three years was not more distinguished by his success in arms, than by the virtues of his domestic administration.*

While the native dominion of the Greeks was reviving under these two heroes, the Latin empire had become a prey, after the death of Henry, to all the disorders of a feeble government. By the decease of the last of the two Flemish princes who had worn the crown of Constantinople, the male line of their house was extinct: the daughter of Baldwin had succeeded to the possession of his European state; Henry had left no issue, and the feudatories of the Byzantine state offered his throne to Peter de Courtenay, [A. D. 1217,] a French baron who had married his sister, and whose regal pedigree has been illustrated by a

---

* Gibbon, ch. lxii., whom, for the Annals of the Greek Empire of Nice, we shall be contented to abridge.

great historian.* Peter accepted the tempting but fatal honour, incautiously traversed the dangerous passes of Greece with a train of French knights, and, being entrapped into a perfidious truce with the despot of Epirus, the second of a race of Comnenian princes who had established an obscure independence on the ruins of the Greek empire, was thrown into a dungeon, in which he ended his life. [A. D. 1219.] Meanwhile the wife of Courtenay, Iolanta, the new Latin Empress of the East, had reached Constantinople by sea; and during the short residue of her life, the government was administered in her name as regent for her captive or deceased lord.†

On her death, and the refusal of her eldest son to abandon his French fief, Robert, his next brother, was summoned to ascend the Eastern throne, [A. D. 1221,] and his arrival at Constantinople was followed by his coronation. The chivalrous qualities of the House of Courtenay, which had been signalized in Europe and in Palestine, were ill sustained by Robert. He proved himself at once pusillanimous, indolent, and licentious; and, during his reign of seven years, the Latin empire, shaken on either side by the rude assaults of the Greeks of Nice and Epirus, rocked to its foundations. So corrupt was the spirit of the

---

* Gibbon, xi. 287. The English branch of this ancient family is represented by the Courtenays, Earls of Devon.

French adventurers who sought employment in the East, that the Greek Emperor Vataces found no difficulty in enlisting whole bodies of them into his service against their countrymen. With such aid, his arms were everywhere successful; the fleets which he equipped commanded the seas, and reduced several of the islands on the coast of Asia Minor; and, in a disastrous attempt to check his victorious career, most of the hardy veterans of the Fourth Crusade, who had survived the storms of the Bulgarian and Grecian wars, were numbered with the slain. A disgraceful feud in the Byzantine palace finally drove Robert from a throne which he wanted courage to defend against either foreign or domestic enemies. To revenge his seduction of the affianced bride of a Burgundian gentleman, the infuriated lover burst with a band of his friends into the imperial retreat, barbarously mutilated the beauty of his fair mistress, cast the mother, who had pandered to her falsehood, into the Hellespont, and openly braved the power of her paramour. When Robert demanded the assistance of his barons to punish this unpardonable outrage upon the laws of humanity and the majesty of the purple, they justified the act, and made common cause with the criminal; and the craven prince, too impotent to enforce retribution for the cruel offence and affront which he had provoked, abandoned his throne, and appealed to the judgment of the Papal Court. [A. D. 1228.] But the pope was unwilling to

Baldwin II.

commit his authority to the hazard of so profitless a quarrel; and the imperial exile was hurried by grief or pride to a premature grave.*

As Robert died without issue, the succession to his crown devolved upon his younger brother, Baldwin II., who was born at Constantinople shortly after the arrival of the Empress Iolanta and the capture of her husband, and who was still a minor. But, as the

---

* Du Cange, *Hist. Constant.* lib. iii. c. 1-12.

necessities of the state demanded a defend r of maturer years, the barons of the empire offered a share of the imperial dignity to a valiant nobleman of Champagne, John de Brienne, who had already, as we shall hereafter observe, been raised by his merit to the titular crown of Jerusalem, and had resigned that visionary diadem, with the hand of his eldest daughter, to Frederic II., Emperor of the West. Although this regal adventurer was already far advanced in life, he accepted the proposal of the Byzantine barons that he should ascend the imperial throne of Constantinople, upon condition of marrying his second daughter to his young colleague and destined successor, Baldwin II. During nine years, the aged hero nobly sustained the arduous duties of his station against the increasing resources and energies of the empire of Nice; but Vataces had now permanently re-established the Greek standard in Europe, and had recovered the greater portion of the ancient possessions of his nation in Thrace; the Latin territories were gradually circumscribed within the environs of the capital; the alliance of the Greek emperor with the King of Bulgaria threatened total ruin to the falling state; and the last exploit of John de Brienne was the repulse of their combined army and navy of one hundred thousand men and three hundred galleys from the walls of Constantinople.* [A. D. 1237.]

---

* Du Cange, *Hist. Constant.* lib. iii. c. 18, *ad fin.*

The strength of the capital and the prowess of John de Brienne had deferred for twenty-four years the total extinction of the Latin empire; but the sceptre of all its territories was already held by the Greek conqueror. During his active and glorious career, Vataces had compelled the Comnenian sovereign of Epirus to resign the imperial title; and, reuniting Western Greece to the Eastern Provinces, he had consolidated his dominion over the whole expanse of country, from the Euxine to the Adriatic, and from the Danube to the Mediterranean. In a brief reign of only four years, his son and successor, Theodore Lascaris II., carried his victorious arms into the recesses of Bulgaria, [A. D. 1255,] and reduced that wild kingdom within its natural limits, and into its ancient submission to the Eastern Empire. The infancy of his son John made way for the rise of another hero of noble Greek family, Michael Palæologus. [A. D. 1259.] On the death of the second Theodore Lascaris, the guardianship of the infant emperor was wrested by a conspiracy from the hands of an unpopular favourite of the last reign, and obtained by Palæologus, whose martial reputation and post of constable of the French mercenaries gave him the command, and had secured him the affections, of the imperial troops. The new regent soon aspired to a higher dignity, to which his pretensions were founded not only on his personal merit, but on the superior right of hereditary descent over the reigning dynasty;

since his mother was a daughter of the last Alexius, and an elder sister of the princess whom Theodore Lascaris had espoused. In the usual progress of such usurpation as the Eastern Empire had often witnessed, Palæologus was first declared the guardian, next the colleague, of his young sovereign; and, finally, he was crowned as sole emperor, and John Lascaris was condemned to an empty title of honour and a harmless obscurity. The personal claims and the public services of Palæologus might extenuate his conduct in thus seizing the sceptre; but the guilt of his usurpation was subsequently deepened by an act of unpardonable cruelty toward his unfortunate pupil; and in order that Lascaris might be for ever incapacitated from reigning, he was deprived of his eyesight by command of his jealous oppressor.*

It was in the second year of the reign of the vigorous usurper, that the success of a desultory and almost an accidental enterprise terminated the feeble existence of the Latin Empire of the East. Since the death of John de Brienne, his son-in-law and colleague Baldwin II., upon whom the sole sovereignty devolved, had proved himself utterly incapable of defending his throne; and had spent a lesser portion of his nominal reign of twenty-five years in the Eastern capital, than in traversing Western Europe with vain supplications for pecuniary and military aid, and in exposing to public scorn his necessities and his weakness.* As the catastrophe of his inglorious fortunes approached, he slumbered in his palace, neither conscious of the imminence of his danger, nor prepared for one generous effort of despair. The repulse of an attack by Palæologus in person upon the suburbs of Constantinople, in the preceding year, might indeed have awakened him to the designs of that active and ambitious enemy. But such was the blind security of his government, that the squadron of galleys which the Venetians maintained in their Byzantine colony was suffered to carry away the flower of the French chivalry on a rash maritime expedition into the Euxine, at the very juncture when a body of the Greek troops was hovering about the gates of the capital. The commander of this hostile force was Alexius Strategopulus, the favourite lieutenant of the Emperor Michael, upon whom that prince had bestowed the title of Cæsar, and who now amply justified the confidence of his sovereign. By his knowledge of the weakness of the Latin garrison, and of the disposition of the inhabi-

---

* His two mendicant visits to England are noticed by the Monk of St. Alban's, p. 396, 637. In the first, he was first repelled with insult for presuming to land without permission, and afterward, on explanation, received and dismissed by Henry III. with a charitable collection of some seven hundred marks. In the second, he is contemptuously numbered by our uncourtly monk as *pauper*, profugus, *inglorious*, &c. (a beggar, a vagabond, and a craven,) among the herd of princely beggars who were attracted to England, by the weak

tants, he was encouraged to attempt the surprise of Constantinople. He was assisted by the concert or the favour of the native Greek population; by the hatred which the Genoese settlers bore to their Venetian rivals; by the cowardice of Baldwin; and by the general terror of the Latins. His troops were secretly admitted into the heart of the city, before their presence was discovered; at the first alarm Baldwin, escaping from his palace, sought safety on board the returning squadron from the Euxine, which arrived only in time to protect his flight to Italy; and the Greeks of Constantinople joyfully hailed the deliverance of their capital from a subjection of fifty-seven years to the Latin yoke.* [A. D. 1261.]

The Emperor Michael Palæologus hastened to make his triumphant entry into the ancient and recovered seat of the empire of his nation; and the remainder of his reign was laboriously occupied in securing his dominion against the vengeance or ambition of the Latin Powers. From his fugitive rival Baldwin, in person, he had, indeed, little to dread; and that craven prince closed his worthless life in an indigent exile. But his empty offers had meanwhile seduced the cupidity of Charles of Anjou, king of the Sicilies, to bestow a daughter upon his son Philip as the heir to the titular diadem of the East, and to undertake the reconquest and partition of the Greek

Empire. The mingled prudence and good fortune of Palæologus defeated this design. His measures to conciliate the papacy by an acknowledgment of its spiritual supremacy, and a union of the Greek and Latin churches, belong to ecclesiastical history, as does also his success in averting a formidable invasion of his dominions by the French chivalry under Charles of Anjou, through the subsidies with which he supported the revolt of Sicily against that prince. The domestic reign of Palæologus was disturbed by a cruel persecution of his reluctant subjects, to enforce their submission to the papal authority; which, as his own insincerity in that cause was notorious, rendered his hypocritical policy the more atrocious. [A. D. 1282.] On his death, after a memorable reign of twenty-three years, of which the last nine had been shared by his son Andronicus, the dissolution of the hollow union of the two churches was indignantly demanded by the unanimous voice of the Greek clergy and people, and proclaimed by the willing or constrained assent of the surviving emperor. Of that prince, the long and inglorious reign, succeeding to a period of comparative vigour, may be said to open a new period of decline in the Byzantine annals, which will hereafter lead us to survey the last agony and fall of the Greek Empire.*

---

* Du Cange, *Hist. Const.* lib. v. c. 34; n ad c. 14 G.bbon, ch. lxii

SECTION II.

THE FIFTH CRUSADE.

MEANWHILE, having pursued to its catastrophe that great and singular episode in the history of the Crusades which was produced by the diversion of the Latin arms to the siege of Constantinople, we may here with propriety resume our general narrative of the progress of those Christian efforts for the recovery of the Holy Sepulchre, which

conquest of the Byzantine Empire [A. D. 1204.] While the cupidity and ambition of the leaders of the Fourth Crusade seduced them to employ in that enterprise the forces which Pope Innocent III. had designed for the relief of Palestine, the state of the Mohammedan Empire justified his reproach, that their disobedience had ruined the fairest occasion of re-establishing the Christian fortunes in that country. By continued dissensions among the princes of the house of Saladin and the emirs who struggled for independence, the Mussulman power in Syria was reduced to its lowest ebb; and a dreadful famine and consequent pestilence in Egypt would effectually have paralyzed all opposition from that dangerous quarter to the success of the crusading arms. The hopes excited for the Christian cause by the division and weakness of its enemies, were completely lost in the diversion of the Fourth Crusade against the Eastern Empire; and a truce for six years with Saphadin was the only advantage derived by the Latins on the Syrian coast from the distresses and alarm of the infidels. During this interval of repose, the titular crown of Jerusalem devolved, by the death of Almeric and his queen Isabella, upon Mary, her daughter by a prior marriage with Conrad of Tyre; and the clergy and barons of Palestine delegating to Philippe-Auguste of France the choice of a husband for the young heiress, that monarch named John, son of the Count de

who was worthy of sharing, and capable of defending, her throne. [A. D. 1210.] Having accepted the proffered honour, John de Brienne arrived in Palestine, and received the hand of Mary with the royal title.*

Soon after this event, on the expiration of the truce with Saphadin, the peace of Palestine was broken, less by the ambition of the Mussulman prince, than by a rash refusal to renew the treaty with him, which had apparently been dictated in the Christian councils by the anticipation of powerful aid from France. But the new King of Jerusalem brought with him from Europe only a slender train of three hundred knights; though his personal prowess in the fields of Palestine sustained his previous reputation, his most strenuous efforts to withstand the progress of the infidels were ineffectual; and he was reduced to address to Pope Innocent III. a pressing solicitation for succour, as the only means of saving from destruction the poor remains of the Latin kingdom. Although Innocent had already engaged in an object of nearer and deeper interest to the papal supremacy—the extirpation of the alleged heresy of the Albigenses—he was not unmoved by the danger of the Christian cause in Palestine; and he immediately and earnestly answered the appeal of John de Brienne by proclaiming throughout

---

* Abulfeda, lib. iv. p. 182–194. *Contin.* Will Tyr. (in Martenne

William Longespee, Earl of Salisbury.

Europe a new Crusade to the East. He not only despatched a circular letter to all the princes of Christendom, in which they were urged, by the usual arguments, to embark in the sacred enterprise, but he instructed his legates and the clergy in every country of the West to add their spiritual exhortations to the laity in the same cause. To give the greater unity and solemnity to the design, a general council of the church—the fourth of Lateran—was at the same time convened;* and by that assembly, in which

---

* *Contin.* Will. Tyr. p. 668–680. Matthew Paris, (Ed. Watts,

all the principal monarchs of Christendom were represented by their envoys, the design of arming Europe anew against the Eastern infidels was zealously adopted.

The FIFTH CRUSADE, the result of this resolution, was divided in the sequel into three maritime expeditions: [A. D. 1216;] the first consisting principally of Hungarians under their king, Andrew; the second composed of Germans, Italians, French, and English nobles and their followers; and the third led by the Emperor Frederic II. in person. Of each of these enterprises, none of which were attended with many novel or interesting features, the events may be briefly distinguished and dismissed. Though the King of Hungary was attended by the flower of a nation which, before its conversion to Christianity, had been the scourge and terror of Western Europe, the arms of that monarch, even aided by the junction of numerous German crusaders under the Dukes of Austria and Bavaria, performed nothing worthy of notice: and after a single campaign in Palestine, in which the Mussulman territories were ineffectually ravaged, the fickle Andrew deserted the cause, and returned with his forces to Europe. His defection did not prevent the Duke of Austria, with the German crusaders, from remaining, in concert with the King of Jerusalem, his barons, and the knights of the three religious orders, for the defence of Palestine; and, in the following year, the constancy of these faithful champions of the Cross was rewarded by the arrival of numerous reinforcements from Germany.*

This accession of strength gave a new energy and direction to the Christian councils; and it was resolved to change the scene of warfare from the narrow limits of the Syrian shore to the coast of Egypt. Several motives impelled the crusaders to this resolution; the wealth of the latter country, which tempted their greediness of spoil; the dispiriting impression of repeated failures in direct assaults upon the Mussulman power from the Christian garrisons of Palestine; and a conviction—which calamitous experience alone had forced upon so rude an age of warfare, but which a juster appreciation of the principles of martial science will confirm—that, in a military sense, Egypt, by its position and resources, is the key of Syria. By the conquest of Egypt, therefore, it was believed that the true seat of the Mussulman power† must be overthrown, and the recovery of Jerusalem effected; and the situation of Damietta, at the mouth

---

* *Cont.* Will. Tyr. p. 680, 681. Abulfeda, p. 260–263. Jacobus a Vitriaco, *Hist. Hierosol.* (*in Gestis Dei per Francos,*) p. 1129–1131. Bernardus Thesaur. (*apud* Muratoria, *Scrip. Rer. Ital.* vol. ii) p. 820–822. Matthew Paris, p. 244, 245. Godefridus Monachus, *Annales* (*apud* Freher Marguard, *Rer. German. Scriptores*, vol. i. Ed. Tertia, 1718,) p. 384–387.

† Matthew Paris ascribes the design of carrying the war into Egypt to the advice of Pope Innocent III.

of the Nile, pointed out that city as the first object oi attack.*

The short passage from Acre to the Egyptian coast was effected by sea; and the crusading army, being safely landed under the walls of Damietta, immediately formed the siege of the place. [A. D. 1218.] In a furious assault from the galleys of the crusaders upon a castle in the river which defended the port, the Duke of Austria and the flower of the Christian knighthood were completely repulsed; but the walls of a tower were so shattered by the engines of the besiegers, that the garrison of the castle were terrified into a surrender. The hopes with which this first success inspired the Christians were shortly increased to the highest degree, by intelligence of the death of their most formidable enemy, the Sultan Saphadin; and by the opportune and successive arrival of new bands of crusaders from Italy, France, and England,

---

* The Monk of Cologne describes in a remarkable passage the commercial wealth and importance of Damietta:—" Hac via exeunt naves cum speciebus oneratæ, venientes ab Indiâ, et tendentes versus Syriam, Antiocham, Armeniam, Græciam et Cyprum; et ab hoc transitu Rex Babyloniæ maximos recepit reditus. Hæc civitas quasi caput et clavis est totius Ægypti; præcellit enim in munitione Babyloniam, Alexandriam, Tanaim (?) et cunctas civitates Ægypti. Godefridus Monachus, p. 388. (Ships laden with spices (from India,) and proceeding toward Syria, Antioch, Armenia, Greece, and Cyprus, pass out by this way; and the king of Babylon receives great returns by this route. This city is, as it were, both the head and the key of all Egypt; for it far surpasses in strength Babylon, Alexandria, and every other city of Egypt.)

headed respectively by the papal legates, by the Counts of Nevers and La Marche, and by the Earls of Salisbury, Arundel, and Chester. But these numerous accessions of force served only to augment the blind confidence of the besiegers, and to introduce disunion and discord into their camp, through the jealous and conflicting pretensions of so many chieftains of various nations. The intrigues of the papal legates to arrogate to themselves the general direction of the host, fomented, instead of healing, these dissensions; and while the unexpected desperation with which the defence of the city was protracted, converted the presumption of the crusaders into anxiety and despondence, the usual horrors of famine and pestilence completed their distress. At length the still heavier pressure of similar calamities within the walls of Damietta utterly exhausted the strength of its defenders; out of a population of near fourscore thousand souls, nine-tenths had perished of disease and hunger; [A. D. 1219;] and after a siege of seventeen months, the assailants forced their way into a city, which was filled only with the dead and the dying.*

---

* *Cont.* Will. Tyr. p. 682–688. Abulfeda, p. 264–271. Jac. a Vitriaco, p. 1131–1134, &c. Godefridus, p. 387–391. Bernardus, p. 822–838. Matt. Paris, p. 253–259. This last writer gives a long and particular account of the siege of Damietta, and of the operations before the place. He draws a harrowing picture of the effects of the pestilence in Damietta, and exhibits a power of description which will bear no unfavourable comparison with more celebrated historical passages on the same horrid theme.

Both during the siege and after the capture of Damietta, the invasion of Egypt had filled the infidels with consternation; and the alarm which was betrayed in their counsels proved that the crusaders, in choosing that country for the theatre of operations, had assailed the Mussulman power in its most vital and vulnerable point. Of the two sons of Saphadin, Coradinus and Camel, who were now uneasily seated on the thrones of Damascus and Cairo, the former, in despair of preserving Jerusalem, had already demolished its fortifications; and the brothers agreed in repeatedly offering the cession of the holy city and of all Palestine to the Christians, upon the simple condition of their evacuating Egypt. Every object which had been ineffectually proposed in repeated Crusades, since the fatal battle of Tiberias, might now have been gloriously obtained by the acceptance of these terms; and the King of Jerusalem, the French and English leaders, and the Teutonic knights, all eagerly desired to embrace the offer of the sultans. But the obstinate ambition and cupidity of the surviving papal legate, Cardinal Pelagius, of the Italian chieftains, and of the knights of the other two religious orders, by holding out the rich prospect of the conquest and plunder of Egypt, overruled every wise and temperate argument in the Christian councils, and produced a rejection of all compromise with the infidels. After a winter of luxurious inaction, the legate led the crusading host from Damietta toward Cairo; [A.D. 1220;]

but the infidels had employed the interval in vigorous preparation for a renewal of hostilities; the whole Mussulman force of Egypt and Syria was collected under Camel to oppose the Christian advance up the Nile;* and the cardinal legate showed himself as incapable of conducting the war as he had been clamorous for its prosecution. While he hesitated to attack the sultan's army which obstructed the road to Cairo, and suffered the infidels to straiten his quarters, the Nile rose; the Egyptians, by opening the sluices in the canal of Ashmoum, inundated the Christian camp;* and the crusaders found themselves suddenly enclosed on all sides by the waters and the enemy. In this calamitous situation, which equally precluded their further advance or their retreat to Damietta, there remained only the choice of extermination by hunger, the elements, and the sword, or the disgraceful alternative of purchasing a peace, which they had lately refused to sell, by the surrender of Damietta. The legate, therefore, sent a suppliant embassy to the

---

* A curious letter in Matthew Paris from an English crusading knight, Philip d'Aubeney, to the Earl of Chester, (who had returned home after the capture of Damietta,) rates the force of the Christian army which advanced up the Nile at a thousand knights, five thousand other cavalry, and forty thousand foot, p. 264.

† The letter last quoted states that the water reached "usque ad braccarios et cinctoria, ad magnam miseriam et dolorem," (up to their hips and waists, causing great discomfort and pain.) And another letter from the Grand-Master of the Templars, which immediately follows, quaintly describes the army as enclosed by the waters, " sicut piscis reti includitur," (like as a fish enclosed in a net.)

Mussulman camp with an offer of this price for permission to evacuate Egypt in safety; and the Sultan of Cairo acceded to the prayer. The King of Jerusalem himself became a hostage for the performance of the treaty; a free retreat to Damietta was allowed to the humbled and perishing remnant of the crusading host; and, on their embarkation, that city was delivered up to the infidels. The King of Jerusalem, with his barons and the knights of the three religious orders, then sailed to Acre; and the rest of the crusaders, assuming the failure of the Egyptian war for a sufficient discharge from their vows, gladly separated from their eastern brethren, and retraced their homeward voyage to the shores of Europe.*

Amid the sorrow and indignation excited throughout Europe by the abortive and disgraceful result of so hopeful an enterprise, its calamitous issue was loudly attributed by the crusaders, not without justice, to the presumption and incapacity of the legate Pelagius. But the new pope, Honorius III., laboured to transfer the public reproach from his servant upon the Emperor Frederic II., by charging to that monarch's continued evasion of repeated vows to join the Crusade, all the disasters which his presence in the East might have prevented. Frederic, however, was deaf to the papal censures, until an occasion was afforded

Emperor Frederic II.

to Honorius of stimulating his zeal by the arrival from Palestine of Herman de Saltza, grand-master of the Teutonic knights, with a proposal for the marriage of the emperor with Iolanta, daughter and heiress of John de Brienne: who, wearied of the ineffectual struggle against the infidels, was willing to

abdicate in her favour his titular crown of Jerusalem
The ambition of Frederic was dazzled by the prospect
of adding this new, though little more than nominal
honour to his other dignities; and the young princess
being brought to Italy by her father, the emperor received her hand, and with it, for her dower, a solemn
transfer from John of his rights to the sovereignty of
the Holy Land. As a condition of this renunciation, Frederic on his part had previously engaged his
honour to the pope and the grand-master of the military orders, [A. D. 1225,] that he would within two
years lead a powerful army to Palestine, to achieve
the reconquest of his new kingdom. The real or
pretended impediments which for five years delayed
his fulfilment of this pledge; his quarrel with the
papacy and excommunication by Gregory IX., the
successor of Honorius; and his final departure for the
Holy Land, while still labouring under that sentence,
and in defiance of the hostility of the pontiff; all belong to the history of Italy, and must be sought in
the annals of that country.

The slender force with which Frederic embarked
for Palestine, in a squadron of only twenty galleys,
seemed so inadequate to the maintenance of his dignity, and the object of his voyage, as to excite the
wonder of his own age at the attempt; and the causes
of his subsequent and rapid success, amid every
obstacle which the pope with unrelenting enmity con-

still be numbered among the unsolved problems of history.* The Mussulman power, indeed, was now weakened by the fraternal dissensions of the Sultans of Cairo and Damascus; [A. D. 1228;] and it has been conjectured that Frederic, from the outset of his expedition, trusted to the effects of secret negotiations with the former of those potentates. But the death of his brother soon relieved Camel from the jealousy or dread with which the ambition of Coradinus had inspired him; and Frederic had thenceforth to contend with the undivided hostility of the Mussulman Empire. Meanwhile, he was deserted by the flower of the Christian chivalry in Palestine, and his weakness was betrayed to the infidels. The pope not only prohibited the knights of the religious orders from serving under the banners of an excommunicated prince, but actually despatched envoys to the sultan to dissuade him from negotiating with a leader whom the Christians disowned. Undismayed by this iniquitous persecution, which perhaps, more than any event of the times, exposes the unprincipled policy of the Papal See, Frederic boldly took the field against the infidels. The Knights Templars and Hospitallers obeyed the prohibition of the pope, until their natural thirst for enterprise, or a generous sense of shame, induced them first to follow his march, and finally, to

---

* The Monk of St. Alban's can account for the astonishing success of Frederic only by the direct interposition of Heaven in exciting dissensions "in gentibus Saracenis." (among the Saracenic races.)

co-operate indirectly with the force which acknowledged his command. But the national affections of the Teutonic knights had more effectually and unscrupulously prevailed over their dread of papal censures; and at their head, with the scanty force of his own soldiery, the emperor advanced from Acre, occupied and refortified Jaffa, and approached Jerusalem. At this juncture, and without any signal defeat of the infidels, or any explicable motive on the part of the sultan for concessions so important, we are surprised by the authentic record of a treaty, by which free access to the Holy City, together with the possession of Bethlehem, Nazareth, and other places, was restored to the Christians, and a peace for ten years was concluded between them and the Moslems. To signalize the acquisition of these honourable terms, Frederic resolved to celebrate his coronation at Jerusalem. Under a plea that he still remained excommunicate, the patriarch refused to perform, and the Templars and Hospitallers to attend, the ceremony; but, accompanied by the Teutonic knights and the officers of his train, the emperor entered the Holy City, proceeded to the Church of the Sepulchre, and himself taking the crown from the altar, placed it on his head.* [A. D. 1229.] Immediately after this act,

---

* Abulfeda, p. 336-358. Matt. Paris, p. 300-304. Godefridus, p. 396-397. But the most interesting account of Frederic's proceedings is given in a letter from himself to Henry III. of England

the state of affairs in Italy warning him of the necessity of his presence in that country, he returned to Acre, and there embarked for Europe,—having brought the Fifth Crusade to a successful conclusion, and obtained for the Christian cause in Palestine more than the arms of any other prince had been able to achieve since the conquest of Jerusalem by Saladin.*

These valuable fruits of the emperor's daring and ability were, by the mere wanton insolence or venomous hostility of faction, immediately neglected, and ultimately lost. The return of Frederic to Europe

---

* It is difficult to determine what were the real conditions on which Frederic obtained access for the Christians to Jerusalem. The papal party laboured to deny that he had redeemed the Holy Sepulchre from the hands of the infidels; and a letter from the Patriarch of Jerusalem, (also in Matt. Paris,) among other charges, accuses him of having left the sacred places in their possession. But the inveterate hostility which the Patriarch, the Templars and Hospitallers, and other papal adherents in Palestine, as well as in Europe, bore to Frederic, is sufficient to deprive their statements of all credit; and his own public letter declares expressly that the Saracens were only to have the liberty of visiting the Temple of Solomon as pilgrims and unarmed, and adding, "civitatem Hierusalem, sicut melius unquam fuit, reædificare nobis liceat secundum pactum"—(we are allowed by treaty to rebuild the city of Jerusalem, so that it shall be better than it ever was.) He farther states, that he had given orders accordingly for the rebuilding of the towers and walls of the Holy City; but his intentions were evidently frustrated by the necessity for his hasty return to Europe; and it does not appear that any attempt was made to renew them by the resident Christians in Palestine. It is observable, however, that the Mussulman version of the treaty in Abulfeda

was the signal for the open outbreaking of that disaffection to his person and authority which had only been repressed through the awe excited by his presence; and resistance to the imperial title was now made the convenient pretext for the revival of the same spirit of internal discord and intrigue which had ever been the bane of the Christian fortunes in Palestine. The Empress Iolanta having died in giving birth to a son, the enemies of Frederic insisted that her rights to the sovereignty of Jerusalem had devolved, notwithstanding the existence of her child and the matrimonial title secured by treaty to her husband, upon her half-sister Alice, daughter of Isabella, by the third marriage of that queen with Henry of Champagne. Alice, the widow of Hugh de Lusignan, king of Cyprus, having arrived on the Syrian shore from that island, to assert her title to the throne of Palestine, a furious civil war commenced between her partisans and those of Frederic. [A. D. 1230.] If the former were more numerous, their advantage was counterbalanced by the fidelity and courage with which the knights of the Teutonic order defended the cause of their national monarch until he was able to despatch reinforcements to his officers. The revolt of Palestine was at length composed, and the imperial authority restored, chiefly by the good offices of Pope Gregory IX., during the hollow reconciliation between that pontiff and Frederic, which had

dissensions of the Christians had meanwhile prevented any union of forces for their common security against the infidels; no use had been made of the season of pacification obtained by Frederic's treaty, to improve the defences of the Holy Land; and finding the strength of the Latin kingdom consumed in intestine strife, the independent emirs of Syria were encouraged to disclaim any share in the peace which the Sultan had concluded, and began to renew their predatory hostilities from every quarter. In one of these incursions, they surprised and slaughtered a body of several thousand pilgrims of the Cross on the road between Acre and Jerusalem; and upon another occasion the Templars, who arrogated to themselves the right of making war and peace on their own account, were defeated in a campaign against the emir of Aleppo, with the heaviest loss which their order had suffered since the fatal field of Tiberias.*

Every vessel from the shores of Syria now brought to Europe the intelligence of some fresh disaster, and quickened the public conviction of Christendom that a new Crusade was indispensable for the succour of the Holy Land. At the Council of Spoleto, the authority of the Church was again exerted to promulgate the necessity, and to command the preparation of another general armament against the Eastern infidels; and the Dominican and Franciscan friars were charged by the pope with the duty of preaching the sacred war, and of collecting contributions for its support. But the proceedings of these missionaries neither responded to the impatience of the people, nor to the urgency of the danger. Instead of promoting the equipment of the thousands of warriors who assumed the Cross at their exhortations, the immense sums which they obtained for the service were either absorbed into the papal treasury,* or diverted, in shameless disregard of their own vows of poverty, into the coffers of their orders; and nearly seven years were suffered to elapse without any earnest attempt on the part of the pope or his agents for the relief of Palestine. The expectations of aid which were held out to the Christians in the East, during this interval, served only to hasten the ruin of their affairs; for the Sultan of Egypt, in rage or alarm at the thick-coming rumours of invasion from Europe, resolved to anticipate its object, and marching an army into Palestine, he once more expelled the Christians from Jerusalem.†

---

* " Nec sciri poterat," says " Matthew Paris, "in quam abyssum tanta pecunia, quæ per Papales procurationes colligebatur, est demersa," (nor could it be ascertained into what abyss so great a sum of money, collected by the papal government, was plunged,) p. 339.

† Labbe, *Concilia*, vol. xi. p. 481. Matt Paris, p. 837-840, 864, 865. Sanutus, *ubi supra*.

CHAPTER III.

THE SIXTH CRUSADE.

HE news of this event completed the indignation which the dilatory and sordid evasions of the pope and his ministers had long excited in Europe, [A. D. 1238;] and the martial and religious enthusiasm of the Western chivalry was too ardently roused by the danger of the Christian cause in the East, to be longer restrained and deluded from its object by

of the papal court. Despite, therefore, of the facilities for commuting their vows for gold, the dissuasions, and even the direct prohibitions which were opposed by the papal authority to their enterprise, the nobles of France and England, who had now taken the Cross, were resolved at once to proceed to the Holy Land; and in the latter kingdom the crusading barons, meeting at Northampton, solemnly bound themselves to each other at the altar, that, lest they should be prevented from their design by any pretext of the Roman See, or cajoled to divert their arms to the effusion of Christian blood against the pope's enemies in Europe, they would within the year lead their forces direct to Palestine.* The French Crusaders were the earliest to reach the Syrian shores. Thibaud, Count of Champagne—a celebrated Troubadour, and by marriage king of Navarre—the Duke of Burgundy, the Counts of Bretagne, Montfort, and Bar, and many barons of distinction, safely landed with numerous bands of followers at Acre; and offensive warfare was immediately commenced against the infidels, by an advance to Ascalon. In this expedition the French were at first successful; and the Count of Bretagne with his followers bursting away from his confederates into the Mussulman territory,

---

* Matt. Paris, p. 461–463. "Et ne per cavillationes Romanæ Ecclesiæ honestum votum eorum impediretur .... juraverunt omnes (and they all swore that they would not be hindered from fulfilling their honourable vow by the cavils of the Roman Church.)

Richard, Earl of Cornwall.

and ravaging it to the gates of Damascus, safely rejoined the army with immense spoil. But there was little concert in the operations of the crusaders; and the example of the Breton chivalry soon entailed upon their French compeers a disastrous defeat near Gaza, in which, during a similar incursion, the Count de Bar and other lords were slain, and Amoury de Montfort, with many nobles and knights, made captive. This reverse so dispirited the king of Navarre, that he retreated with the whole army to Acre; and thence the French leaders, accusing the Templars and Hospitallers of having deserted them in their need, for the most part returned to Europe.*

---

* Sanatus, lib. iii. pars xi. c. 15. Matt. Paris, p. 474–488 bulfeda, lib. iv. p. 488, 489

Such had been the abortive result of the French Crusade, when Richard, Earl of Cornwall, brother of Henry III., landed at Acre, accompanied by the flower of the English chivalry. The renown of this prince for personal prowess, the lineage of a Plantagenet, even the very name of Richard, which he bore in common with his uncle of the Lion Heart,* all seemed at his approach to inspire confidence into the Christians, and to strike the infidels with terror. On his arrival in Palestine, he seems to have been placed at the head of the Latin councils and forces almost by acclamation; and the weight of his presence was immediately felt in the intimidation of the Mussulmans. He found that the Templars on the one hand, and on the other the Hospitallers and French Crusaders, had concluded discordant treaties with the Emir of Karac, a vassal of the Court of Damascus, and with the Sultan of Cairo; and his first act was to de-

---

* So great was the awe inspired by the achievements of Cœur de Lion in the East, that, at the distance of half a century, his dreaded name was still used by Mussulman women to hush their refractory children. "Be quiet, be quiet, here is King Richard coming to fetch you." And if a horse started at a bush or a shadow, the infidel rider would chide his steed with the exclamation, "What! dost think King Richard is there?" Joinville (Johne's Translation,) p. 109. So also says Matthew of Westminster of the respect obtained among the Moslems for Richard of Cornwall by the very memory of the name which he bore. " Cæperunt nimis prudentiam et potentiam Comitis formidare, tum quia hoc nomen Richardus adhuc Saracenis inimicum ipsum intitulavit," &c., p. 304. (They began to fear greatly the prudence and power of the count, also because the very name Richard

mand from the former chieftain the fulfilment of a promise to release the Christian captives who had been taken at the battle of Gaza. On the hesitation or inability of the emir to restore these prisoners, the earl advanced with the Christian host to Jaffa; and this single movement sufficed to obtain all the objects of the war. Both the Sultans of Damascus and of Egypt hastened to negotiate with him; and so ably did he avail himself of the dissensions between these princes, and their common awe of his name and reputation, that he extorted from one or both a solemn and absolute cession of Jerusalem, and the greatest part of the territory of which the Latin kingdom, in its best days, had ever consisted. He had at the same time the satisfaction of receiving from the hands of the infidels all their Christian captives, among whom were thirty-three nobles, many Templars and Hospitallers, and five hundred knights and other crusaders of inferior rank. Finally, having remained in Palestine until the banner of the Cross was once more planted on the ruined walls of Jerusalem, the Earl of Cornwall then, and not before the execution of the treaty, quitted the shores of Palestine, and in his homeward progress through the State of Europe, was everywhere welcomed with honour as the deliverer of the Holy Sepulchre.*

---

* Sanutus, *ubi supra et* c. 16. Matt. West, p. 302–304. Matt. Paris, p. 479, 486, 511, also p. 503–505. The pages last quoted ontain the public despatch of the Earl of Cornwall himself, giving a

Frederic II.

The services which the Earl of Cornwall thus rendered to the Christian cause in Palestine did not, perhaps, excel in degree, and closely resembled in their form, those which the Emperor Frederic II. had accomplished twelve years before. [A. D. 1240.] But the English prince was more fortunate than the German monarch in not having provoked the opposition of the papal see, or the disaffection of the Latin chieftains of Palestine; and while Frederic had been shunned and deserted in the East by the sworn champions of the Cross, and was basely defrauded of the well-earned fame of unassisted success by the malice of his enemies in Europe, Richard had been

---

very clear and interesting account of his conduct, and of the treaty which he had extorted from the infidels

aided by the zealous co-operation of the crusading chivalry, and was rewarded with the undivided applause and gratitude of Christendom. The Templars, indeed, both before and after his departure from Palestine, displayed that proud and factious spirit of contention which forms the greatest, if not the only just reproach upon the memory of their illustrious order. To show their independence, they had refused to become parties to the late treaty with the Sultan of Egypt, and continued their hostilities against his subjects; but with this exception, unanimity for once prevailed in the Christian councils. While the patriarch resumed the ecclesiastical charge of Jerusalem, the Hospitallers undertook, at their own cost, to rebuild the fortifications of the Holy City; and the government of Frederic, as the feudal sovereign of Palestine, was established in the capital of the kingdom.* But no leisure was afforded for the completion of these salutary measures of organization and defence; and the recovery of Jerusalem had scarcely been achieved, before the feeble Latin kingdom was once more and suddenly overwhelmed by the violence of one of those tremendous tempests of barbarian war, which have, in various ages, overcast and desolated the face of Asia. The remote gathering of the storm, which now broke upon Palestine, must be observed in the far distant plains of Tartary; and before we

---

* Matt. Paris, p. 534–543.

hasten to the term of the present chapter, we shall be led, by no unnatural connection with its principal subject, to take a brief survey of the revolutions of Asia during that epoch in the history of the world, which is defined by the commencement and close of the Crusades.

Every vicissitude of conquest which afflicted the vast continent of Asia throughout the middle ages, had its origin among those restless and wandering tribes which overspread its central extent from the frozen deserts of Siberia to the banks of the Indus, and from the shores of the Caspian to the frontiers of China. Under various appellations, of which that of Tartars is the most recent and familiar, these same pastoral and predatory nations have at several periods, as often as some master-spirit has arisen to impel and guide their migrations, burst the bounds of their wild native regions, and inundated the more civilized seats of mankind with a terrific deluge. From this source had successively swept toward the West, the irruptions of the Huns at the downfall of the Roman Empire; of the Hungarians five centuries later; and of the Seljukian Turcomans in the following age. The establishment of a great empire, embracing Persia, Syria, and Asia Minor, by these Seljukian Tartars, and the terror which their successes excited in the Greek Emperors, have already been related among the proximate causes of the Crusades; and in the Ottoman descendants of the same race, after the apparent extinction of its power and a long interval of obscurity in the mountains of the Lesser Asia, we are hereafter to discover the conquerors of Constantinople.* In the course of the period marked by the Crusades, all the original dynasties of the Seljukians were overwhelmed and utterly obliterated by domestic revolution or foreign violence. On the aspect of Syria, indeed, this change impressed no new features; for in that country the Turcoman cavalry was continually recruited by fresh swarms from the pristine seats of the nation; and it was at the head of these kindred hordes that Saladin founded his empire on the common subversion of the Atabec sovereignty of Damascus and the Fatimite khalifate of Egypt. But in Persia and in Asia Minor, or Roum, the catastrophe was more violent; and the ruin of the monarchies, founded by the Seljukians in those countries, was among the desolating effects of a new

---

* The Kharizmians, from whom the Ottomans are descended, were in fact of the same race as the Seljukian Turcomans, but issued two centuries later from their native plains. After their expulsion from Persia by the Moguls, a body of these Kharizmian Turcomans under Soliman Schah sought refuge in Asia Minor, and entered into the service of the Seljukian Sultans of Roum or Iconium. On the ruin of that dynasty by their old Mogul enemies, the Kharizmians under Othman, the grandson of their original leader Soliman, preserved an independent existence in the mountains of Bithynia; the remains of the Seljukians were gathered to the same standard; and these Turcoman nations became blended into one people, and known in history by the name of Ottomans from that of their Kharizmian

and mighty irruption from the farthest recesses of Tartary.*

About the first years of the thirteenth century, the formidable name and victorious progress of a new conqueror and nation of Tartarian race first broke upon the astonished world. From the wide upland plains beyond the great eastern desert which extend to the Chinese wall, issued a race described as countless in number, and as more horridly inhuman in aspect and spirit, and more utterly devoid of all civilization, than any of the destroyers of mankind who had been let loose from the Tartarian regions to desolate the earth. Their earliest appearance in authentic history is under the general term of Moguls; and under the guidance of a leader, whose proper designation of Temudgin has almost been lost in the national title, which was arrogated for his grandeur, of Zingis Khan, or the Mightiest of Lords. He was the son of a khan who had reigned over thirteen hordes; and it is probable that the immense masses of the same generic features, who were drawn to his standard by the results of conquest or the thirst of rapine, derived their common term of Moguls from the original distinction of his own tribe. The early fortunes of a barbarian conqueror, the founder of his own greatness,

---

* In Persia the *original* dynasty of the Seljukians had already been supplanted by that of the Sultans of Korasm; but the conquerors, as above observed, were of kindred Turcoman stock. De

Zingis Khan.

are always obscure; the unlettered* traditions of nomadic savages must be equally destitute of authenticity and interest; [A. D. 1206;] and we may at once dismiss the tale of vicissitudes, whether fabulous or real, which are ascribed to the youth of Zingis. He first burst the limits of his native Tartar reign, to precipitate his myriads upon the plains of China; the great wall proved but a feeble barrier against his innumerable cavalry; and after a desolating warfare he tore five great provinces of the north from

---

* Zingis himself could neither read nor write, and it was not until the lapse of near a century, that the traditions of his life were collected by order of a Persian khan, his great-grandson. De la Croix, *Histoire du Grand Genghizcan*, (Paris, 1716,) p. 536–539

the huge but ill-cemented fabric of the Chinese dominion.

The complete conquest of that empire seems only to have been suspended by a diversion which was given to the Mogul arms. The murder of his ambassadors by command of Mohammed, the Kharizim Sultan of Persia, afforded Zingis a just cause of war; and, traversing the wide expanse of Tartary, he descended into Western Asia at the head of an incredible force of seven hundred thousand Moguls and Tartars. On the great plains which are intersected by the Sihon or Jaxartes, and the Oxus, he was encountered by the Turcoman Sultan with an inferior host of four hundred thousand men; and in the stupendous conflict, the victorious Moguls slaughtered nearly the half of their enemies. This success laid all Persia open to the destroyers; and, stimulated by vengeance to even more than their ordinary inhumanity, they spread a frightful devastation, from the effects of which those regions have perhaps never recovered, from the shores of the Caspian to the banks of the Indus. [A. D. 1224.] The Sultan Mohammed, flying from the storm which he had provoked, found an inglorious safety and obscure death in one of the desert islands of the Caspian; but his valiant son Gelaleddin, whose exploits became the darling theme of Persian song, still opposed, with the remnant of the Turcoman bands, a heroic though fruitless resistance to the progress of the victors. In many a well-sustained combat, his long retreat to the banks of the Indus was tracked by the blood of his pursuers; and boldly plunging with his steed into the broad and rapid current of that river, he was suffered, by the admiration which his prowess extorted from Zingis—the only trait of generosity in the recorded actions of the barbarian—to escape unmolested. The Indus was for a season the term of Mogul devastation; and, unable to command the further progress of his satiated hordes, or recalled to Tartary by a revolt of some chieftains, whom he easily subjugated, Zingis slowly led back his myriads, laden with the spoils of Persia, to their native plains. In these regions he shortly closed his destructive career by a natural death, enjoining his children, as his last command, to complete the conquest of the Chinese empire.*

This injunction was imposed upon a race to whom repose was intolerable, and motion and rapine the dearest qualifications of life. The four sons of Zingis— Octai, Toushi, Tooti, and Zagatai—were the inheritors alike of his wild genius and expansive dominion;†

---

* D'Herbelot, *Bibliotheque Orientale*, Art. Genghizcan, Gelaled din. De la Croix, *Hist. du Grand Genghizcan, passim*. De Guignes, *Hist. Gen. des Huns*, vol. iv. lib. xv.

† " He had many other sons, but these were the only princes employed in great stations, and destined by their father for monarchy— probably on account of their high descent by their mother, Burta Koutchin, the daughter of Zei Nevian, chief of the tribe of Konharat, the first in rank among the five principal wives of Chenghiz, all of whom were of high birth.—*Malcolm's Persia*, 1. f. p. 260. (Note.)

and with a spirit of fraternal or prudential concord more remarkable than their native ability, the latter three were satisfied to enjoy dependent sovereignties under their brother Octai, who was elevated by their consent to a general supremacy, under the title of Great Khan, over the Mogul and Tartar nations. By these sons of Zingis and their immediate successors, the Mogul arms were carried from the shores of the Pacific Ocean to the banks of the Euphrates, the Danube, and the Vistula; in little more than half a century had conquered or overrun nearly all Asia, and no inconsiderable part of Europe; and, at the close of the period embraced in this chapter, their descendants reigned over China, Tartary, Persia, Russia, and Siberia. The total subjugation of the first of these countries was reserved for Kublai, one of the grandsons of Zingis; but of the two empires into which it had been divided, the northern, already dismembered during the life of Zingis, was completely swallowed up in the Mogul dominion five years after his death. Other enterprises suspended the fate of the southern dynasty of the Chinese for about forty years; and when Kublai had achieved its fall and extinction, the unity of the Mogul power was already broken by the separation of its vast branches. Meanwhile, the race of Zingis were seated on independent thrones in Russia, Western Tartary, and Persia. Only eight years after his death, another of his grand-

with the command of a host of five hundred thousand Moguls, for the invasion of Russia. [A. D. 1235.] In the resistless progress of such swarms, the princes of that devoted land were overwhelmed; the country devastated, its capitals of Moscow and Kio burned to ashes; the rude national independence destroyed; and the Mogul yoke permanently fastened on the people for two hundred years. With continued violence the Tartar invasion swept over Poland, Hungary, and the circumjacent regions, from the shores of the Baltic* to those of the Euxine and Adriatic. In the battle of Legnitz, the Duke of Siberia, the Teutonic Order, and the Polish Palatines were routed with tremendous slaughter; [A. D. 1242;] in a single conflict, the King of Hungary, Bela IV., was so utterly defeated, that he abandoned his realm to its ruin. Amid the consternation of Christendom, Germany, and perhaps all Western Europe, was only saved by the firmness and energy with which the Emperor Frederic II. exhorted its princes and chi-

---

* A singular example of the effect of the Mogul conquests has been noticed by Gibbon, from a passage in Matthew Paris, p. 398. The destruction caused by the approach of the Moguls to the Baltic prevented the inhabitants of that coast from sending their vessels to England, in 1238, to take in cargoes of herrings as usual; so that, as there was no exportation, forty or fifty of those fish sold for a shilling. "It is whimsical enough," as the historian observes, "that the arms of a Khan, who reigned in China, should have affected the price of fish in the English market:" but the passage is also curious, as illustrating the existence of a regular herring fishery, and of so active a commer

valry to arm for the general defence against a common and merciless enemy.* The progress of the Moguls was first arrested by the gallant defence of a few knights and soldiers in the Austrian city of Neustadt, by their own distrustful ignorance of the art of sieges, and probably by respect for the experienced prowess and superior skill of the gathering chivalry of the West. From its first obstruction at Neustadt, the huge inundation of Tartar warfare began slowly to recede, and at last rolled back its waves to the deserts of Asia.†

---

* See the version of his circular letter in Matthew Paris, p. 496–498, addressed to the King of England, and exhorting him as well as other princes, by the arguments of a common religion and danger to unite in despatching succours for the defence of the frontiers of Germany—"velut Christianorum januam"—the gate, as it were, of the Christians.

† A lively picture of the terror of Christendom at the progress of the Tartars is afforded by many passages and letters in the History of the Monk of St. Alban's, especially in p. 487, 496–498, 538–540, and *Additamenta*, p. 1128–1131. A frightful estimate of the numbers of a Tartar host is given in the assertion, that it covered twenty days' journey in length, and fifteen in breadth! One description—which, it is curious, (p. 539,) was obtained from an outlawed Englishman, who had wandered eastward from Palestine, fallen among those barbarians, and entered Europe with them as interpreter—accurately presents the genuine lineaments of the Mongolian race. " Habent autem pectora dura et robusta, facies macras et pallidas, scapulas rigidas et erectas, nasos distortos et breves, menta proeminentia et acuta, superiorem mandibulam humilem et profundam, dentes longos et raros, palpebras à crinibus usque ad nasum protensas, oculos inconstantes et nigros, aspectus obliquos et torvos, &c." (They have large and strong bodies, thin and pale faces, high and stiff shoulders, short and misshapen

The state, meanwhile, of the Mogul power in the central expanse of that quarter of the globe—which in the triple partition of the dynasty of Zingis formed the Empire of Western Tartary—may be overlooked in its uninteresting obscurity; [A. D. 1258;] but the second invasion and conquest of the southern regions of Asia had some effects, more important and durable, upon the aspect of the civilized world. The permanent subjugation of Persia was the work of Holagou, a third mighty victor among the grandsons of Zingis. That kingdom was again bravely defended by the hero Gelaleddin, who, on the first withdrawal of the Moguls to their native plains, had returned from India, and resumed the possession of his ruined throne. But his efforts were again fruitless against the innumerable Tartarian swarms; and after sustaining a contest of eleven years and the vicissitudes of fourteen great battles, he closed a career, which was worthy of a better termination, by a sluggish old age and an inglorious death in the fastnesses of Tur-

---

black and unsteady eyes, and a doubtful and fierce look.) Their ferocity could hardly be exaggerated, for assuredly they spared neither age, sex, nor condition; yet their cannibalism, though asserted by eye witnesses, and easily credited throughout Europe, may be doubted. "Victi quoque non supplicant, et vincentes non parcunt," (when vanquished they ask no quarter, and when victors they give none,) is the emphatic evidence of a war of extermination; and their very women, warlike and ferocious as themselves, were wooed for their powers of destruction. "Et quæ melius pugnat, concupiscibilior habetur" (and

kestan. After the subjection of Persia, the crowning triumph of Holagou was the capture of Bagdad, the extinction of the once splendid Khalifate of the Abassides, and the death of the last sovereign pontiff of a religion which the idolatrous conquerors were at a subsequent period to embrace and extend. The feeble Mostasem, the representative of the long line of Khalifs, who boasted their descent from the kinsman of Mohammed, and who had reigned in Asia for five centuries, was hunted from his throne, and murdered by command of Holagou; and with him expired the union of spiritual and temporal supremacy, long become, indeed, more nominal than real, which the reverence of the Moslem world had constantly recognised, and the ambition of usurpers had as perpetually violated, in the family of their prophet. While the Turcoman dynasty of Persia and the Abassidan Khalifate were thus finally swept away, the ravages of the same tempest spread over Asia Minor and Armenia, and approached the confines of Syria. In the former country, the Seljukian dynasty of Roum was overwhelmed in the deluge of Mogul invasion; the Christian principalities of Armenia shared the same fate; and it was only some unexplained change of course in the barbarian movements, rather than any foreign resistance opposed to their progress, that delayed their appearance on the shores of the Bosphorus and the Mediterranean.*

But even the secondary consequences of their victories were fatal to the Christian power in Syria; and we are recalled to the History of the Crusades by the effects of their conquest of Persia. When the fall of Gelaleddin dispersed the Turcoman or Kharizmian hordes which he had gathered to his standard for the defence of his realm, one of these tribes, flying before the Moguls, in the second year after the recovery of Jerusalem by the Earl of Cornwall, approached the frontiers of Palestine with the purpose of demanding a settlement in Egypt. Alarmed at their appearance, the sultan, to divert such unwelcome guests from his own states, and irritated against the Christians by some unprovoked hostilities of the Templars, advised them to establish themselves in Palestine; and, guided by an Egyptian emir with a body of his master's troops, Barbacan, the Kharizmian chief, entered the Holy Land at the head of twenty thousand cavalry. The ruined defences of Jerusalem had not yet been sufficiently restored to sustain a siege; the city was abandoned by the knights of the military orders on the approach of the invaders; [A. D. 1242;] and the savage Kharizmians, bursting into the place, made a horrid and indiscriminate massacre of all the remaining inhabitants. By the rapacious or wanton fury of these barbarians, both Christian and Moslem sanc

---

‘he successors of Zingis has been abridged chiefly from De Guignes, vol. iv. lib. xvi.-xix., &c., with references to the mere modern text of

tuaries were profaned and pillaged with equal alacrity; the very sepulchres were violated, the remains of the dead disinterred and rifled; and the most sacred and valuable relics of Jerusalem involved in a general destruction.*

To arrest the progress of invaders more fierce and inhuman than any by whom Syria had previously been desolated, the Christian chivalry made common cause with the Moslems of Damascus, Aleppo, and Ems; and the sultans of all these territories sent succours to the knights of the military orders. But the united force of these confederates was still inferior to that of the Egyptians and Kharizmians; and when the rash exhortations of the patriarch of Jerusalem induced the knights to hazard a battle, they suffered a terrible defeat. Their Syrian allies were routed and dispersed; the grand-masters, both of the Hospital and Temple, fell on the field; and of the whole Christian chivalry, only twenty-six Hospitallers, thirty-three Templars, and three Teutonic knights, escaped from the general slaughter.† Tiberias, Ascalon, and other fortresses of the Latin kingdom, successively fell, either carried by storm or abandoned to the victors; [A. D. 1244;] the whole country was left a prey to their ravages; and the remains of the Christian chivalry and inhabitants shut themselves up in their last

---

* Matt. Paris, p. 546–549, 556–558. Makrisi, (in Joinville, Johne's Translation,) vol. ii. p. 235.

stronghold of Acre. By subsequent dissensions between the Egyptians and Kharizmians, Palestine was delivered from the presence of the latter; the Moslems of Syria and Egypt felt the necessity of reuniting to crush intruders so destructive; the barbarians, after capturing Damascus, were utterly defeated in a general engagement by the Sultan of Egypt; their leader Barbacan was slain; and their whole horde was slaughtered or dispersed, or driven back upon the Eastern deserts. But this expulsion of the Kharizmians produced no relief to the Christian cause in Palestine. The Holy Sepulchre still remained in the hands of the Syrian or Egyptian infidels; the Latin kingdom had again well nigh dwindled into the single fortress of Acre; and the extremity to which its defenders were reduced, once more suggested to the martial and religious feelings of Europe the necessity of a new Crusade.*

---

* Matt. Paris, *ubi supra et* 599-639. Joinville, p. 209-211, and Makrisi, (*ibid*.,) p. 236-238.

View on the Nile.

SECTION IV.

THE SEVENTH CRUSADE.

THE design of this sacred enterprise was ratified, as usual, in a general assembly of the Latin Church; and at a council, which was convoked at Lyon for this among other purposes, by Pope Innocent IV., it was resolved that a Crusade should be preached, [A. D. 1245,] and all temporal wars suspended for four years throughout Chris-

Germany and Italy, and the renewed quarrel between the Emperor Frederic II. and the papacy, seem to have prevented the missionaries of the Holy War from meeting with much success in those countries; but the effects of their preaching extended to remoter regions, and Haco, King of Norway, assumed the Cross.* It was in France and England, however, that the flame of enthusiasm was most ardently and effectually rekindled, chiefly through the example of Louis IX., whose character was almost equally revered by both nations; and on the intelligence of whose purpose William Longsword, (the former crusading companion of the Earl of Cornwall,) with the Bishop of Salisbury, the Earl of Leicester, Walter de Lacy, and many other English nobles and knights, vowed to serve under his standard. The Norwegian monarch having been diverted from his enterprise by some unexplained causes, the prosecution of the Holy War was abandoned to the chivalry of France and England; and the events of the Seventh Crusade are confined to the expedition of St. Louis and his insular auxilaries.†

---

* Matt. Paris, p. 648.

† Our sufficient guide, for the events of the Seventh Crusade, will be that good knight John, Lord de Joinville, grand-seneschal of Champagne, the faithful companion of St. Louis, and actor in the scenes which he describes, whose memoirs have been enricned, both by the notes and dissertations of Du Cange, and by extracts from such Arabian MSS. as illustrate the subject before us. The text of the contemporary national historian, Matthew Paris, will also, how-

Blanche of Castile.

During his absence on the Crusade, Louis IX. left his kingdom under the administration of his mother, the celebrated Blanche of Castile.

In Cyprus, the general rendezvous of the expedition, Louis was joined by a long array of the baronage of France, with their knights and men-at-arms, and,

---

ever, supply some notices of the share of the English crusaders in the expedition. But the perfect good faith which breathes through the narrative of the Marshal of Champagne, the affection with which he describes the virtues and cherishes the memory of the excellent prince whom he followed, and the unaffected simplicity with which he confesses every emotion of a spirit, too truly brave for concealment of its fears, and too pious, with all his superstition, not to claim our respect, altogether give a charm and value to his lively relation, which is scarcely to be found in any other authority of the times, and fill the realities of chivalric adventure with more delightful and

Haco, King of Norway.

among others, by the noble historian of the Holy War.* [A. D. 1248.] Eight months were consumed with little necessity or prudence, it should seem,

---

* Nothing can be more touching than Joinville's expressions of his feelings on quitting his native land and kindred on so distant and perilous an enterprise. "But as I was journeying from Bliecourt to St. Urban, I was obliged to pass near to the Castle of Joinville; I dared never turn my eyes that way for fear of feeling too great regret, and lest my courage should fail on leaving my two fine children, and my fair castle of Joinville, which I loved in my heart." His descriptions always bring the scene before our eyes. "They all with a loud voice sang the beautiful hymn of *Veni Creator* from the beginning to the end; and while they were singing, the mariners set their sails in the name of God. Instantly after, a breeze of wind filled our sails, and soon made us lose sight of land, so that we saw only sea and sky," &c., p. 118, 119. (Johnes's Translation.) His naïve reflection immediately afterward, on the prudence of carrying a

Ships of the 18th Century.

before the congregated host finally proceeded to its destined scene of action. In imitation of the plan of the Fifth Crusade, Egypt, as the principal seat of the Moslem power, was again selected for the theatre of operations, the capture of Damietta for the first enterprise of the war; and by a strange blindness or fatality, the very errors which had entailed destruction thirty years before upon a Christian army on the same shores, were now faithfully copied or repeated. The armament with which Louis sailed from the shores of Cyprus covered the sea with eighteen hundred vessels, great and small, and contained full two thousand eight hundred knights, with their horses and an attendant cavalry of six or seven thousand men-at-arms, and a force of infantry which has been variously estimated at from fifty to above one hundred thousand.* But a violent tempest, blowing from the Egyptian coast, so dispersed this immense armada that, when the French king made the port of Damietta, he had not with him above seven hundred knights. The numerous forces of the sultan lined the shore, and so awed and astounded the French by

---

* If an Arabian historian may be credited, Louis afterward declared to one of the officers of the Egyptian Sultan that he had landed with nine thousand knights, five thousand horse, and one hundred and thirty thousand foot, including workmen and servants. See *Arabic Extracts* appended to Joinville, p. 262. But this is doubtless an exaggeration of Moslem vanity; and a passage in Makrisi, (*ibid.*, p. 254,) which estimates the whole force at seventy thousand men. is probably

their imposing array, and the clang of their trumpets and kettle-drums, that the councillors of Louis advised him to defer his landing until the junction of his absent knights; but the gallant monarch, who dreaded a continued exposure of his armament to the perils of the sea much more than the numbers of the infidels, resolved on an immediate attack; and himself, in complete armour, with his shield pendent from his neck, his lance on his wrist, and the oriflamme borne before him, leaping into the waves breast high, was among the foremost who reached the shore. The Mussulmans were so panic-stricken at the boldness of the Christian debarkation, that they not only fled from the strand, but abandoned the city of Damietta, though it had been furnished with a numerous garrison, and was more strongly fortified than when, in the former Crusade, it had sustained a siege of eighteen months. [A. D. 1249.] Before the infidels fled, however, they set fire in many places to the trading quarter of Damietta,* which, with much valua-

---

* In consequence of this destruction of merchandise, the booty captured, although Damietta had long been the emporium of Egypt, was small, not exceeding six thousand livres in value; and Louis incurred great obloquy by appropriating the whole of it to himself, contrary to "the good and ancient customs" observed in the Holy Land, by which one-third of all spoil went to the king, and the remaining two-thirds were shared among the crusaders. To this act, which seems

ble merchandise, was utterly consumed; and the French, astonished at their own success, took possession of the deserted city, and impatiently awaited the arrival of the remainder of their scattered armament.*

The crusaders, however, soon discovered that it was no more than a transient panic which had delivered Damietta into their hands; and they themselves were shortly besieged within its walls by the army of the sultan. The throne of Egypt was at this epoch filled by Nedjmeddin, grandson of Saphadin, brother of the great Saladin, a prince of courage and ability; who, on intelligence of the meditated invasion of the French, had been recalled from his career of conquest in Syria to the defence of his kingdom; and who, though afflicted with a mortal disease, had succeeded in reaching the banks of the Nile some time before the Christian descent. His first act, on learning the flight of the garrison of Damietta, was to punish fifty of their officers with the death which their cowardice deserved; his next, to hasten, ill as he was, to the scene of danger, assume the personal command of all the levies of Egypt, which he summoned to his standard, and invest on all sides the Christian position. The gathering numbers of the infidels already began to straiten

---

* Joinville, p. 116–128. Makrisi, p. 238–242. See also several letters in Matthew Paris from the Count d'Artois, the master of the Templars, and others, announcing the capture of Damietta. *Addita*

Louis and his followers in Damietta, when their anxiety was relieved by the junction of those parts of their expedition which had been dispersed on the voyage from Cyprus, and driven into Acre, together with a body of English nobles and knights, under William Longsword. Notwithstanding the arrival of these reinforcements, however, much time was lost in mischievous inaction at Damietta, interrupted only by skirmishes with the infidels; and the crusading host fell into licentious excesses and disorders,* which their victorious leader wanted either power or energy to repress, and to which their pious historian does not hesitate to ascribe the wrath of God and the subsequent ruin of their enterprise.†

At length it was resolved to advance to Cairo; and the Christian army began to ascend the branch of the Nile from Damietta towards that capital.‡ The

---

* After describing the debaucheries of the nobility, Joinville adds, *Et le commun peuple se print à forcer et violer femmes et filles. Dont de ce advint grant mal. Car il failut que le roy en donnait congié* (was obliged to wink) *à tout plain de ses gens et officiers. Car ainsi que le bon roy me dist, il trouve jusques à ung gect de pierre près et à l'entour de son paveillon plusieurs bordeaux, que ses gens tenoient.* (The commonalty likewise gave themselves up to debauchery, and violated both women and girls. Great were the evils in consequence, for it became necessary for the king to wink at the greatest liberties of his officers and men. The good king even told me, that at a stone's throw round his own pavilion were several brothels.) Ed. Paris, 1668, p. 32.

† Joinville, p. 128–132. Matthew Paris, p. 664.

‡ There is an inexplicable tale in Joinville of the treacherous con-

march along the bank of the river, notwithstanding the resistance of the Moslems, was successfully though slowly accomplished, as far as Mansoura; but with the capture of that town commenced the disasters of the Crusade. At the head of the flower of the French and English chivalry, the Count d'Artois, one of the brothers of Louis, being detached to effect the passage of the Ashmoum canal,* near that place,

---

ian army, and thus led his enemies into a snare! The French were enjoined not to injure any of these Mussulmans, who, however, suddenly turned upon the Templars in the van, attacked them by surprise, and were immediately cut to pieces by that fiery chivalry. It seems inconceivable that the "good king" should have been gulled by so clumsy a stratagem, and may rather be suspected that the infidels were deserters, who were sacrificed to some suspicion of the impetuous Templars. P. 132.

* We omit a long account in Joinville of some unavailing efforts of the French, under cover of their *chas-chatails*, or wooden towers, to throw a causeway over the canal of Ashmoum. These machines, as fast as they were built, the infidels destroyed with the Greek fire, of the appalling effects of which the brave knight gives a woful description. The whole passage (p. 134–138) forms a valuable illustration of middle-age warfare, but is unimportant to our present narrative, as the French were unsuccessful in all their efforts, and were at last enabled to pass the canal only by the treason of a Bedouin, who betrayed to them the existence of a ford through the current. But it may be observed as a curious fact, that, throughout the operations of this disastrous campaign, the superiority of the Orientals over the Latins in martial science is very evident. Of the composition of the celebrated Greek fire, to the marvellous effects of which the mediæval historians and annalists bear such ample and such frequent testimony, nothing whatever is known with certainty. It was invented or discovered by Callinicus of Heliopolis in Syria, in

rashly pursued the flying infidels into the town, without deigning to listen to the experienced counsel of William Longsword, and the grand-master of the Templars, to await the support of the main body of the army. The conduct of the French prince was marked by the same vaunting temerity which, in so many previous and subsequent combats of the Middle Ages, led the national chivalry of France into headlong destruction. Stung by his insolent reproaches, Longsword and his English brethren, the masters of the Temple and Hospital, with the knights of both orders, vied with the French in the blind precipitation of their valour; they burst into the town of Mansoura; and when the fury of their charge had thrown the whole body into confusion, they were enveloped in the place by the rallying infidels, and totally

---

was preserved by them for four centuries, when, by some means or other, it was procured by the Moslems, who, as we see above, employed the Greek fire with destructive force against the army of King Louis. Asphalt, or mineral bitumen, sulphur, and petroleum, or mineral oil, are all supposed to have been used in its composition, though in what proportions it is impossible now to ascertain; and Anna Comnena expressly mentions the pitch obtained from evergreen firs. It was projected in various forms, and from various kinds of instruments, and was inextinguishable by water, but extinguishable by sand, vinegar, and other liquids. It was undoubtedly the most formidable material of war known to the Middle Ages, though its employment would seem to have been confined wholly to Eastern Europe and Asia Minor; but after the discovery of gunpowder, in

routed. The Count d'Artois himself—the author of the calamity—William Longsword, and the master of the Templars, the victims of his presumption, and a host of other gallant knights, were all slain on the spot, or grievously wounded; the master of the Hospitallers fell alive into the enemy's hands; and the remnant of the band were rescued from the same fate only by the advance of the main army under the king himself; who, after performing prodigies of personal valour, succeeded in compelling the Moslems to retire.*

This equivocal victory was, however, without advantage to the Christians; and their critical position only served, on the contrary, to inspire new confidence into the infidel host. Nedjmeddin himself was now dead, having lately expired under the incurable malady against which his spirit had bravely striven;

---

* Joinville, p. 132–148. Matt. Paris, p. 672–680, 685. Makrisi, p. 245–248. For the relation in the text of the part taken by the English crusaders in the calamitous action of Mansoura, we are indebted to the monk of St. Alban's. Joinville, from respect probably to the memory of the Count d'Artois, has passed in silence over the tale of the fatal rashness by which that prince brought such ruin on the crusading cause, and has omitted the name of Longsword among the victims of his presumption. It is more remarkable that, from whatever cause, the good seneschal has never once, we believe, directly noticed the share of the English in the crusade; and a single observation, that Louis assigned a certain post to "the Duke of Burgundy and the nobles beyond seas, his allies," (p. 139) is the only

but his death was carefully concealed until the arrival of his son and successor, Touran-Shah, in the Moslem camp; the government was administered by the sultana, in the name of her deceased lord; and the functions of a commander-in-chief were skilfully performed, and the courage of the troops sustained, by Bibars, general of the Mamelukes, who himself, in the sequel, seized the sceptre which he was worthy of wielding. On the arrival of the new sultan, the Egyptian galleys on the Nile were drawn overland from above, and launched below the Christian camp; the communication of the French army with Damietta was thus cut off; and through precisely the same imprudence, and probably on the very ground on which the host of the Fifth Crusade had been enclosed between the canal of Ashmoum and the river, Louis and his army were now intercepted. In this situation, famine and a pestilence, the consequences of unwholesome diet,* soon made frightful ravages in the

---

* "You must know that we eat no fish the whole Lent, but eel pouts, which is a gluttonous fish, and feeds on dead bodies. From this cause, and from the bad air of the country, where it scarcely ever rains a drop, the whole army was affected by a shocking disorder, which dried up the flesh on our legs to the bone, and our skins became tanned as black as the ground, or like an old boot that has long lain behind a coffer. In addition to this miserable disorder, those affected by it had another sore complaint in the mouth from eating such fish, that rotted the gums, and caused a most stinking breath. Very few escaped death that were thus attacked," &c.—Joinville, p. 159. "The disorder I spoke of, very soon increased so much in the army, that the barbers were forced to cut away very large pieces of

Christian camp; a further advance was impossible, and after a period of calamitous inaction, broken only by the assaults of the infidels and some vain overtures of peace, no other resource remained for the enfeebled and wretched army of the crusaders than to attempt a retreat to Damietta. But this movement was the signal of universal disorder and rout; the Mussulmans broke into the camp and murdered the abandoned sick; their galleys cut off all the fugitives who endeavoured to escape down the river; the troops who marched by land were overwhelmed by the innumerable cavalry of the sultan; and Louis himself—who, though sinking under the same illness as the rest of the army, had remained with the rear-guard, and discharged all the duties of a devoted commander and valiant soldier—fell, in a state of helpless exhaustion from disease and wounds, into the hands of the victorious infidels. [A. D. 1250.] His surviving brothers, Charles and Alfonso, Counts of Anjou and of Poitiers, together with all his nobility and knighthood, who escaped the first slaughter of the onset, shared his fate; but no mercy was shown by the infidels to the soldiery and others of inferior condition; and of the Christians of all ranks there fell on this fatal occasion, either slain in the field or massacred in

---

desh from the gums, to enable their patients to eat. It was pitiful to hear the cries and groans of those on whom this operation was performing; they seemed like to the cries of women in labour and I cannot express the great concern all felt who heard them," p. 162.

cold blood, at the lowest computation, upward of
thirty thousand men.*

The situation of even the captive king and his
nobles was for some time extremely critical, and their
ultimate safety was placed in imminent hazard, by a
domestic revolution in Egypt, which almost immediately followed the Moslem victory. The new sultan, Touran Shah, is accused by the Oriental writers
of debauchery, favouritism, and cruelty; but it is only
certain that his impolitic conduct alienated the affection of the formidable bands whose services, under
Bibars, had been mainly instrumental in achieving his
triumph over the Christian invaders. These troops,
whose renown is so familiar to European ears under
the designation of Mamelukes, had been organized by
the late Sultan Nedjmeddin, and had proved themselves the firmest support of his throne. Their ranks
had been originally filled, as they continued ever after
to be recruited, by slaves, principally of the hardy
Turcoman stock, purchased at an early age, and educated in the camp; but their fidelity to the house of

* Joinville, p. 149–170. Matt. Paris, p. 685, 686. Makrisi, p.
248-251. The numbers which perished in this retreat and capture
of the crusading host, it is, as usual, difficult to estimate. Joinville
is silent on this point; Makrisi says, one hundred thousand—doubt-
'ess an exaggeration; but it appears that not one of the crusaders,
except the garrison of Damietta, escaped; and of the Christian captives in Egypt, afterward released, the numbers are declared, with
uncommon precision by the same Arabic historian, p. 254, to have
been only twelve thousand one hundred men, and ten women.

St. Louis in captivity.

their founder expired with his death, and they now revolted and murdered his son. With Touran Shah ended the Curdish dynasty, which, commencing with the great Saladin, had reigned in Egypt and Syria for eighty years; under sultans who sprang from their own ranks, the Mamelukes held independent possession of those countries for nearly a century and a half, until their nominal subjection to the Turkish power; and it has been reserved for our age to witness the final extinction of their bands.*

By Touran Shah, the King of France had at first been treated with generosity; and a negotiation for

---

* For the origin of the Mamelukes, see Joinville, p. 156. Makisi, p. 244, with Du Cange's note, &c.

his ransom and that of his followers was speedily concluded; but not until some menaces of torture had been ineffectually tried upon the brave spirit of Louis, to obtain the surrender of the Christian fortresses in the Holy Land. It had, however, been agreed that he should yield up Damietta as the price of his own liberty, and pay a sum of gold, equal in French money to four hundred thousand livres, for the deliverance of his army, when the murder of the sultan suspended the fulfilment of the treaty. In the subsequent confusion, Louis and his nobles narrowly escaped death* from the fanaticism of some of the Moslem chieftains; but more humane or avaricious suggestions finally prevailed in their councils, and the completion of the treaty was resumed. Finally, Damietta was surrendered by its French garrison in exchange for the persons of the king and his nobles; the Templars were reluctantly compelled to make a loan from the treasurers in their galleys to complete

---

* Joinville himself, when a party of Saracens with drawn swords and menacing aspects entered the galley in which he was confined, imagined that his last hour was come. "With regard to myself, I no longer thought of any sin or evil I had done, but that I was about to receive my death; in consequence I fell on my knees at the feet of one of them, and making the sign of the cross, said, 'Thus died St. Agnes,' Sir Guy d'Ebelin, constable of Cyprus, knelt beside me, and confessed himself to me, and I gave him such absolution as God was pleased to grant me the power of bestowing; but of all the things he had said to me, when I rose up, I could not remember one of

the required discharge of the first instalment of the pecuniary ransom; and Louis, with the sad remnant of the proud host which had debarked at Damietta, bade adieu to the shores of Egypt.*

On their liberation, the greater number of the surviving nobles, with their followers, gladly availed themselves of the plea, that the disasters and sufferings which they had already undergone were a sufficient acquittance of their crusading vows; and, abandoning all idea of further service in the sacred cause, they sailed direct for France. But the religious and chivalrous scruples of their king were less easily satisfied. His devotional feelings, and his sensitive conviction of the disgrace with which defeat and captivity had sullied his arms,† equally impelled him to continue his efforts, in the hope of achieving some happier enterprise for the redemption of the Holy Sepulchre, and the recovery of his fame. He therefore proceeded to Acre, (Ptolemais,) and, after some hesitation in his councils, announced a settled purpose to remain in Palestine, and to employ whatever treasures and forces he could still supply or raise in the

---

* Joinville, p. 170-184. Matt. Paris, p. 686-689. Makrisi, p. 251-255.

† 'Rex autem apud Achon tristis remansit et inglorious, jurans in cordis amaritudine maximâ, quòd nunquam in dulcem Franciam sic confusus remearet." (But the king, sad and inglorious, remained at Acre, swearing in very bitterness of heart, that thus dishonoured he would never return to fair France.) Matt. Paris. p. 690

St. Louis entering Ptolemais.

defence of the Christian garrisons.* During four years he persevered in this design, unable, indeed, with his exhausted resources and scanty levies, to perform any signal action, yet still reluctant to return ingloriously to his native realm. As the whole force which he succeeded in assembling under his standard during this long period, never amounted to above four thousand men, he was prevented from pursuing any offensive operations against the infidels; but his treasures were lavishly expended in refortifying Jaffa, Cæsarea, and Sidon, and in making great additions to the strength of Acre; and his presence and exertions not only deserved and obtained the gratitude of the Christian chivalry and people of Palestine, but contributed to suspend for forty years the fall of the last bulwarks of the Latin kingdom on the Syrian shores.†

Among the circumstances which favoured his labours, and protected the weakness of the Christians,

---

* Among the nobles who had remained with him was the faithful Seneschal of Champagne, who had originally maintained his train of knights at his own expense, but having lost every thing in Egypt, was now compelled to become the stipendiary soldier of the king. When, however, his first term of hired service expired, and Louis proposed a new pecuniary engagement, "I replied," says Joinville, "that I was not come to him to make such a bargain; but I would offer other terms: which were that he should promise never to fly into a passion for any thing I should say to him, which was often the case, and I engaged that I would keep my temper whenever he refused what I should ask." The good saint laughingly assented to these quaint and cheap conditions. Joinville, p. 205.

may be numbered the dissensions of their enemies. The usurpation of the Mamelukes, and the struggle of their leaders for the possession of the Egyptian throne, had encouraged the revolt of Damascus under a sultan, the relative of the murdered Khalif of Cairo; a furious civil war between the Moslems of Egypt and Syria interrupted their assaults upon the Christians, and both parties sought either to gain the alliance or to avert the hostility of the French king. Louis profited by their mutual fears and jealousies, to obtain from the Mameluke rulers of Egypt the release of all the surviving Christian captives whom he had left in that country, and a remission of the moiety, which was still unpaid, of the stipulated ransom for his army. He received a promise even of the cession of Jerusalem itself; and the intelligence of the Moslem dissensions and of his successful negotiation, again excited the hopes of Europe for the recovery of the Holy Sepulchre and the re-establishment of the Latin kingdom. But these sanguine expectations were blighted by the conclusion of peace between the Egyptian and Syrian infidels; and their reunited forces were immediately turned against the Christians. The ravage of the Latin territory by a combined army of various Moslems, under the Sultan of Damascus, and their advance to the gates of Acre, at last revealed to Louis the vanity of his fondest aspirations, and the utter hopelessness of ultimate success.

capture of the strong Christian fortresses; and by their retreat Louis remained at liberty to withdraw without dishonour from the suspended contest. The news of his mother's death, by which his kingdom was left without a regent, quickened his increasing desire to escape from a scene of continued disappointment and mortification, and justified the announcement of his purpose to return to France. The clergy and barons themselves of the Latin kingdom, perceived and acknowledged that his prolonged residence could not be attended with any advantage; and, offering him their humble thanks and praise for the great good and honour which he had conferred on Palestine, they gratefully counselled him to think rather of ensuring his safe passage to Europe than of continuing among them. Louis accepted their advice, and adopted a measure so congenial to his altered wishes and so necessary to the welfare of his kingdom. Embarking at Acre, he reached France after a perilous voyage, marked by more than one trial of his brave and generous nature. [A. D. 1254.] It was, however, but in shame and sorrow that he abandoned the cause still dearest to his pious feelings; and he closed the Seventh Crusade with the melancholy reflection and self-reproach, which even the consciousness of his own virtuous intentions could not assuage, that he had in vain sacrificed his chivalry and people to defeat and destruction; and that, in exchange for the best blood and treasures of his kingdom, he had been able to accomplish nothing either worthy of his name, or suitable to the general honour and service of Christendom.*

The residence of St. Louis, however, in Palestine, had at least put some check upon the eruption of those bitter feuds among the Christians themselves, which had ever been the bane of their cause, and which broke out anew immediately after the departure of their royal leader. Among the most turbulent and irreconcilable communities of the Latin State, were the colonies of the three maritime Italian republics, and the military orders. In their insolent disdain of all control by the local government of the feudal kingdom, the Venetians, the Genoese, and the Pisans extended their pernicious spirit of commercial and political rivalry from Europe to the Syrian shore; openly fought with each other in every seaport of Palestine for the possession of exclusive privileges and quarters, and even violated the sanctity of Christian churches by impious and bloody struggles for their occupation. With more flagrant dereliction of duty the religious chivalry of the Hospital and Temple forgot their vows in the indulgence of their mutual hatred, and employed in their fierce rivalry the arms which they had sworn to use only in the common service of the Cross. [A. D. 1259.] To decide their quarrel, the two orders drew out their forces in the field for a general and formal engagement; the prowess or numbers of the Hospitallers prevailed; and so sanguinary and merciless was the encounter, that of all the militia of the Temple then serving in the Holy Land, scarcely one knight escaped the carnage. From every commandery of the Temple in Europe the most strenuous exertions were made to despatch its effective members to Palestine, both for the purpose of replenishing the vacant posts of their slaughtered brotherhood, and of inflicting a signal vengeance upon the Hospitallers; and nothing short of a war of extirmination was meditated between the two orders; when their deadly feud was suddenly smothered under the overwhelming violence of a new tempest of Mussulman invasion, which threatened to bury them, with the whole Christian State, under a common ruin, and awoke them to the duty or necessity of uniting their exhausted forces against the general enemy.*

After a revolutionary period of disorder and bloodshed, Bibars, styled also Al Bonducdari or Bondocdar, the same Mameluke chieftain who had distinguished his ability in the defence of Egypt against St. Louis,

---

* Matthew Paris, p. 846, who describes in strong terms the events of the unnatural warfare between these devoted champions of the Cross, and the purpose with which the Templars in Europe hastened to the Holy Land, "propter ultionem horribilem hostiliter in Hospitalarios retribuendam," (for the purpose of taking a horrible revenge

was raised by the suffrages of his fellow-soldiers to the throne of that kingdom; [A. D.1263;] and had now commenced an enterprising reign of seventeen years, which proved nearly fatal to the remains of the Christian power in Palestine. No sooner had he consolidated his authority in Egypt, than he carried his arms into Syria, reduced the Mussulman states in that country into subjection, and poured the united forces of the infidels into the Christian territories. In the open field, the numbers of the invaders rendered all resistance to their ravages hopeless; but the few and scanty garrisons of the Latins made a gallant and desperate defence; the military orders gave many a noble example of heroism; and, by that singular admixture of religious constancy with every fierce and unholy passion which distinguished their times and their associations, the same men who had so lately stained their swords with the blood of their Christian brethren, now vied with each other only in the generous devotion of their lives to the common cause, and in the inflexible preference of martyrdom to apostacy. [A. D. 1265.] Upon one occasion, the last of ninety Hospitallers who had defended Azotus, died in the breach; on another, the prior of the Templars with his companions, who had been reduced to extremity, and surrendered Saphoury on a capitulation which Bibars treacherously violated, were offered the alternative of a cruel death or instant conversion to Islamism, [A. D. 1266,] and unanimously sealed the sincerity of their faith with their blood. But all the heroic efforts of the two orders failed to arrest the progress of the infidels, or to awaken the timely sympathy and succour of Europe. In the course of a few years, not only the inland castles of the two orders, but Cæsarea, Laodicea, Jaffa, and many maritime fortresses successively fell before the Mameluke arms; and the capture of Antioch, and the extinction of its Latin principality, which throughout the vicissitudes of the Crusades had hitherto preserved an obscure and uninteresting existence, completed the triumph of Bondocdar.

The fall of Antioch, which was basely surrendered without resistance, was attended by the massacre of ten or even forty thousand Christians; above one hundred thousand more were sold into slavery; [A. D. 1268;] and the once proud capital of Syria was abandoned to desolation and solitude.* Acre was preserved from the same fate only through the succour of the King of Cyprus, and the destruction of the Egyptian navy by the elements;

---

* "Eo anno," says Rishanger, the continuator of the *Chronicle of St. Alban's,* "Soldanus Babyloniæ vastatâ Armeniâ, Antiocham, unam de famosioribus orbis civitatibus abstulit Christianis, et tam viris quam mulieribus interemptis, in solitudinem ipsam reduxit." (In that year the Sultan of Babylonia, having laid waste Armenia, took Antioch, one of the most famous cities on the globe, from the Christians, and both the men and women being slain, he reduced it to a solitude.) p. 857. It may, however, be doubted whether its

and at this juncture the fall of that last Christian bulwark on the Syrian coast was suspended for twenty years by an expiring effort of the crusading spirit.*

---

* Sanutus, *Secret. Fidel. Crucis,* lib. iii. pars. xii. c. 6, *ad* part xiv
 8. De Guignes, *Hist. Gén. des Huns,* &c., lib. xxi., *passim.*

SECTION V.

THE EIGHTH CRUSADE.

THE appalling intelligence of the dreadful catastrophe which had extinguished the Christian State of Antioch, roused the Papal Court from a long and selfish apathy to the affairs of the East; and the unabated zeal with which Louis IX. of France had already contemplated a renewal of his pious services on the imaginary cause of Heaven, was now quickened by the approbation of Clement IV.

The piety of Louis was sincere and ardent, and in another age it would, doubtless, have taken a more rational direction, but in the thirteenth century it was the mere embodiment of a passion for the delivery of the Holy Sepulchre, which neither his past experience nor his sufferings, great as the latter had been, could eradicate; and after thirteen years spent at home in the wise and temperate exercise of his regal functions, he resolved again to devote his mental energies and his material resources to the organization of a new Crusade. Three years were consumed in preparations for this final effort to recover Palestine, and on the 4th of July, 1270, he set sail with his fleet from the port of Aigues-Mortes, and in a few days reached the roadstead of Cagliari in Sardinia, where he anchored, and called a council of war of his barons and counts to deliberate on the course it was most proper to pursue; when it was determined by a majority, and in obedience to the king's secret wishes, to attempt the reduction of Tunis, the king of which country and his people Louis hoped to convert to Christianity. The circumstances which led to this extraordinary resolution are but imperfectly known, though they may probably be as safely referred to the intensely devotional temperament of the monarch, as to the interested representations of his brother, Charles of Anjou, King of Naples and Sicily, whose subjects were molested by the piratical practices of the Moors; but however this may be, the desire to visit Tunis, and to reclaim its inhabitants had taken so deep a hold on the mind of Louis, that he was heard to say, before he left France, that he would willingly spend the rest of his life in a dungeon, away from the light of the sun, if, by such a sacrifice, he could accomplish this cherished object.* Many of his wisest advisers tried to turn him from this fatal determination, but in vain; and the good but mistaken king landed his army on the Tunisian territory on the 24th of July, and encamped it on the site of the ancient Carthage. The Moors did not oppose its debarkation, but on the approach of the fleet fled in dismay, and the Saracenic prince, for whose special benefit this *detour* had been made, treated the Frankish monarch as an enemy, and threatened, at the head of a hundred thousand men, to drive him into the sea. No encounter, however, took place between the hostile troops, for, beside that Louis avoided one as incompatible with the spiritual design of his mission, the Moors had no wish to measure swords with the Christian chivalry; but they harassed the Christian army by desultory attacks on outposts and stragglers, and by intercepting their supplies; and these distractions, aided by the heat of the climate, the want of water, and the necessity of feeding on salted provisions under an African sky, caused a pestilence to break out in the crusading camp, which, in a few short weeks, nearly decimated

---

* Michaud, iii. p. 85.

the hapless army. Night and day the Frankish soldiers were under arms, but the enemy was fugitive, and when sought was nowhere to be found. Meanwhile death sped his way through the ranks. Fatigue, famine, and disease did their work but too surely. The dead were so numerous that it was found impossible to bury them. The ditches of the camp were filled with carcasses thrown in by the heap. The stench emitted corrupted the air, and despair and misery overwhelmed the unhappy crusaders. The Count de Vendome, the Count de la Marche, Gaultier, de Nemours, the Lords de Montmorency, de Pienne, de Bressac, and many others of the highest condition, fell before the fatal epidemic; and when the Duke de Nevers, the king's son, who had been born at Damietta during the captivity of his father, died, the hero and the monarch yielded to the man and the father, and he wept bitterly. At length the king himself fell ill; the rude medical art of the age did its best for him, but in vain—the hand of fate was on Louis of France—and he expired tranquilly in his camp, on the shores of the ancient Numidia, on the afternoon of the 25th of August, 1270.—Let us now return to the progress of the Eighth and last Crusade.

In the defence of a land and a cause which, during two centuries, had continually exercised the valour, and prodigally wasted the blood of the chivalry of Christendom, the last successful exploits of heroism

Edward I. of England.

were reserved for an English prince, the descendant of those illustrious houses of Normandy and Plantagenet, whose prowess had so often been signalized on the same ensanguined field. Prince Edward, the future monarch of England, accompanied by his faithful consort Eleanor, and attended by his kinsman Edmund Crouchback, Earl of Lancaster, four other earls, four barons, and a gallant but slender train of knights and soldiers, which did not exceed one thousand men, had joined the French army in Africa before the death of Louis IX.; and the abandonment of the Crusade by their allies, which followed that event, might have absolved the small English force from the

magnanimous leader swore, that though every other follower should desert him, he would still proceed to Palestine, attended only by his groom;* his spirit was emulated by every English heart; and after refreshing their strength during the winter in Sicily, he sailed in the spring with his gallant band to Acre.†

The arrival of Edward in that port once more rekindled the hopes of the desponding Latins; and the long memory of the prowess of Cœur de Lion had still retained sufficient influence in the East to appal the spirit of the Moslems at the intelligence, that another hero of the lion-hearted race approached to uphold the banner of the Cross. The Sultan Bondocdar, who had carried his ravages to the gates of Acre, immediately retired in discouragement at the report.‡ The broken remains of the Latin chivalry of Palestine eagerly gathered around the standard of Plantagenet; and though the total force which the Christian State

---

* "Juravit solito Juramento per sanguinem Domini, inquiens; Quamvis omnes commilitiones et patriotæ mei me deserant, ego tamen, Fowino custode palufridi mei, (sic enim vocabatur curator equi sui,) intrabo Tholomaidam." (He swore by his usual oath, the blood of the Lord, saying:—"Although all my fellow-soldiers and compatriots desert me, yet I, with Fowin, the keeper of my palfrey, will enter Tolamais.") Rishanger, *Contin.*, Matt. Paris, p. 859.

† Rishanger, p. 858, 859. Matt. Westminster, (Ed. Francofurti, A D. 1601,) p. 400. *Chronica de Matlros, (apud* Gale *et* Fell, vol. iii.,) p. 241. *Chronicon* Thomæ Wikes, p. 94. *Chronica* Walteri Hemingford, p. 590. (Both in Gale, vol ii.)

‡ Both Rishanger and Matthew of Westminster (*ubi supra*) declare that, but for the opportune arrival of Edward, Acre was to have

could muster, including his English followers, did not exceed seven thousand men, Edward boldly marshalled this scanty army for offensive hostilities against the infidels. Advancing from Acre. his achievements justified the general expectation both of his enterprising courage and of his military skill. His first exploit, the surprise and defeat of a large body of the Mussulman forces in the field, was succeeded by the assault of Nazareth; and in the dreadful slaughter which preceded and followed the capture of that city, he equally emulated the chivalric valour. and the fanatical cruelty of the earlier champions of the Cross.* But the reduction of Nazareth closed his brief career of victory; his English followers fell rapid victims to the Syrian climate, and the hero himself was already stretched on a sick couch, when he narrowly escaped death from the poisoned dagger of an assassin. Whether the villian was the mere hired emissary of a Mussulman emir, or one of the few survivors of that fanatical sect of the mountain chief, which the Moguls were supposed to have extirpated,†

---

* In his first surprise of the infidels, Edward "invenit Sarraconos et uxores eorum cum parvulis suis in lecto: quos omnes," coolly continues the chronicler of Melrose, "ut hostes Christianæ fidei occidit in ore gladii,"—(he found the Saracens with their wives and little ones in bed—all of whom, as enemies of the Christian faith, he slew with the point of the sword.) P. 242.

† The destruction of the Syrian assassins by the Tartars is noticed by Matt. Paris, p. 821, (*ad an.* 1257.) "Circulo ejusdem anni, Tartari detestabiles Assassinos detestabiliores, &c., destruxerunt,"—

THE EIGHTH CRUSADE.

Attempt to assassinate Edward.

is uncertain; but he easily obtained a private audience of Edward under pretence of a confidential mission; and, while the prince was reading his credentials, he drew a hidden poniard, and aimed a blow at his intended victim. The attack was so unexpected, that Edward received several wounds before he recovered from the surprise, when, vigorously struggling with the assassin, he felled him to the floor, and instantly despatched him with his own

---

(In the course of this year the detestable Tartars destroyed the more detestable assassins.) In the first part of a tedious Dissertation on the Assassius, by M. Falconet, read before the French Academy of Inscriptions, and of which a translation is printed in Johnes's Joinville, (vol. ii. p. 287–328,) an attempt is made to prove that Paris was in error; that it was only the assassins of Persia, a kindred and more numerous sect, which the Tartars destroyed; and that those of Syria, according to Abulfeda, were extirpated by the Mamelukes about A. D. 1280.

dagger. As the weapon had been poisoned, the life of the prince was for some time in imminent danger; but a leech in his service undertook to cut away the infected flesh from his wounds, and the operation was successful.*

After his own restoration to health, the wasting effects of disease among his followers; the total inadequacy of his remaining force to any further enterprise of importance; the failure of other Christian princes to despatch their promised succours to his aid; and intelligence from England of his father's dangerous illness and anxiety for his return:† all conspired in inducing Edward to listen to overtures for peace, which were extorted from the Sultan of Egypt, not less by the experience of his prowess than by some new troubles which had broken out in the Mussulman

---

* Rishanger, p. 859, 860. Matt. West. p. 401. *Chron. de Mailros*, (which suddenly breaks off in the midst of its tale of the attempt to assassinate Edward,) p. 241, *ad fin.* Wikes, p. 96–98. Hemingford, p. 590–592.

Not one of these writers, who were contemporary, or nearly so, with the event, knew any thing of that beautiful fiction, the creation of a much later age, which ascribes the recovery of Edward to the affectionate devotion of his consort Eleanor in sucking the venom from his wounds. Hemingford, whose account is very circumstantial, and has principally been followed in the text, notices the presence of Eleanor, the demand of the leech that she should be removed from the chamber of her lord before the operation was performed for his cure, and the gentle violence which was necessary to withdraw her from the scene. P. 591.

† The letter from Henry III., pressing his son's return, may be seen in Rymer, (Ed. by royal command, 1816,) vol. i. p. 487.

States. The mutual necessities of the sultan and of the English prince, therefore, produced the conclusion of a truce between the infidels and the Christians in Palestine for ten years; and after a residence of fourteen months in the Holy Land, and the accomplishment of a seasonable treaty, which had alone arrested the progress of the Mameluke arms and prolonged, for another brief period, the precarious existence of the Latin State, Edward bâde adieu to the Syrian shores, and sailed, with his few surviving followers, for his native land.* [A. D. 1272.]

After the departure of the English prince, and while the remaining Christian possessions on the coast of Palestine were left in the peace which he had won, some last abortive efforts were used to interest Europe in their preservation. Pope Gregory X., who was residing in Palestine when he was surprised with the news of his elevation to the tiara, [A. D. 1274,] and who had been a sorrowing witness to the helpless condition of the Latin State, made an earnest endeavour, immediately after his arrival in Europe, to arouse the sovereigns and nations of Christendom to the preparation of a new Crusade. But the solitary example, given by one pontiff, of a deep sincerity in the cause, only served to prove the utter extinction of the crusading spirit. Notwithstanding his labours, seconded by the authority of a general council of the church which he assembled at Lyon, he could only obtain hollow promises of devotion to the service of the Cross from those princes who desired to perpetuate his favour, and who, after his death, evaded the fulfilment of their reluctant vows. Meanwhile, however, the Christians in Palestine, during eight years, were permitted, by the good faith or distraction of the Mussulman councils, to enjoy unmolested a peaceful respite of their fate; and that interval was filled only by the struggle of royal pretensions in the expiring Latin kingdom. Since the death of the Emperor Frederic II., the baseless throne of Jerusalem had found a claimant in Hugh de Lusignan, King of Cyprus, who, as lineally descended from Alice, daughter of Queen Isabella, was, in fact, the next heir, after failure of issue by the marriage of Frederic and Iolanta de Brienne. His claims were opposed by the partisans of Charles of Anjou, King of the Sicilies; that wholesale speculator in diadems, who, not contented with the iniquitous acquisition of his Italian realms, and the splendid dream of dismembering the Greek Empire, extended his grasp to the ideal crown of Palestine. He rested his claim upon the double pretensions of a papal title to all the forfeited dignities of the imperial house of Hohenstauffen, and of a bargain with Mary of Antioch; whose rights, although she was descended only from a younger sister of Alice, he had eagerly purchased. But the prior title of the house of Cyprus was more generally recognised in

Palestine; the coronation of Hugh had been celebrated at Tyre; and the last idle pageant of regal state in Palestine was exhibited by the race of Lusignan.*

At length the final storm of Mussulman war broke upon the phantom king and his subjects. It was twice provoked by the aggressions of the Latins themselves, in plundering the peaceable Moslem traders, who resorted, on the faith of treaties, to the Christian marts on the Syrian coast. After a vain attempt to obtain redress for the first of these violations of international law, Keladun, the reigning sultan of Egypt and Syria, revenged the infraction of the existing ten years' truce by a renewal of hostilities with overwhelming force; yearly repeated his ravages of the Christian territory; and at length, tearing the city and county of Tripoli—the last surviving great fief of the Latin kingdom—from its dilapidated crown, dictated the terms of peace to its powerless sovereign. [A. D. 1289.] The example of this punishment, and

---

* Mr. Hallam, following Giannone, has fallen into some inaccuracy, on no very important matter, indeed, in stating (*Middle Ages*, vol. i. p. 871, 8vo. ed.) Mary of Antioch to have been the legitimate heiress of Jerusalem in 1272, while the royal line of Cyprus, descended from Alice, eldest sister of *her* mother, Melesinda, had, of course, a better title. Until that race should be extinct, the house of Anjou could only rest their pretensions on the lapsed rights of Frederic II.; but these had expired with his posterity; and, in short, as observed by Mr. Mills, (*Crusades*, vol. ii, p. 269,) "the House of Anjou had no juster claim to the throne of Jerusalem, than they had to the throne

the authority of a feeble government, were insufficient to prevent a repetition, two years later, on the part of the lawless inhabitants of Acre, of similar outrages upon the property and persons of the Mussulman merchants; and the Sultan Khatil, the son of Keladun, was provoked, by a new denial of justice, to utter and enforce a tremendous vow of extermination against the perfidious Franks. At the head of an immense army of two hundred thousand men, the Mameluke prince entered Palestine, swept the weaker Christian garrisons before him, and encamped under the towers of Acre. [A. D. 1291.] That city, which, since the fall of Jerusalem, had been for a century the capital of the Latin kingdom, was now become the last refuge of the Christian population of Palestine. Its defences were strong, its inhabitants numerous; but any state of society more vicious, disorderly, and helpless than its condition, can scarcely be imagined. Within its walls were crowded a promiscuous multitude, of every European nation, all equally disclaiming obedience to a general government, and enjoying impunity for every crime under the nominal jurisdiction of independent tribunals. Of these there were no less than seventeen; in which the papal legate, the king of Jerusalem, the despoiled great feudatories of his realm, the three military orders, the colonies of the maritime Italian republics, and the representatives of the princes of the West, all arrogated sovereign rights,

fenders. When, therefore, the devoted city was invested by the infidels, we need not wonder that, amid the common danger, her councils were without concert, and that, with an immense population, the vast circuit of her walls was inadequately manned. All the wretched inhabitants who could find such opportunites of escape, thronged on board the numerous vessels in the harbour, which set sail for Europe; and the last defence of Acre was abandoned to about twelve thousand men, for the most part the soldiery of the three military orders.*

From that gallant chivalry, the Moslems encountered a resistance worthy of its ancient renown and of the extremity of the cause for which its triple fraternity had sworn to die. But the whole force of the Mameluke empire, in its yet youthful vigour, had been collected for their destruction. During thirty-three days, the beseigers incessantly plied a long train of balistic and battering engines of huge dimensions and prodigious power against the defences of the city; various parts of its double wall were beaten down or undermined; and at length the fall of a principal work, of which the fatal importance is expressed in the original relations of the siege by its title of "the Cursed Tower," opened a yawning breach into the heart of the place. At this awful crisis, the recreant Lusignan, who wore the titular crown of Jerusalem,

---

* De Guignes, lib. xxi. Sanutus, lib. iii., pars. xiii., c. 20. Gio-

basely abandoned his duty, and proved himself destitute of the only qualities which might have conferred lustre upon his ideal dignity. Secretly withdrawing in the night from his post, he seized a few vessels in the port, and sailed away with his followers to Cyprus. Even his cowardly flight could not shake the constancy of the Teutonic knights whom he had deserted in the Cursed Tower, and who continued to guard its ruins. But, with the following dawn, their post was attacked by the infidels in immense force; several times were the assailants repulsed with dreadful carnage, and as often were the slain replaced by fresh bands of the Moslems. At length, after most of the German cavaliers had fallen in the breach, the infidels, in overpowering numbers, forced a passage over their lifeless bodies; a torrent of assailants pouring into the place swept its few surviving defenders before them; and Acre was irretrievably lost. Bursting through the city, the savage victors pursued to the strand the unarmed and fleeing population, who had wildly sought a means of escape, which was denied not less by the fury of the elements than by the want of sufficient shipping. By the relentless cruelty of their pursuers, the sands and the waves were dyed with the blood of the fugitives; all who survived the first horrid massacre were doomed to a hopeless slavery; and the last catastrophe of the Crusades cost life or liberty to sixty thousand Christians.

Even in the fatal hour in which Acre fell, the he-

ries of the Hospital and Temple preserved and displayed their unconquerable spirit. Led by their grand-master, the knights of St. John sallied from the devoted city, carried havoc into the heart of the infidel leaguer, and when, overpowered by numbers, all but seven of their order, with a few followers, had been left on the field, this gallant remnant fought their way to the coast, and effected an embarkation. Meanwhile, for three days after the fall of the city, the Templars continued to defend their monastic fortress within its walls. Their valiant grand-master, Pierre de Beaujeu, whose military skill and personal heroism had been conspicuous throughout the siege, was killed by a poisoned arrow; but the obstinate resistance of his brethren obtained from the sultan the promise of a free and honourable retreat. When the Red Cross-Knights issued from their fortress on the faith of this assurance, they were assailed by the lawless insults of the Mussulman hosts; they impatiently renewed the contest; and most of their number were slain on the spot. The few who escaped forced a passage with their swords through the Mameluke lines, fled into the interior country, and even there resumed the war, until they were ultimately driven again to the coast, and effected their escape by sea to Cyprus. Theirs was the last effort for the defence of Palestine; the Christian population of the few maritime towns which had yet been retained fled to Cyprus, or sub-

yoke; and, after a bloody contest of two hundred years, the possession of the Holy Land was FINALLY abandoned to the enemies of the Cross.*

The fall of Acre closes the annals of the Crusades. But the mere loss of that last possession of the Latins on the Syrian shore would not have put a term to the hopes and efforts of Christendom for the recovery of the Holy Sepulchre, if the spirit itself which prompted every preceding enterprise for the same object had not already expired. A century earlier, the capture of Jerusalem by Saladin had sufficed to fill all Europe with grief and horror, and had impressed the three greatest monarchs of the age with the conviction that the demands of religion and honour rendered it equally imperative upon them personally to revenge the disgrace of Christendom, and to chastise the insolence of the enemies of God. At a still later epoch, even the fall of a remote dependency of the Latin kingdom of Jerusalem had awakened the most intense anxiety and alarm in Europe for the safety of the Holy Sepulchre; and the catastrophe of Edessa had attracted the sovereigns and national chivalry of France and Germany to the plains of Asia. At every cry for succour from the Christians in Palestine, until the fatal issue of the Fifth Crusade, myriads of warlike and fanatical volunteers, of the noblest as well the meanest blood of Europe, had eagerly responded to

---

* Sanutus, lib. iii. pars. xii. c. 21-23. De Guignes and G. Villani,

the call; and their devotion to the cause was much more frequently chilled and diverted from its support by the tortuous and sordid policy of the papal see, than by any lack of sincerity or change of purpose in themselves. Yet, after the fall of Acre, no exhortations which succeeding pontiffs strenuously repeated for fifty years, could rouse the princes and people of the West to any earnest design for the revival of the Crusades.* Nor was it that Europe had become less martial or restless in the fourteenth than it had been in the twelfth century. Warfare still constituted the only serious occupation of her princes and nobles—its pursuit the only path of honourable distinction, its image almost their only pastime; and the flame of chivalry—which we have elsewhere characterized, after a great writer, as at once a cause and consequence of the Crusades—never burned so brightly as in the age which immediately succeeded the extinction of those enterprises.

The cessation of the Crusades was assuredly, then, not produced by any abatement of the love of arms, or of the thirst of glory in the chivalry of Europe. But the union with these martial qualities of that fanatical enthusiasm which inspired the Christian

---

* An enumeration of these abortive efforts of the popes to rekindle the enthusiasm of Europe would be superfluous in this place, but may be found in Mr. Mill's *History of the Crusades*, vol. ii. ch. vii —a work to which we take this last occasion of expressing our great obligations.

warriors of the eleventh century, had been slowly dissolved; and the abandonment of Palestine to the undisturbed possession of the Moslems is clearly to be traced to the gradual but total exhaustion in the European mind of the same superstitious phrensy which, pervading every rank of society, had wrought such stupendous efforts for the possession of the Holy Land. The long duration of this wild passion, indeed, is far more astonishing than its final decay; and, instead of being a subject of surprise that it at length expired, it may rather provoke our wonder that so strange an enthusiasm should so tenaciously have survived all experience of disappointment and calamity. In the thirteenth century, however—a full generation before the fall of Acre—we begin clearly to discern the decline of the crusading spirit in the evidence both of historical and poetical literature; and when the pious follower of St. Louis, and faithful chronicler of his deeds, refused to accompany him in his second expedition,*—when the religious obligation of wresting

---

* "The King of France and the King of Navarre pressed me strongly to put on the Cross, and undertake a pilgrimage with them; but I replied, that when I was before beyond sea, on the service of God, the officers of the King of France had so grievously oppressed my people that they were in a state of poverty, insomuch that we should have great difficulty to recover ourselves; and that I saw clearly, were I to undertake another Croisade, it would be the total ruin of my people. I have heard many say since, that those who had advised him to this Croisade had been guilty of a great crime, and had sinned deadly." Joinville, (Johnes's Edition,) vol. i. p 241

the sepulchre of Christ from the hands of the infidels became the subject of bold and jocular denial in a popular poem,*—we may feel assured that the noble and the minstrel already spoke the altered sentiments of their times.

The causes to which this extinction of fanatical zeal in Europe may be referred are obvious, and have often been exposed. Among them, the most immediate was, assuredly, a growing conviction of the hopelessness of success. After the signal and tremendous failure of the Fifth Crusade in Egypt, it may be doubted whether any mighty armament could ever again have been directed to the same scene, if the personal character and influential example of St. Louis, rather than the spontaneous ardour of his nobles, had not produced his two calamitous expeditions. In the intermediate enterprise of the Emperor Frederic II., his tardy if not reluctant voyage to the Holy Land, as well as the whole tenor of his conduct respecting the affairs of his Eastern kingdom, was evidently induced

---

* In the *Fabliaux* of Le Grand d'Aussy, (vol. ii. p. 168,) translated in the kindred work of Way, (vol. ii. p. 227,) is preserved a very curious specimen by Rutubœuf, a French rhymer of the age of St. Louis, in which a crusader and non-crusader are made to discuss the duty of assuming the Cross. Throughout this dialogue, under pretext of rebuking the levity of the non-crusader, it is evident that the sly minstrel intended to ridicule the expiring folly of his times; nor would it be easy, in more serious terms, to offer a better exposure of the practical evils which the Crusades had inflicted upon their votaries, than is presented in this lively satire.

much more by political than religious considerations; and the efforts of our two English princes, Richard of Cornwall, and his nephew Edward, if inspired by a more generous motive of glory or devotion, were unsustained examples of individual heroism, which served only to prove that their spirit was no longer supported by the popular enthusiasm and hopes of their age. None of those leaders were followed by the immense and various array of the Western nations, which had thronged around the consecrated banners of their precursors in the first five Crusades; the defence of Palestine itself was abandoned almost entirely to the military orders; and perhaps it was only the institution of those martial and religious fraternities, and the revolutions and consequent weakness of the Mohammedan States, which protracted the struggle through the last seventy years of its duration.

But, beyond all question, the primary cause which both defeated the object of the Crusades, and awakened Christendom from its long dream of fanatical madness, was the conduct of the papal see. Sincere as Pope Urban II. and some of his successors undoubtedly were in the promotion of these undertakings, the temptation of diverting the general enthusiasm to the profit of its own spiritual and temporal power soon became too strong to be resisted by the selfish ambition and cupidity of the court of Rome. Accordingly, the service of the Cross became the frequent pretence for pecuniary exactions to fill the papal coffers;* next, crusaders were allowed and even encouraged to commute their vows for money; and, finally, the same spiritual indulgences, or pardons for sin, which had been the great inducement to persons of all ranks to engage in the earlier Crusades,† were openly and shamelessly sold. Moreover, by an easy enlargement of the crusading principle, the sacred duty and merit of combating the infidel foes of God was first extended to the extirpation of heresy among Christians by the sword; and this doctrine required to be stretched but a point further, to reach all the temporal enemies of the church, or, in other words, every political opponent of the reigning pontiff.

Innocent III. was the first of the popes who applied the religious enthusiasm of Europe to this double object of taxation and persecution. The Crusade which he directed against the Albigenses, was the earliest diversion of the martial fanaticism of the Middle Ages from its original object; and the indulgences which he lavished upon all who assumed

---

* Sufficient examples of this fact, in the case of England, have already been cited in the present chapter from Matthew Paris, p. 389, 461, 463, &c.; nor can it be doubted that the same conduct was pursued in other parts of Europe.

† The promise of spiritual indulgences and pardons is expressly mentioned by Villehardouin as among the primary motives of the warriors who engaged in the Fourth Crusade. *Et mult s'en croisi-*

the Cross in that atrocious warfare, were more extensive than any which had been promised for the deliverance of the Holy Sepulchre. The conduct of Innocent in converting the Saladine tithe, which had been first levied by general and voluntary consent throughout Europe, into a compulsory tax upon the clergy, was, indeed, more legitimate in its purpose. But though, as we formerly observed, that loftiness of spirit which characterized that celebrated pontiff may redeem his memory from any suspicion of mean or sordid motives, the example which he thus set had very important results under his successors, not only in disgusting the ecclesiastical orders with the prosecution of holy wars, which were made the pretext of plundering their revenues, but also in encouraging that spirit of resistance to the papal exactions which may be numbered among the remote causes of the Reformation.*

It can scarcely be necessary, in this place, to remind the reader of the more flagrant abuses of the crusading principle which were so frequently committed by the successors of Innocent III. During a period of forty years, every war in which they pursued their

---

* This is evidently the opinion of a writer of great research and celebrity, though he shrinks from stating it broadly: *Peut-on en conclure que les Croisades soient la cause de la guerre des Hussites et de la Réformation de Luther?* (May we not then conclude that the Crusades were the cause of the war of the Hussites, and of the Reformation of Luther?) Heeren, *Essai sur l'Influence des Croisades*, Paris, 1808, p. 176.

unrelenting hostility against the imperial house of Hohenstauffen, from the first excommunication of Frederic II. until the fall of his grandson Conradin, was audaciously invested with the title of a Crusade, and its supporters were rewarded with the same privileges as the Christian warriors in Palestine. One of these pontiffs, Clement IV., during the contest between Charles of Anjou and Manfred for the crown of the Sicilies, even prevented large bodies of crusaders from proceeding to the Holy Land, by inviting them, with the promise of equal indulgences, to exchange the perilous fulfilment of their vows in the East, for the lighter service of attacking his political enemy in Italy.

It would be a waste of words to enlarge upon the serious injury sustained by the Christian cause in Palestine through these abuses, or to describe the ridicule and scandal which were thrown upon the crusading principle itself, by its prostitution to purposes too grossly temporal long to delude even the blindest superstition. Nor were the shameless expedients less palpable by which the papal court and its agents, in the same age, frequently impeded the religious enterprises, and disappointed the zeal of society, in order to embezzle the immense sums which were collected for the ostensible service of the Cross. Of the extent of these frauds we have cited abundant evidence, even from the monastic annalists of our own

in disgust the last fitful gleams of the crusading fanaticism, since such fruitless exactions fell less severely on the poor and ignorant commonalty, than on those ecclesiastical and noble orders who, by their riches and intelligence, were more interested, and better qualified to expose and resent the dishonest artifices of the papal policy.*

---

* The popular belief, which held that pilgrimages to various shrines of Europe were scarcely less efficacious than the more arduous journey to the Holy Land, has sometimes been numbered among the causes of the decline of the crusading spirit; but it seems to have been rather a consequence of the impossibility of visiting Jerusalem. At least, the institution of the sacred festival of the jubilee by which Pope Boniface VIII. drew an immense concourse of pilgrims to Rome, in the last year of the thirteenth century, to receive a general pardon for their sins, must be regarded only as a profitable expedient consequent upon the loss of the holy places in the East, which had previously attracted the stream of devotion.

CHAPTER VI.

Consequences of the Crusades.

HE causes which produced and extinguished the Crusades are so evident, as to have led most inquirers to a common conclusion on their nature and operations; but, in their estimate of the consequences of these memorable expeditions upon the political, moral, and religious aspect of society, scarcely two historians of eminence are agreed.

If we are to believe one celebrated writer, the most sanguinary and destructive wars which fanaticism ever produced, were the sources of unmingled good;* if we are to adopt the judgment of another, yet more distinguished, the principle and effects of the Crusades were analogous in their baneful tendency, and equally injurious in their influence upon knowledge and civilization.† According to a third reasoner, those enterprises enormously augmented the papal power, and aggravated the prevailing superstitions;‡ by a fourth they are numbered, with some hesitation, indeed, among the beneficial causes of the great reformation of religion.|| Again, though the first writer to whom we have here alluded thought he could discern in these wild expeditions the earliest gleams of light, which tended to dispel barbarism and ignorance, and was led to discover in them the dawn of all social improvement in Europe, the ablest historian of the Crusades in our own times has denied almost all permanence to their effects.¶ And lastly, while a disciple of the blind school of fatalism has seen in the con-

---

* Robertson, *History of Charles V. &c.*, *Introduction*, sec. 1.
† Gibbon, *Decline and Fall*, &c., ch. lxi.
‡ Mosheim, *Eccles. History*, Cent. xi. p. i. c. 1. sec. 8.
|| Heeren, *Essai sur l'Influence des Croisades*, p. 139–176.
¶ Mills, *History of the Crusades*, vol. ii. c. 8. Such seems also to be the opinion of Mr. Hallam; although it is to be gathered less from expressed reasoning than from the absence of much reference to the effects of the Crusades, in his View of the Progress of Society during Middle Ages.

dict of Europe and Asia only some fortuitous advantages,* the eloquent champion of a religious philosophy of history has, with a far happier spirit of reverential inquiry, been contented to trace the beneficial designs of Omnipotence through the mingled evil and good of this, like every other, convulsion of the political and moral world.†

The value of these various and conflicting opinions may perhaps best be ascertained by a distinct, though, within our narrow limits, necessarily a brief examination of the forms in which the Crusades were likely to act upon the condition of Europe; in their influence upon religion, upon international power, upon internal government, upon commerce and learning, and lastly upon social morals and civilization in general.

I. With respect to religion, when we consider that the Crusades were the sources of a vast increase of power and wealth, and consequently of luxury and corruption, in the Romish Church; when we remember that the detestable establishment of the Inquisition, and the scandalous traffic of indulgences for sin at least originated in the perversion of the crusading enthusiasm; it is impossible to deny the conclusion, that the immediate effects of that fanatical spirit were extremely pernicious. And it is probably the superficial view of these temporary evils which has misled many writers who, in natural and well-founded disgust at the cruelty and impurity with which they stained the holiness of Christianity, have overlooked the salutary reaction which they necessitated. Such inquirers, in fact, in passing an unqualified judgment on the mischievous results of the Crusades, have not distinguished between the proximate and ultimate consequences of those enterprises. For if, as they undoubtedly did, the corruptions of the Church of Rome produced the reformation of religion, the very evils engendered by the Crusades, in nurturing and maturing the intolerable growth of ecclesiastical abuses, must have essentially hastened the season of their correction.

II. The consequences of the Crusades, in affecting the distribution of international power, is a question which admits of less doubt. The opinion, once entertained, that those expeditions were instrumental in arresting the progress of the Mohammedan arms, seems universally exploded; nor can it be proved that they ultimately produced the least change in the external disposition of any of the European states, except the maritime Italian republics. We have seen, indeed, that applications from the Greek Empire to the pope and the western potentates, for succour against the Seljukian Turks, preceded the First Crusade; and it is true that Alexius Comnenus profited by the successes of the Latins, to recover a con siderable part of Asia Minor from the infidels. But, before the crusaders traversed that region, the Seljukian power had already obeyed the usual fate of Asiatic dynasties, in internal decay and partition; and the real peril of Constantinople from the Turks in that age was already past, when her emperor was oppressed by the arrival of allies scarcely less dangerous. The temporary advantages which the Greek Emperor extracted from the victorious passage of Godfrey of Bouillon and his compeers were never renewed; and we may agree with a judicious historian,* that whatever obligations might be due to the first crusaders from the Eastern Empire, were cancelled by their descendants one hundred years afterwards, when the fourth in number of those expeditions was turned to the subjugation of Constantinople itself. Certain it is, that the Byzantine Empire never recovered from the shock and dismemberment which attended the Latin conquest; and the silent revival and growth of the new Turkish power in the mountains of Asia Minor, which finally overthrew the Greek Empire and planted the banner of the Crescent on the towers of Constantinople, were in no degree connected with, and could not be retarded by, the contest of the crusaders with the Sultans of Damascus and Cairo for the possession of the Syrian shore. In Western Europe itself, the Crusades left absolutely no consequences in the political connection of the Latin kingdoms; and we have only to compare their extent at the close of the 11th and of the 13th centuries, to assure ourselves that neither the fate of a single dynasty, nor the boundaries and relative strength of nations, had at all been affected by the vicissitudes of the fanatical contest in which they had shared.

III. The influence of that contest on the internal government and constitution of the feudal kingdoms of Europe is a distinct and more difficult problem. Among the benefits, in these respects, which had been attributed to the Crusades, are the firmer establishment of regal authority, the depression of the feudal aristocracy, the gradual deliverance of the rural population from predial servitude, and the growth of municipal freedom. The era of the Crusades was assuredly one of active and rapid improvement in social order and civilization; but, so far as opposite changes are discernible in the feudal kingdoms at the close of the Crusades, such results can scarcely, upon any sound principle of reasoning, be referred to a single and common cause in the influences of those enterprises. Now, the same period witnessed the triumph of the crown over feudalism in France, the foundation of constitutional freedom upon the ruins of royal tyranny in England, and the completion of the aristocratic and municipal privileges of Germany. In the first of these countries, it has been proved, that of all

the great and arrière fiefs, the annexation of which to
the crown consolidated the royal power during the
Crusades, not one lapsed by the extinction of a feudal
house in those wars, and only one, the county of
Bourges, appears clearly to have been acquired by
purchase from a chieftain who had taken the Cross.*
In England, on the contrary, if the Crusades had any
effect upon the regal authority, it was injurious. The
sale of the royal domains by Richard I. to defray the
cost of his expedition to Palestine, tended, indeed, to
throw the crown, by the dimunition of its revenues,
into dependence upon the aristocracy; but the circumstances which favoured the struggle of that body
against his successors—the mingled tyranny and pu-
sillanimity of John, and the total incapacity of his
feeble son—were altogether foreign to the present
subject of inquiry. In Germany, it is needless to remind the reader, that the fall of the house of Hohenstauffen, and the consequent extinction of the imperial
authority, were as totally unconnected with the result
of the Crusades. In a word, how is a belief in the
general depression of the feudal aristocracy, through
their share in those costly and distant enterprises, to
be reconciled with their triumph, in the same ages,
over the royal and imperial power in England and in
Germany?

---

* Heeren, *Essai sur l'Influence des Croïsades*, p. 181–185; Mills, *History of the Crusades*, vol. ii. pp. 351–354; and the authorities there cited.

Equally difficult would it be to show any perceptible amelioration in the condition of the peasantry of Europe through the influence of the Crusades; for, at the close of the 13th century, the chains of feudal tyranny remained unbroken; the mass of the rural population was still in bondage to the soil, and, in the following age, the frightful insurrections of the populace in France and England reveal the continuance of that wretched state of servitude which goaded their order to desperation.* There is, therefore, neither a shadow of evidence, nor even a probability, to warrant the hypothesis, that the condition of the serfs of the feudal system was improved by the events of the Crusades; scarcely any contemporary though accidental changes, in this respect, can be traced in the same period; and the relaxation of predial servitude must be referred altogether to later ages.

There is, however, more reason to conclude, though

---

* It is singular that Gibbon, while denying in general all beneficial consequences to the Crusades, and contending that they checked rather than forwarded the maturity of Europe, should number them "among the causes which undermined the Gothic edifice" of Feudalism; and assert that the poverty of the barons, whose estates were dissipated in these expeditions, extorted from them "those charters of freedom which unlocked the fetters of the slave, and secured the farm of the peasant." Of such manumission there is no evidence whatever. It is no less singular that the great historian, in adopting this fanciful theory, should have overlooked, or at least omitted, all consideration of the real and positive benefits which accrued to commerce from the Crusades.

rather from general deductions than special proofs, that the growth of municipal independence was at least favoured by the Crusades. Not that even this assertion is to be received without great qualification; for the liberties of the inland cities of Northern Italy arose before the commencement of those enterprises, and were lost before their conclusion;* in Germany, also many towns on the Rhine had already, in the 11th century, obtained important privileges from Henry IV., in reward for their fidelity to that emperor, during his disastrous contest with the papacy;† and in our own country, the chartered rights of cities flowed exclusively from the crown under circumstances which bear no imaginable relation to crusading incidents. But, throughout the continent north of the Alps, and in Germany especially, during the 12th and 13th centuries, there appears so remarkable an advance in the liberties and consequent prosperity of numerous towns, that it is natural to attribute some share in the successful struggle of their inhabitants against aristocratic oppression to the frequent absence of the most active and enterprising of their feudal seigneurs and neighbours in the holy wars; and still more to the com-

---

* " At the latter end of the 13th century, there were almost as many princes in the north of Italy, as there had been free cities in the preceding age." Hallam, *Middle Ages*, vol. i. p. 407.

mercial impulse which was excited by those enterprises.

IV. If on any point, indeed, we may safely dissent from the conclusions of those historians who have seen no beneficial results in the Crusades, it will be in remarking the obvious effect of the Latin expeditions to the East, in enlarging the commerce of Europe.

The rapid extension of the trade of the maritime Italian republics is clearly referable to their share in the Crusades, not only in the mere transport of warriors and pilgrims for hire, but in the warlike naval co-operation which won for them numerous lucrative establishments in the Levant. Thence they drew and poured into Europe the rich products of the East, and accumulated a commerce which, though not previously altogether unattempted, had acquired little activity until the commencement of the Crusades. Nor were its benefits by any means confined to Italy, or even to the shores of the Mediterranean; for, by inland communication, they were spread among the free cities of Germany, and, through the Straits of Gibraltar, to those English and Flemish ports, which formed the only entrepôts for the merchandise of the Italian republics, and of the Hanse Towns of the North. It is not, therefore, too strong an assertion, that the Crusades were more instrumental in the dissemination of commerce throughout

covery of the New World, and the accomplishment of a maritime passage to India.

V. But no kindred influence of the Crusades can be traced in the diffusion of lettered knowledge. If, indeed, those enterprises had enriched the Western World with the precious stores of the ancient Greek literature, the result would more than have compensated for the political injuries which the crusaders inflicted upon the worthless and tottering edifice of Byzantine power. But the spirit of the ignorant Latins was still too barbarous to profit by a collision with the more cultivated, though perverted, intellect of the Greeks; the mutual hatred and contempt of the two races disdained all communion; and so far were the literary treasures of Constantinople from awakening the curiosity of her French captors, that the destruction of many of the Greek classics, still extant in the 13th century, is notoriously ascribable to the three calamitous conflagrations which attended the Latin conquest of the Eastern capital.* Nor, even, was any knowledge of the language of Greece imported into the West by the crusaders; and the true restorers of Greek learning in the Latin world were Petrarca and Boccaccio, whose exertions, in the next century after the Crusades, were aided by circumstances upon which those wars could have left no control. Nor

---

* See the authenticated catalogue of these losses in Heeren, pp. 413, 414.

can any part of the illumination for which Europe was indebted in the Middle Ages to the letters and science of the Arabians, be more correctly ascribed to the occupation of Palestine by the Franks. For the intellectual splendour of the eastern khalifate was extinct before the First Crusade; the rays of light diffused from that source had long previously penetrated into the West through Spain and Italy; many Latin translations of the Arabic writers had been prepared in those countries; and Toledo, Salerno, and Cassino were flourishing schools for the transmuted philosophy and learning of the Mohammedans.* Lastly, if the Crusades had exercised any decided influence on letters, we might expect to find its traces in the native and romantic poetry of the West, of which the darling theme was most congenial to the chivalric spirit of such enterprises. Apart, however, from the general and connecting link of chivalry, the subjects even of Trouveur and Troubadour contemporary song do not much abound with references to the adventures of Paynim war. Some oriental colouring was, no doubt, transfused through the strains of the numerous minstrels who followed their lords to Palestine; but it is a singular fact, that, except in two, which relate the deeds of Godfrey of Bouillon and Richard Cœur de Lion, the Crusades do not form the subject of the romances of chivalry.† It has

---

* Mills, *Crusades*, vol. ii. pp. 860–864.

† *Idem*, vol. ii. p. 867, and Dunlop, *History of Fiction*, vol. ii. p. 140

been acutely remarked, that those expeditions were, perhaps, too recent, and too much matters of real life, to admit the decorations of fiction;* but neither do they appear to have engrossed more attention, as subjects of authentic narrative, than the other political events of the times; nor to have particularly quickened that fervour of historical composition which is usually awakened by great events, and tends by its excitement to stimulate the intellect of an age.. In this respect, notwithstanding the natural interest and richness of their materials, and the spirit-stirring character of their details, the Crusades did not elicit any striking improvement; and though there is no lack of chroniclers of the Holy Wars, they are scarcely more numerous, or of higher merit, than the contemporary national annalists of the same ages.

VI. That the new blending of so many masses of men of various climes and manners in a common cause—the commingling, as it were, for the first time, of the great family of nations—and the general habit of foreign and distant travel—must altogether have given a mighty impulse to society, and dispelled many clouds of ignorance, in which the previous stagnation of intercourse had thickly shrouded the countries of the West—can hardly, we think, be doubted by any inquirer whose judgment has not been misled to the maintenance of some preconceived and favourite

---

* Dunlop, *ubi suprà.*

theory. But, it has been triumphantly asked,* if some benefits were thus necessarily communicated to Europe, what were they? Specific proof may, in this spirit, be vainly demanded of a general consequence, which, from its very nature, admits of none. Yet no man has denied the striking and steady progress of civilization after the 11th century; and our historian of the Middle Ages, in his view of society, has even marked the close of that century which is identical with the commencement of the Crusades, as the point which separates the extreme darkness of barbarism in Europe, from the dawn of a progressive renovation.*

If the Crusades, by the stimulus which they gave to the commercial and general communion of nations, were *not* the principal causes of this nascent improvement during the 12th and 13th centuries, what other attributes, peculiar to the times, can be pointed out, which may be believed to have exercised so strong and universal an influence, as those enterprises with all their attendant circumstances? It has been said that the Crusades were altogether pernicious to morality, and that the absurd and cruel principles of superstition and fanaticism which they fostered were equally detrimental to religion. But here again is room for a caution against the confounding of proximate and ultimate consequences. As the dissolute, as well as the pious, enlisted under the banner of the

---

* Berington, *Literary History of the Middle Ages*, p. 269.
† Hallam, *Middle Ages*, vol. iii. 372.

Cross, the habits of the worst portions of society were not likely to be improved by the license of crusading camps; but the myriads, who perished amid their excesses in the East, at least relieved their native lands of the burden and curse of their presence. The stern spirit of religious persecution, encouraged by an exterminating warfare against infidels, is the darkest feature in the operation of the Crusades upon the feelings and happiness of their times. The justice of the principles upon which those enterprises were either originally undertaken or subsequently perverted, is utterly indefensible upon all the laws of God and man; nor were there, perhaps, ever any human contests, in themselves more thoroughly misguided and iniquitous than those holy wars. But in their fruits when time had purified the soil in which the wild and bitter stock of superstition was planted, they became very salutary to mankind. The union of a religious with a martial spirit, however incongruous in its origin, has tended, more than any other combination of sentiment, to humanize not only warfare itself, but the ordinary relations of civilized life; and, as the institutions of chivalry were matured and perpetuated by the Crusades, we owe to those enterprises the cultivation of all the moral qualities, of personal honour and fidelity to obligations, of courtesy to the one sex and respectful tenderness to the other, which have descended upon the modern gentleman, and survive to dignify and adorn the intercourse of polished society.

In conclusion, then, we may venture to affirm, of the influence and consequences of the Crusades, that, upon the state of religion, they were at first pernicious, but ultimately beneficial; that, upon the distribution of national power in the European system, they were, altogether, or nearly, immaterial; that upon the internal government and constitution of the feudal kingdoms, they are no otherwise discernible than in favouring the growth of municipal freedom; that, in the diffusion of commerce, they were most important and valuable, but in that of learning absolutely null; that, in the commingling of nations, they must have given a strong and general impulse to the progress of civilization; and, finally, that, at least by the promotion of chivalric sentiment, they were an obvious, though indirect and distant means of ameliorating the social morals and manners of Europe.

CHRONOLOGY OF THE CRUSADES.

The predisposing causes of those famous enterprises are generally attributed to the impulsive influence of religion upon the barbaric mind, the institution of chivalry, the union of martial and superstitious feelings, and the influence of fanatical enthusiasm. But the proximate causes are seen in the persecuting frenzy of Hakem, the third Fatimite khalif, and in the fanatical cruelties of Seljukian Turks. The reports of returned pilgrims respecting the insulting and savage cruelty of the latter, as well as the destruction of the Church of the Resurrection by the former, excited general indignation; but it was not till the return of Peter Gautier, an officer of Amiens, who had renounced his profession in order to undertake a pilgrimage, that any proposal was made for attempting the expulsion of the infidels from the Holy Land. Peter (the Hermit) laid before Pope Urban II. a project he had formed for expelling the infidels from Palestine; which, being backed by the complaints of the Greek emperor, Alexis, and the urgent appeals of Peter, the pope was induced to espouse the projected enterprise; accordingly he recommended to all Christian princes, first at the Council of Placentia, and afterward at that of Clermont, the duty of zealously engaging in this holy war. At the latter council the pope obtained from the ambassadors present a commission for Peter Gautier to proceed forthwith in the prosecution of his chivalric design. The ensuing spring (1096) was appointed for the departure of the first army.

A. D.
The Crusades—Abortive Expeditions.
1096 Peter the Hermit, issues from the western frontiers of France, leading an immense concourse of the lowest orders.
The rabble multitude is divided:—
The first division, of 20,000, is led by Walter, the Pennyless, through Hungary.
In Bulgaria they are all destroyed, except Walter and a few who escape to Constantinople.
The second division, of 40,000, under Peter the Hermit, advance into Hungary.

A. D.
1096 They are nearly all cut off by the Turks in the plain of Nice; only 3000 escape.
Fall of Walter, the Pennyless.
Third division, of 15,000, from Germany, under Gondenschal, a German monk.
Their atrocious wickedness in Hungary ends in their ruthless massacre at Belgrade.
Fourth division, of 200,000, composed of one huge mass of the vile refuse of France, Flanders, the Rhenish Provinces, and England. They are guided by two "divinely

spirit of crusading was roused into action by the Council of Clermont, and before a single advantage had been gained over the infidels, the fanatical enthusiasm of Europe had already cost the lives, at the lowest computation, of 250,000 of its people. But while the first disasters of the Crusade were sweeping this mass of corruption from the surface of society, the genuine spirit of religious and martial enthusiasm was more slowly and powerfully evolved. With maturer preparation, and with steadier resolve, than the half-armed and irregular rabble, the mailed and organized chivalry of Europe was arraying itself for the mighty contest; and a far different, a splendid and interesting spectacle opens to our view."—*Procter.*]

THE FIRST CRUSADE.

Though not undertaken by any of the crowned heads of Europe, was eagerly embraced by the most distinguished feudal princes of the second order, viz. :—
Godfrey of Bouillon, with his two brothers, Eustace and Baldwin, and a kinsman also named Baldwin; Hugh, Count of Vermandois, and Robert of Normandy, brothers of the French and English Kings; Robert of Flanders, Stephen of Chartres, and Raymond of Thoulouse—the first temporal prince who assumed the crown; Boemond, son of Robert Guiscard, Prince of Tarento, and his cousin Tancred.

Order of Departure.

The *first division*, under Godfrey consisted of the nobility of the Rhenish provinces and the North of Germany.
Godfrey receives assistance from Carloman of Hungary and the Emperor Alexius; he peaceably arrives with his army on the fertile plains of Thrace.
The *second division*, under the Counts of Vermandois and Chartres, embraced the chivalry of Central and Northern France, the British Isles, Normandy, and Flanders.
Their passage from Italy is opposed by the Emperor Alexius,

and Hugh is made prisoner at Durazzo.

1096 Thrace ravaged by the Crusaders, under Godfrey, in retaliation for the opposition offered Hugh of Vermandois, by the Emperor Alexius.
The *third division*, under Boemond and Tancred, composed of Southern Italians—10,000 horse, and 20,000 foot.
The *fourth division*, under the Count of Thoulouse, includes his own vassals and native confederates, comprehended under the general appellation of Provencals.

1097 Godfrey at open war with Alexius: seizure of the bridge of Blachernae; attack upon Constantinople.
Hugh of Vermandois mediates.
Messages from Boemond and the Count of Thoulouse, requesting Godfrey to defer negotiations till they should arrive.
Godfrey submits; hence an Accommodation between the wily Alexis and the crusading princes; the latter swears fealty, the former delivers his son as hostage.
Approach of the third division to the Byzantine capital.
Boemond at first refuses to do homage to Alexius, but afterward submits.
The fourth division next approaches—its leader, Raymond, sternly refuses homage to Alexius whom he menaces.
Alexius craftily gains the ascendency over the mind of the aged, though stern, Raymond.
Muster of the several divisions in the plain of Asia Minor; numbers estimated—including 100,000 mailed cavalry, and a prodigious number of priests, women, and children—at about 700,000.
Siege of Nice, June 20; it falls into the hands of the Greeks by stratagem.
Battle of Dorylæum in July; ultimate victory of the Crusaders.
Evacuation of Asia Minor by the Sultan of Roum.
Triumphant entry of the crusading hosts into Syria.
Battle between Tancred and Baldwin.
Baldwin separates from the main body and proceeds eastward, victoriously overrunning the

CHRONOLOGY OF THE CRUSADES. 471

A. D.

whole country as far as the Euphrates.

1097 The Crusaders lay siege to Antioch.
Famine and pestilence in the Christian camp; desertion of great numbers to Baldwin in Mesopotamia, &c.; cowardice of the Duke of Normandy, Count of Chartres, the Viscount of Melun, and Peter the Hermit.

1098 *The Latin principality of Edessa founded* by Baldwin.
Siege of Antioch renewed; the Turks defeated, through the treachery of Phirous; city surprised and captured; the Turkish garrison escape within the citadel.
The Sultan of Persia unites the Turks against the Christian invaders; twenty-eight emirs lead a force of from 3000 to 4000 cavalry to relieve the garrison in the Citadel of Antioch.
Blockade of the Crusaders in the city.
Second famine; horrible distress, attended by cannibalism, and vice of every kind.
Alexius abandons their relief.
The despairing Crusaders are called into action by superstition and the imposture of a priest.
Great battle of Antioch; the Turks routed with terrible slaughter.
Foundation of the Latin principality of Antioch; Boemond its ruler.
Disunion among the crusading princes.
Third famine and pestilence in Antioch, which sweep off 100,000 persons—cannibalism again resorted to.

999 The Crusaders, now numbering only 1500 cavalry and 20,000 infantry, and an equal number of unarmed camp followers, &c., proceeded from Antioch to Jaffa by sea.
Jerusalem invested by the Crusaders, June.
Sufferings of the besieged from thirst.
Arrival of Genoese galleys in Jaffa; the mariners are brought to the camp to construct three movable towers.
Jerusalem taken by the Crusaders, July 15; frightful massacre of the Mussulmans and Jews.

A. D.

habitants; the law of conquest supplies to Jerusalem a new and Christian population.

1099 *Foundation of the Latin kingdom of Jerusalem;* its first king is *Godfrey* of Bouillon, elected by th. army.
He modestly declines the title of king, accepting only that of "Defender of the Tomb of Christ."
[Thus the great design of the *first Crusade* had been accomplished, in the triumphant recovery of the Holy Sepulchre.]
Foundation of the *Knights of St. John of Jerusalem*—the origin of which was an hospice founded in Jerusalem in 1048, by a few merchants of Memphis, for the accommodation of pilgrims from Europe. An hospital for the sick was afterward added, hence the term—knights hospitallers; the members of which are also known as the Knights of Rhodes.
When the Crusaders entered Jerusalem, many of the chevaliers determined on joining the order—Godfrey granted a donation, which example was followed by other princes. To the usual vows of chastity, poverty, and obedience, was added a vow to be always ready to fight against Mohammedans, and all who forsook the true religion. Thus was the chivalric institution—the offspring of feudalism—made subservient to the interests of the church. See 1118.
Flourishing period of chivalry.
[On the continent, the lowest tenant, by military service, was fully included in the pretensions and privileges of nobility, except in the case of imperial fouds, which were not accounted noble beyond the third degree of subinfeudation. Hence the land which bristled with fortresses afforded as many titles of nobility; and every country was filled with a numerous order of minor counts, barons, and vavasors—the vassals of the greater feudatories, and themselves each the chieftain of a train of knightly dependants. The least of these last, who was bound or entitled to serve his lord as a horse-

are derived the original distinction, and the very name of CHIVALRY—was a member of the same aristocracy as the duke or count, the privileges of which order, according to feudal customs, formed an impassible line between it and the commonalty. The exact epoch at which Chivalry acquired a religious character, it is not easy to determine. In the age of Charlemagne, the form of knightly investiture was certainly unattended by any vows or ecclesiastical ceremonies; but in the eleventh century, it had become common to invoke the aid of religion in the inauguration of the knight. There is abundant proof, however, of the success of the church, before the Crusades, in infusing some religious principle into the martial spirit of Chivalry. The original obligations of this institution included loyalty and honour, courtesy and benevolence, generosity to enemies, protection to the feeble and the oppressed, and respectful tenderness to woman.]

1099 Approach of a great Fatimite army, swelled by Turks and Saracens.
Battle of Ascalon; the Crusaders victorious; they acquire much booty.
The princes depart for Europe, except Tancred, who remains with Godfrey.
Daimbert, patriarch of Jerusalem.

1100 Capture of Boemond, prince of Antioch, by an Arminian chieftain.
Death of Godfrey, aged 40, five days preceding the first anniversary of his reign.
Baldwin I. prince of Edessa, elected king of Jerusalem: he resigns to Baldwin du Bourg, the brother of Godfrey, the principality of Edessa.

1101 First Crusade by land; or Supplementary Crusade under Counts Vermandois and Chartres.

1102 Vermandois is wounded in a battle with the Mussulmans of Cilicia; dies at Tarsus;
Rash assault by a vanguard upon the Egyptian invaders; Chartres taken and murdered; Baldwin rescued from death by a grateful

1103 Azotus reduced by Baldwin; the siege of Acre formed.
1104 Arrival of 70 Genoese ships with Crusaders, which results in the Conquest of Acre by Baldwin I.
1106 The Count of Tholouse is joined by several French princes, who had arrived in the Supplemental Crusade, (1101.)
Tortosa taken by Raymond.
1108 Bertrand, son of Raymond, effects the conquest of Tripoli.
1109 Tripoli and its vicinity erected into a county, by Baldwin, for the house of Thoulouse. Hence "County of Tripoli."
1111 The Crusaders take Berytus.
Sidon captured by the Crusaders. [With an interval of four years, two fleets of Scandinavian cruisers, who had performed the long voyage from the Baltic, through the Straits of Gibraltar, to the Syrian shores, co-operated with the Christian forces of Palestine, in the siege of Sidon. Although the first attempt was repulsed, the second proved successful.]
1112 Critical position of the State of Edessa, surrounded by Armenians and Turks.
Heroic exploits of its prince, Baldwin du Bourg, and his relative, Joscelyn de Courtenay.
Arrival of large numbers of pilgrims and Crusaders from Europe.
1113 The order of Knights Hospitallers of St. John confirmed by Papal Bull.
The Suljuk Turks of Aleppo, Damascus, and Iconium, aided by Mohammedans of Arabia, Egypt, and Persia, harass and often defeat the Crusaders.
1117 Birth of Noureddin, the younger son of Zenghi, second of the Attabek princes.
1118 Expedition against Egypt conducted by Baldwin.
Death of Baldwin I. (in March) on his march toward Egypt; his cousin.
Baldwin II. (Prince of Edessa) King of Jerusalem.
The order of *Knights Hospitallers* of the order of St. John (called also Knights of Malta) becomes a military order. Hence
Knights Templars: institution of the order of the Temple of Solo

CHRONOLOGY OF THE CRUSADES. 473

[The object of the institution of this order was to act in a military capacity to protect pilgrims. See 1099.

[The military orders were, in the first instance, subjected to the rule of St. Augustin; modified, of course, in some degree, by the peculiar object of their institution. The most ancient of these was the order of the Knights Hospitallers of St. John of Jerusalem, established in the first instance (1048) for the reception and care of pilgrims visiting the holy city. This order became monastic in 1092, and in 1118 added the military qualification.]

1120 Zenghi, governor of Mosul, (1145, 1146.)

1124 Tyre reduced by Baldwin II., aided by the Doge of Venice, who obtains the sovereignty of one-third of the city.

[All the maritime republics of Italy, with their characteristic mercantile cupidity, extorted great commercial advantages, as the price of their services to the Crusaders. And throughout the Christian possessions in Palestine and Syria generally, the three republics of Genoa, Pisa, and Venice contended, often with bloodshed, for the right of establishing places of exchange, and enjoying the common or exclusive privileges of trade.]

Archbishopric of Tyre established. Extension of the Latin kingdom of Jerusalem, from the sea-coast to the deserts of Arabia, and from the city of Beritus, on the north, to the frontiers of Egypt, on the south, forming a territory about 60 leagues in length, and 30 in breadth; and exclusive of the county of Tripoli, which stretched northward from Beritus to the borders of the Antiochian principality.

1131 Abdication of Baldwin, with the consent of his nobles and prelates, in favour of his son-in-law.

Fouiques (of Anjou) King of Jerusalem.

Baldwin retires to a convent.

1144 *Baldwin* III., King of Jerusalem, (13 years old,) in conjunction with his mother, Melesinda.

[Soon after the martial sceptre of

volved upon a woman and a minor, the Christian power in the East began to decline.]

1145 Fall of Edessa; Zenghi, the Turkish emir of Aleppo, takes it by storm.

Indignation excited in Europe by the event.

St. Bernard preaches a Second Crusade, which is promoted by Louis of France.

[At the soul-stirring exhortations of St. Bernard, the great feudatory princes of Bavaria, Bohemia, Carinthia, Piedmont, and Styria, with a crowd of inferior chieftains, assumed the cross; and the conversion of the emperor Conrad III., after some struggle between the sense of political interest and religious duty, completed the triumph of the pious orator.]

Decline of the power of the Crusaders.

1146 Zenghi murdered by his own troops at the siege of Jabbar; his son, *Noureddin*, the third of the dynasty of the Attabeks of Syria, becomes King of Aleppo and Damascus.

He maintains war against the Crusaders.

1147 *The Second Crusade;* led by the Emperor Conrad III., and by Louis VII., King of France.

[The number of the Crusaders has been estimated as approaching near to a million; of which 70,000 were mailed cavalry, and 250,000 were trained infantry, the rest were clergy, pilgrims, women, and camp followers.]

Treacherous policy of Comnenus, the Greek emperor; he harasses the crusaders in their march through Bulgaria.

Conrad, on arriving at Constantinople, indignantly refuses to have an interview with Comnenus.

Louis arrives at Constantinople after the departure of Conrad; he accepts the apologies, and is induced to delay his march, by the treacherous emperor.

Almost total destruction of the imperial army in the passes of Lycaonia by the Sultan of Iconium.

Louis encamps at Nice; here he is joined by Conrad and the rem-

A.D.
1147 The united forces come to Ephesus; here they separate—the Germans proceed by sea to Palestine; the French by land.
Sanguinary defeat of the Turks by Louis, on the banks of the Meander.
1148 Surprise and defeat of Louis in the mountains between Pisidia and Phrygia; narrow escape of the king.
Retreat upon the port of Attalia.
Louis transports his nobles and knights by sea to Palestine.
The infantry and pilgrims left behind perish, either by the cimetars of the Turks, or the unnatural cruelty of the Greeks.
The sovereigns of Jerusalem, Germany, and France, resolve on reducing Damascus.
1149 Great victory of Saladin over the Christians at Antioch; Raymond is killed, Joscelyn de Courtenay made prisoner.
Unsuccessful siege of Damascus.
Return of Louis; he lands at St. Gilles on the Rhone, in October.
[Louis left Metz in 1147, at the head of 70,000 knights, mounted and armed, and a band of infantry and camp followers, amounting to about 200,000. He returned a fugitive, with about 300 followers, in barks furnished by Sicily.]
1150 Return of Conrad with the miserable remnant of his army.
[Thus ended abortively the second Crusade, leaving the Christian cause in Palestine again deserted, save by the scanty bands, but enduring courage of its habitual defenders.]
1151 Increasing danger of the Latin kingdom of Palestine from the arms of Noureddin, the Attabek of Aleppo.
Victory of Baldwin III. over the Turks at Jericho.
1153 Ascalon falls by the chivalry of Baldwin.
1152 Death of Baldwin III.; his brother talent was unrelieved by the same virtues.]
1162 Almeric neglects immediate dangers, and wastes his energies in projects for the conquest of Egypt;
Victory of Almeric over Shiracouch.
Pelusium besieged and taken.
1163 Surprise and sanguinary defeat of Almeric, near Artesia, by Noureddin.
1167 Second signal defeat of Shiracouch on the Egyptian frontiers; the Turks capitulate and engage to evacuate Egypt.
1168 Project of Almeric for the permanent subjugation of Egypt.
Pelusium taken, and cruelly sacked by Almeric.
He advances before the wall of Cairo.
Death of Noureddin.
1169 Failure of the project of Almeric, owing to the faithlessness of the Greek Emperor and the craft of the vizier Shaweer.
Retreat of Almeric into Palestine.
Rise of Sallah-u-deen, or Saladin— the scourge of the Christian fortunes in Palestine.
1171 Saladin deposes the sons of Noureddin, and unites under his sway all the Mussulman states from the Nile to the Tigris.
Dissensions and weakness of the Latin kingdom of Palestine.
1173 Death of Almeric; his son *Baldwin* IV. (a leper) King of Jerusalem.
Regency of the king's sister, Sybilla, and her husband, Guy de Lusignan.
Disaffection of the barons of Palestine.
1176 Siege of Alexandria.
1177 Defeat of Saladin before Jerusalem.
1183 Abdication of Baldwin IV.; his nephew *Baldwin* V. (an infant) under the protection of Joscelyn de Courtenay.
Raymond, regent of the kingdom.

CHRONOLOGY OF THE CRUSADES. 475

A. D.

outrage perpetrated by Reginald de Chatillon.
Lusignan refuses justice, whereupon
Saladin invades Palestine with an army of 80,000 horse and foot.
Battle of Tiberias; sanguinary defeat of the Crusaders; Guy de Lusignan made prisoner; Chatillon decapitated by Saladin himself, and 230 of the Knights of St. John taken prisoners and inhumanly murdered by his orders.
[The Christians were betrayed by the Count of Tripoli. See 1086.]
Fall of Cæsarea, Acre, Jaffa, and Beritus.
Tyre besieged; Saladin abandons the siege and marches against Jerusalem.
Saladin takes Jerusalem, October 2.
[Thus after a possession, by the Christians, of 88 years, Jerusalem was again defiled by the religion and empire of the votaries of Mohammed.]
Fall of Bethlehem, Nazareth, Ascalon, and Sidon.
Tyre, defended by Conrad of Montferrat, holds out against Saladin.
[The news of the fall of Jerusalem, &c., filled all Western Christendom with horror and grief.]
A "Saladine" tithe is exacted in Europe for fitting out armaments for Palestine.

1138 Popular expeditions preceding

THE THIRD CRUSADE—by sea.

["All the principal sovereigns of Europe, except those of Spain, vowed to lead their national forces to the recovery of Jerusalem; but even their earnest preparations were too tardy for popular impatience."]
Myriads arrive in Palestine from the ports of Italy, the Baltic, the North Sea, England, and the Mediterranean, at their own expense.

1189 Siege of Acre commenced; 100,000 Crusaders, led by many noblemen and prelates under Lusignan appear before the city.
["On both sides the frightful consumption of human life was fed by new arrivals; and during nearly two years the strength of Christendom and Islam was con-

A. D.

indecisive conflict before the single city of Acre."]
1189 Departure of King Richard from England, Dec. 11.
1190 Richard I. of England, and Philip Auguste of France, assemble their forces (amounting to 100,000 men) on the plain of Vezelay, July 1.
Louis departs from Genoa for Sicily.
Richard's army sails from Marseilles.
Violent proceedings of King Richard toward Tancred, &c., in Sicily.
Dissensions between Louis and Richard.
Frederic (Barbarossa) defeats the Sultan of Iconium, who sues for peace.
Death of Frederic—drowned while attempting to swim across the river Calycadnus in Cilicia, June 10.
The Duke of Suabia takes the command.
Antioch taken by the imperial army.
Fearful destruction of life in the army of the German Crusaders.
Institution of Teutonic Order of knights.
[About 60 years before this time, a German crusader and his lady founded hospitals in Jerusalem for poor pilgrims, of both sexes, of their nation; and when subsequent endowments had enriched these houses, the male brethren devoted themselves to military, as well as charitable services. But their efforts had obtained little distinction; and their fraternity was dissolved by the expulsion of the Christians from Jerusalem. Its purposes were now recalled to the national attention by the private charity of some individuals among the German army, who opened their tents for the reception of their sick and wounded countrymen. A number of knights having joined this benevolent association, the Duke of Suabia seized the occasion to incorporate them into a regular order of religious chivalry. Note to 1099.
Arrival of Philip of France before

Conquest of Cyprus by King Richard.
Richard's fleet dispersed by a storm.
1191 A Mussulman troop-ship, manned by 1,500 hands, destroyed by Richard.
Arrival of the English before Acre, June 10.
King Richard insults Leopold of Austria before Acre.
Acre capitulates, July 12; 5,000 hostages left by Saladin, till the ransom money of 200,000 pieces of gold should be paid.
[The conquest was dearly acquired by the loss of 100,000 Christians.]
Cold-blooded massacre of the Mussulman hostages; followed by the retaliating slaughter of the captive Christians by Saladin.
Open rupture between Richard and Philip.
Philip of France retires from the crusade, leaving 10,000 of his troops under the Duke of Burgundy.
Conrad, Prince of Tyre, King of Jerusalem.
Assassination of Conrad; followed by
Marriage of Henry, Count of Champagne, with Conrad's widow; hence
Henry. of Champagne, King of Jerusalem.
The kingdom of Cyprus found.
King Richard departs from Acre at the head of the combined army, 30,000 strong.
The Crusaders winter on the coast.
1192 Arrival of the Christian host in the valley of Hebron; terror of the infidels.
The Austrians desert the Crusade; also the Duke of Burgundy and the French.
Unexpected retreat of the Crusaders from before Jerusalem.

1192 Truce for three years between Saladin and Richard; the latter dismantles Ascalon, and the former engages not to molest Tyre, Acre, Jaffa, Antioch, and Tripoli, and to grant free access to all Christians visiting Jerusalem.
Departure of Richard's fleet, having on board his queen, sister, and the daughter of the captive king of Cyprus.
Richard sails from Acre, October, 9.
End of the third Crusade.
Richard lands at Corfu in November, and leaves it about the middle of the same month.
1193 Death of Saladin, March 4.
[He is perhaps, the brightest exemplar in history of an Asiatic hero; and his virtues, like the dark traits which obscured them, exhibit the genuine lineaments of his clime and race.]
Division of Saladin's empire; his brother.
Saphadin reigns in Syria, while his three sons erect distinct thrones at Cairo, Damascus, and Aleppo.
1194 A new Crusade preached in Germany.
1195 Crusade of German chivalry; three great armaments under the guidance of nobles and prelates successively arrive at Acre.
Union of the Mussulman powers of Egypt and Syria against the Crusaders.
1196 Indecisive results of this campaign. Jerusalem still in the hands of the infidels.
1197 Death of Henry, nominal king of Jerusalem.
Almeric of Lusignan marries the widow of Henry, and is recognised King of Jerusalem and Cyprus, (1191.)
A fourth Crusade promoted by Innocent III.

CHRONOLOGY OF THE CRUSADES. 477

A. D.
upon their knees, the maritime aid of Venice.
1200 The Venetians agree to convey the armaments to Palestine for 85,000 silver marks.
1201 The Crusade delayed—1st, by the death of Thibaud; 2d, by dissensions among the leaders; 3d, by the deficiency of 30,000 marks to pay for transhipment.

THE FOURTH CRUSADE.

1202 Departure of the Crusaders, under the Marquis of Montserrat; Zara captured; denunciations of the pope; return of De Mountfort; new destination of the armament, owing to the successful negotiations of the friends of young Alexius with the Latin barons, &c., to replace his father on the throne of the East, which his uncle had usurped.
1203 The Crusaders sail for Constantinople.
Negotiations with Alexius; siege.
Flight of Alexius; Isaac restored.
Disunion between the Latins and Greeks.
Young Alexius induces the Crusaders to defer their expedition till the next year.
Third part of Constantinople burned in a feud.
The Crusaders demand the fulfilment of Alexius's pecuniary agreement; they defy the two emperors, which leads to
Open hostilities; the Crusaders and the Greeks at war.
1204 Revolution in Constantinople; the two emperors deposed by Mourzoufle; Alexius is murdered.
Death of Isaac in prison.
Second siege of Constantinople.
Treaty of partition by the Crusaders.
Capture of Constantinople, April 12.
A second conflagration; destruction of the remains of ancient letters and art, &c.
Pillage; public distribution of the spoils.
Baldwin, of Flanders, the first Latin Emperor of the East.
The Eastern kingdom divided between the Latin barons and the Venetians.
Capture of Mourzoufle; he is thrown from the summit of the

A. D.
to the rescue of his coun'ry from the Latin domination.
1204 *End of the Fourth Crusade.*
[In the division and enjoyment of a conquered empire, the confederated barons seemed to have forgotten the original object of their expedition; and the vain trophies of a victory, not over Paynim, but Christian enemies—the gates and chain of the harbour of Constantinople—sent by the new Emperor of the East to Palestine, were the only fruits of the fourth Crusade, which ever reached the Syrian shores.]
1204 Truce with Saphidin for six years.
["The cupidity of the leaders of the fourth Crusade occasioned the loss of the fairest opportunity of re-establishing the Christian fortunes in Palestine. The dissensions of the Mussulman princes, and the ravages of a dreadful famine, and consequent pestilence in Egypt, would have effectually paralyzed all opposition from that dangerous quarter to the success of the crusading arms. But the hopes excited for the Christian cause were completely lost in the diversion of the fourth Crusade against the Eastern Empire.
1210 *John de Brienne*, King of Jerusalem.
Saphidin applies for a prolongation of the truce, which the Latins refuse.
1211 The Mussulman arms are successful against the Latins, who are in great straits.
1213 Appeal of John De Brienne to the pope for succour against the infidels.
1214 The pope decrees another Crusade.
1215 The 4th Lateran council zealously adopt

THE FIFTH CRUSADE—by sea.

1217 First expedition, the Hungarian Crusaders under their King Andrew.
Second expedition; Germans, Italians, French, English, under Duke of Austria.
1217 Abortive campaign of King Andrew. The Turks expel the Saracens from Jerusalem.
1218 Return of Andrew of Hungary.

A. D.
1218 The Crusaders invade Egypt. Siege and capture of Damietta.
1219 Two of the sons of Saphidin, Coradinus, and Camel, offer the cession of Jerusalem, on condition that the Crusaders evacuate Egypt.
This most acceptable offer rejected, through the cupidity of the papal legate.
1220 Disastrous condition of the Crusaders near Cairo; the legate sues for peace.
Peace purchased by the surrender of Damietta to the Sultan of Cairo.
1221 Disgraceful return of the Crusaders from Egypt to Acre.
1224 Embassy of Herman de Saltza, Grand-Master of the Teutonic knights, to the Emperor Frederic, offering him the hand of Iolanta, daughter and heiress of John de Brienne, King of Jerusalem.
1225 Marriage of the Emperor Frederic and Iolanta; her dower consisting of the transfer of the sovereign rights of her father to Frederic.
Frederic promises to lead an army into Palestine, for its reconquest, within two years.
1228 Frederic (emperor) arrives in Palestine with a reinforcement in 28 galloys.
Difficulties of Frederic, arising from the iniquitous persecution of the pope.
Negotiations with the Sultan Coradinus; peace concluded for ten years; free access to Jerusalem granted to the Christians; with possession of Bethlehem, Nazareth, &c.
1229 Frederic crowns himself in Jerusalem; the patriarch having refused to perform the ceremony.
Return of Frederic to Germany; and *End of the Fifth Crusade.*
Death of the Empress Iolanta in giving birth to a son.
1230 Civil war; struggle for the crown between the partisans of Frederic, and those of Alice, widow of Hugh de Lusignan.
Reconciliation effected by the mediation of Pope Gregory IX.
Renewal of hostilities between the Emirs of Syria and the Latins.
Several thousand pilgrims slaughtered.

A. D.
1230 Sanguinary defeat of the Knights Templars, by the Emir of Aleppo.
1232 Another Crusade projected by the Council of Spoletto: the Dominicans and Franciscans are authorized to preach it.
Appropriation of the moneys collected for the Crusade, by the pope and his agents.
1235 Armenia seized by the Mogols.
1236 The Christians expelled from Jerusalem by the Sultan of Egypt.
1237 Martial and religious enthusiasm excited throughout Europe.
The nobles of France and England take the Cross.

THE SIXTH CRUSADE—two expeditions.
1238 I. Expedition of the French Crusaders under Thibaud, Count of Champagne, Duke of Burgundy, &c.
Defeat of the Crusaders at Gaza; Count de Bar slain, Armory de Montfort, and many nobles and knights taken captive.
Retreat of the King of Navarre upon Acre.
The French leaders, &c. return home.
II. Expedition of Richard. Earl of Cornwall, who lands at Acre, accompanied by the flower of the English chivalry.
His arrival strikes the Mussulmans with terror, and inspires the Christians with confidence.
Richard demands the restoration of the prisoners taken at the battle of Gaza.
He marches upon Jaffa; but
The Sultans of Egypt and Damascus hasten to negotiate for peace.
1240 Jerusalem restored to the Christians.
Restoration of 600 Christian prisoners.
Return of Richard, Earl of Cornwall.
End of the Sixth Crusade.
1241 The fortifications of Jerusalem rebuilt by the Knights Templars.
The ravages of the Moguls in Asia Minor drive several tribes into Syria for settlements. One of these tribes—
The Kharizmian horde, (20,000 cavalry,) under Barbacan, enter Palestine, being guided by an Egyptian emir.
1242 Jerusalem captured by Barbacan, and finally lost to the Christians.

CHRONOLOGY OF THE CRUSADES. 479

A. D.
1242 Indiscriminate massacre of the inhabitants; pillage of the city; general ruin.
The Knights Templars unite with the Moslems of Damascus, Aleppo, Ems, against the Egyptians and Kharismians.
1243 Terrible defeat of the Christian chivalry and their Moslem allies. Fall of Tiberias, Ascalon, &c.
Palestine overrun by the Kharismians.
1244 The Christian chivalry confined to Acre.
Disunion between the Kharismians and Egyptians; the former expelled from Palestine.
Holy Sepulchre in the hands of infidels.
THE SEVENTH CRUSADE.
1245 The new Crusade was resolved upon at the Council of Lyons; temporal wars to be suspended for four years.
Crusade embraced in England and France.
1247 Cyprus the rendezvous of the French Crusaders; here they spend 8 months.
1248 Louis sails for Egypt with 1800 vessels, and 50,000 men.
[In imitation of the plan of the fifth Crusade, Egypt, as the principal seat of the Moslem power, was again selected for the theatre of operations.]
A storm disperses the fleet; only 700 knights, under the king, make the port.
Panic of the Mussulmans; they evacuate Damietta to the French.
Arrival of those dispersed by the storm, with a body of English nobles under William Longsword.
March of the French toward Cairo.
1249 Rashness of the Count d'Artois at Mansora; himself, William Longsword, and a host of knights slain.
Death of Nodjmeddin, Sultan of Egypt.
Louis defeats the Moslems at Mansora.
Crusaders in distress; famine and pestilence make frightful ravages among them.
1250 Total rout of the Crusaders at Man-

A. D.
1250 Revolution in Egypt; Louis in danger.
Surrender of Damietta to the Turks, April 5, in exchange for the king and nobles.
The king proceeds to Acre; but most of his nobles return home.
[During four years, the treasures which Louis was enabled to raise were lavishly expended in refortifying Jaffa, Cæsarea, Sidon, and Acre.]
1253 Dissensions among the Moslem emirs of Syria and Egypt; hence the hopes of the Christians revive.
1254 Renewal of hostilities; the Moslem hordes approach Acre, but soon retire.
The news of the death of the queen-mother of France hastens the
Departure of Louis for Europe.
End of the Seventh Crusade.
1255 Commercial and political rivalry of the Venetian States the cause of troubles in Palestine.
Disunion between the several orders.
1257 Sanguinary battles between the Templars and Knights Hospitallers; complete and merciless destruction of the former.
Preparations of the Templars in Europe for inflicting a desperate vengeance upon the Hospitallers.
1260 Approach of the Mamelukes; occupation of Damascus and Aleppo.
1263 Mameluke invasions, under Bondocdar.
Desperate and unequal battles between the now united orders and the Mamelukes.
1265 Loss of Azotus; Latins put to the sword.
1266 Surrender of Saphoury; Bondocdar (or Bibars) treacherously violates his treaty, and murders all his prisoners.
1267 Loss of Cæsarea, Laodicea, and Jaffa.
1268 Fall of Antioch before Bibars of Egypt: massacre of 40,000 (?) Christians; 100,000 are sold as slaves.
Antioch abandoned to desolation and ruin.
Acre is alone in the hands of the

A. D.
THE EIGHTH AND LAST CRUSADE,
1270 Undertaken by Louis IX., but diverted to Africa. (See France.)
Prince Edward of England separates from the French before Tunis, and proceeds to Sicily.
1271 From Sicily he departs for Palestine at the head of about 1000 Englishmen.
Edward arrives in Palestine in May.
The report of his arrival strikes Bondocdar with terror: he retires from before Acre.
Edward, with only 9000 men, marches against the infidels, and routs them with slaughter.
Assault on Nazareth; capture of the city, and dreadful slaughter of the Moslems.
Edward's army fall victims to disease.
Edward is himself taken ill.
Narrow escape from assassination; Edward kills the assassin, (a Mussulman.)
[None of the writers contemporary with this event knew any thing of that beautiful fiction—the creation of a much later age—which ascribes the recovery of Edward to the affectionate devotion of his consort, Eleanor, in sucking the venom from his wounds.]
Truce for ten years offered by the Sultan of Egypt; accepted by Edward.
272 Edward and his wife Eleanor return home.
End of the Eighth Crusade.

A. D.
1274 Pope Gregory X. endeavours to revive the crusading spirit in Europe.
1276 The Latins twice plunder the peaceable Moslem traders; satisfaction for which Keladun, Sultan of Egypt, vainly demands.
1280 Invasion of Palestine by the Mamelukes, who renew their ravages every year.
1289 Dismemberment of the county of Tripoli from the Latin kingdom, by the Mamelukes.
Tyre and Sidon destroyed by the Turks, so that they might not afford protection any longer to the Christians.
1290 Further outrages on Mussulman merchants by the inhabitants of Acre.
Sultan Khatil demands reparation: denied.
1391 Khatil, having vowed to exterminate the faithless Franks, leads an army of 200,000 men against Acre.
Fall of Acre, the last Christian possession in Palestine.
End of the War of the Crusades.
["The cessation of the Crusades was not produced by any abatement of the love of arms, or of the thirst of glory, in the chivalry of Europe. But the union with these martial qualities of that fanatical enthusiasm which inspired the Christian warriors of the eleventh century, had been slowly, and almost thoroughly dissolved."]